HOUSE OF FAILURE

HOUSE OF FAILURE

William V. Fields

Cupidity Press
Carson, CA

House of Failure
William V. Fields

House of Failure Copyright © 2008
Cupidity Press
All Rights Reserved.
ISBN 13 digit: 978-0-9802480-0-5
ISBN 10 digit: 0-98002480-0-0

Cupidity Press
P.O. Box 4422
Carson, CA 90746
vashawnfields@yahoo.com
(424) 233-6181

Dedication

I want to dedicate this book to Joe Lott, my uncle, and my mother Terri Hunter. Joe thanks for setting the example of greatness for which I strive and never letting me feel alone on this journey. Mother thanks for believing in me. This book is also dedicated to Dee Dee Lawrence, Dr. Malia Lawrence, and Dr. Renford Reese for inspiring me to challenge myself. Lastly, I want to extend my gratitude to all the real life Askaris who make it their mission to remove the crust of ignorance the average inmate has clouding their vision.

TABLE OF CONTENTS

William Fields iii

iv   House of Failure

I Am Not Your Nigga

Do you see a fool?
Are you interacting with a stooge?
Do you see a mistake, a person whose complexion is out of place?
Do you see someone inferior better yet an individual who can't stand
to see their own reflection in the mirror? If not then I can't definitely
be your nigger.
Do you see someone abused?
Who lacks morals or any social clues?
A new with destruction for those with the same hue?
Lacking any type of important tangible realistic or positive views?
I am not your nigga if you don't see any of these traits in me.
I am not your nigga because I am not cursed with a mental or skin
disease.
So why would you want to denigrate me?
Associating me with a word so filthy?
You must be blind or clearly absurd voluntary dementia being your
planned verb.
When I try to correct you, you give me opposition choosing to be
your own races mental mortician.
Who fails to listen to reality instead of opting to mentally battle me
on fruitless issues?
With points as valid as walking on a bridge constructed of wet tissue.
Yes, brother you have issues if you see me as your nigga.
Realer than most in that I harbor deep wants of betterment, while
most are content to operate on another man's settlement, quick to
take a hand out.
How can you be a man while accepting so little for yourself like a
mouse?
Bragging about your clout, caged in here with me.
Your children definitely in neglect out there while you're absent
from the streets.
You love them? So you say so easily.
Yet I have never seen you crack open a book continually to mold
yourself into someone they could aspire to be.
Must say it because it sounds good, palatable to your lips.
Yeah I hear you, but I see your pants constantly riding below your
hips, while memorizing the latest rhymes and justifying your present
and future crimes.

I Am Not Your Nigga (cont.)

With the world is against me mentality constantly on your tongue yet still fascinated with pulling triggers on guns.
I falter at the fact that you fathered a daughter or son. Still getting over on your own thinking you won.
Engaging in life as if its only purpose is self-pleasure and fun.
Witnessing this behavior still leaves me stunned. Leading to thoughts that weigh me down like a ton to whether our race is truly done. When we've reached a point to where we can't control our tongues.
No puns intended only intention for those who can relate to feel it.
Taking the opportunity to bill it to your mind that I am too advanced to be a nigga or your nigga in anyway or of any kind.

Chapter 1

County Blues

"You stupid little boy! Didn't I tell you? Didn't I tell you not to wash the colored clothes with the white clothes?" His mother yelled as she pounded her fist into his upper back, which caused the bottle of bleach he held to fall to the floor, as he received more blows that came routinely following every mistake.

"See what you did now? Spilled my muthafucking bleach on the damn floor! Now clean that shit up off my floor." As he bent down to clean the bleach with a nearby rag she continued to pound into his back with her closed fist over and over again. The sound of her fist against his young hollow flesh made a loud banging sound, as each blow came harder than the previous one, pummeling him in between the washer and dryer.

Bang...Bang...Bang! "Wake your ass up Pink. Pink! Wake up!" Awakening out of his sleep Kevin found himself still entrapped within his decrepit cell. The stench of male body odor filled his freshly awoken nostrils, as the salty musky sweat from not showering in three days, slowly entered his mouth. Disoriented, he reached for his county blues at the foot of his bunk. Sliding his pants on, he struggled to gain his vision as the officer flashed the light of his flashlight in his face. Highly irritated, he raised his arm to shield his eyes, while asking what the officer wanted.

"For your ass to get ready for court, you got ten minutes Pink!" The officer informed him before walking down the tier awakening other inmates for court. Slouched down on his bunk, feet planted firmly to the floor, Kevin "K-Stone" Pink rubbed his face in wonderment. Thinking what the hell have I gotten myself into? Well, he said to himself, it's too late to be asking that question. Reality settled in as the ice cold water from the rusted sink hit his thin brown face. Startled by Freeway Freddy running across his foot, he dropped his face towel on the dirty floor. Picking the specks of food, hair, and dust balls off his towel, he wondered why people would name a rat in jail. Thoughts of his mother also crossed his mind. She wasn't holding up too well. He made a mental note to call her when he came back from court.

"Pick your breakfast up and take it to the holding tank to your right," the officer commanded as he gave each inmate his tray. Grabbing a tray, K-Stone scanned over his breakfast while walking to the tank. Two hard-boiled eggs, a slice of cheese, and two pieces

of stale wheat bread accompanied, by Men Central County Jail
Oatmeal which seemed to always be served cold. Nevertheless,
he ate it greedily, drowning it down with a juice from a company he
had never heard of before.

"Now look, when the other officer calls your name take it to
your assigned court tank pronto. Wisely, Thomas, and Pink you are
all going to CCB. Take it to tank number four." Before entering the
tank inmates' barcodes had to be scanned off their wrist bands.
Taking part in this degrading routine made K-Stone feel equivalent
to a piece of produce at Ralph's check out line. He held rancor for
this process, including the constant dreading he encountered with
every court movement.

Entering the crowded tank, K-Stone did a thorough scan of
all the faces and tattoos of individuals in the holding tank. Going to
court was more than checking the status of how ones case was going.
Most knew they were going to be found guilty. They were just
going through the motions preparing themselves for defeat. It was
more so a meeting ground for gang bangers to meet their homies
who were housed on different floors of the jail. But more so to fight,
jump, and stab rival gang bangers they couldn't get to on different
floors. With that in mind, K-Stone always went into attack mode
whenever he stepped in any tank. Encountering no enemies within
the tank, he relaxed up against an open piece of wall, while watching
the tank door to see who would enter.

"Cuzz!" a voice yelled, over shadowing all the other
conversations, causing K-Stone to push off the wall to put a face
with the oddly familiar voice. When he peered around two inmates
having a conversation in front of him, he saw that it was Uzi, his
closest homie from his turf.

"Cuzz, what's cracking?" Uzi said with much excitement
as they embrace each other. "Looks like where on a mission
together today," Uzi said squeezing K-Stone's shoulder.

"You still on the twenty six hundredth floor?" K-Stone asks.

"Yeah, me by my lonesome. Who's down there with you on
the twenty four hundredth floor?"

"M-Rat, Flat, and X-Ray."

"Sounds like I need to come down there with ya'll. X-Ray
down there doing any of that funny shit?"

"Nope, not since I've been down there."

"Ya'll catch any K4's down there?"

"X-Ray and M-Rat stomped out a fool named Toad a couple of nights ago. He rolled it up last night."

"Toad, that short fat fool?"

"Yeah, that's him. Where you know him from?"

"That fool be whacking the set out in the court tanks."

"Their homeboy still coming to court on you?" K-Stone asked.

"Yeah, that snitch still coming. It's cool though, the case is boo-boo, all they got is that snitch getting on the stand on a young Crip. What's up with your case?"

"Still trying to get some of these charges dropped?"

"Last time I went to court it was a dry run. You know to break a young Ransom down to take a deal?"

"So they offered you a deal?"

"That's if you consider thirty years a deal?"

"Don't feel too bad they offered me fifty to life last month."

"So did you consider it?"

"Do I look like a fool? I told the D.A. to suck my dick! Getting at me like that, she was obviously playing with my intelligence. I meant it too. When I made the comment the judge turned beet red and ordered the bailiff to escort me out the courtroom, that bitch was mad."

"Man, there's something wrong with you."

"What? I'm serious, the bitch was bad, I wanted to jump over the table and show her why they call me Uzi. Know what I mean? Pump some of these hollow tip rounds in her," Uzi said pointing to his crotch, while moving it in a thrusting motion.

"You're a sick dude!"

"I know, I know, the bitches love it."

With all the talking going on in the holding tanks the officers could barely hear their walkie talkies. "Shut the hell up in there!"

"You shut up!" Uzi responded back.

"All right tough guy, get ready to get on the bus. Step into lines of two so you can be shackled together."

As they lined up in the hallway waiting for departure, Bazooka a known K4CB on his way to Torrance court recognized K-Stone and yelled out, "Ransack Killa!" That broke the small chatter between the inmates in line.

K-Stone and Uzi looked on, fuming with anger, but unable to do anything to the enemy that just disrespected their turf.

"Ole busta ass K-Fort, he know we can't do nothing chained up," K-Stone said angrily.

"Cuzz on Ransom, I better not catch one at court," Uzi said with rancor in his voice. "I hope they don't have us sitting out in the cold," Uzi said rubbing his hands together.

"Walk!" yelled the officer behind the line. "Stop when you get to the bus."

"I can feel the breeze all ready K-Stone."

"It's all in your mind."

"Damn that, it's cold out here, my small frame isn't built for this."

K-Stone was never in a hurry to get on the bus. He missed the light of the moon that seemed to dance against the sky and mingled with the crisp cold air that eluded him within the cement walls. Goose bumps started to appear with each shiver his small frame generated, accompanied by his visible breath that came every time he spoke. Giving him the nostalgia of when he was a kid and waiting on the school bus to pick him up down the street from his home, while pretending he was blowing smoke from a cigar until the bus came. He laughed to himself when he thought about how he went from that, to waiting for a county jail bus.

"The first ones on the bus take it to the back," the officer said. As K-Stone and Uzi took their seats they were quiet while adjusting to the cold hard plastic seats in which their thin prison pants gave no protection.

Vroooom! The monster awakened out of its slumber with a loud rumble and white smoke coming out of its rectum, ready to transport its victims to their judgment. Seeing the streets from the inside of the monster was strange; a strangeness that was unspeakable. Every object seemed a blur of empty color. Can emptiness be explained? K-Stone thought to himself, while focusing his attention on the graffiti etched into the seats by former and present victims. Forgotten souls of society, leaving their marks behind like the Egyptians left theirs. For the first time since being locked up, the loss of his freedom was starting to be felt.

"Turn some damn rap on!" Uzi yelled to the front of the bus. "Man nobody trying to hear this soft rock shit! Cuzz, the music is killing me. The bus driver is acting like a little broad. He sees it's nothing but Blacks and Mexicans on the bus."

As usual, the bus driver ignored Uzi's request to change the music. Turning into the garage, the jet black spine of the monster easily slid into the mouth of the court building. All conversation ceased immediately, as reality sank in, of what awaited inside the building.

While waiting to be called off the bus, some one yelled out a joke to crack the stillness of reality, but it brought no reaction. When the officer returned he started to read names off a list. As they were called, the inmates exited the bus one at a time. Once inside the building they were placed on an elevator to their assigned floor. After an hour the court tanks were filled with inmates from L.A. County and Wayside.

"Let the head busting begin!" Uzi yelled out as he saw three of his homies come into the tank.

"Ransom gangstas!" G-Liz, M-Dogg, and Bone-Tone yelled out simultaneously, in response to seeing Uzi and K-Stone.

They immediately embraced each other while speaking their dialect, while a nervous member of K4CB looked on from a corner by the toilet.

"I know you have a smoke?" G-Liz tells K-Stone. Pulling out a cigarette and matches from underneath the pad in his shoe, K-Stone passes G-Liz a smoke and after taking a couple pulls he begins to talk.

"Yeah, Cuzz about to get this twenty year deal today," G-Liz said in a smug tone.

"Is that right?" replied Uzi.

"Yeah, I figure I did the hot one, I might as well take the deal. Besides, the case isn't looking too great."

Sensing someone was ear hustling, G-Liz redirected his attention to Taco.

"Where you from?"

Paralyzed with fear Taco stuttered out, "K-4." Before he could finish his response, M-Dogg struck him in the jaw, instantly breaking it and knocking him to the ground. As he melted to the ground, semi-conscious, the other Ransoms took part in a vicious stomp-out of their most hated enemy. Unconscious and lying in a pool of what he represented, Taco started to come to while the Ransoms stood over him.

"Get your punk ass up!" M-Dogg said kicking him in the side of the rib cage.

"You're not dead yet," Uzi added quickly.

"Enough!" K-Stone said, bored with the extras, "what's done is done." Looking at the others with a solid look, they silently agreed and moved to the other side of the tank. K-Stone lived under certain rules. One was, when you degrade a man without taking his life you were setting yourself up for a future death at his hands. Under those rules, K-Stone would have mercy on an enemy in hand to hand combat, once he was unresponsive. When it was time to kill he would kill. He didn't have the "K" in his name for Kevin.

"Court will be starting in five minutes," the female officer informed the inmates inside the holding cell.

"It's about time. I'm trying to get back to Wayside and lay it out."

"I feel you M-Dogg," G-Liz said yawning, "that early morning leg exercise got me tired." They all started to laugh as G-Liz made jokes about Taco.

"Harris, your lawyer is here to see you." G-Liz exited the court tank to talk to his lawyer before going into court.

"How are you doing Mr. Harris?"

"How does it look like I'm doing?"

"Well Mr. Harris, you look tired. The news I have may brighten you up. The D.A. has accepted your deal for the twenty years, two strikes, and eighty five percent. If you just go in and sign the papers it will be official."

G-Liz looked off blankly seeing his twenty five years of living life flash before his eyes. He quickly calculates the age he would be if he took the deal. In all his gang-banging fantasies, he never thought it would end this way.

"Damn no pussy for twenty years," he said softly as his thoughts escaped his mind through his mouth.

"Mr. Harris... Mr. Harris, are you all right?"

"Yeah I'm cool. Get the paperwork ready."

"All right I'll inform the D.A. of your decision."

As he awaited going into court, Andre "G-Liz" Harris couldn't help but think his life was over. He would be in his forties when he paroled. He asked himself, "What the hell am I going to do at forty something fresh out of the pen?" The only family he had was his grandmother and most likely she would be dead by the time he's finished with his sentence. What a waste was the last thought he had before signing the paper pleading guilty to first degree murder.

After receiving his sentence, G-Liz re-entered the court tank to find K-Stone, M-Dogg, and Bone-Tone in the tank eating lunch.

They handed him his lunch bag. "Good looking." G-Liz said as he started eating his soggy sandwich.

Nobody really said much, the look on his face said it all.

"Well fellas I won't be seeing you'll for two decades."

"Is that right," they said simultaneously.

"Yeah, at least it's over now. I'll be catching the chain in two weeks, straight level four status."

"They can't keep a real lok down!" Uzi yelled entering the tank breaking the monotony. "Who they thought I was? I get fools touched. Why's everybody looking sad and shit?" Noticing the mood had changed since this morning, Uzi put it together.

"Gangsta Lizard, you all right, cuzz? Looks like a thug needs a hug?" Uzi extended his arms to clinch G-Liz who smacked them away. "Don't be like that cuzz. You know how the game works; at least you got get back."

"Huh…that's real. Why are you so amped up anyway?"

"The prosecutor's star witness was found dead this morning on Vermont and Manchester, making it impossible to proceed with the case. Which ultimately means that niggas better handcuff their hoes, because Mr. Uzi is coming to a street near you. For thirteen months, my ammunition has been built up and it's time for release."

The mood quickly changed to slight envy. This was the third murder case Uzi had beaten.

"Pink, your lawyer is waiting for you."

"How's everything going for you Mr. Pink?"

"Just taking it how it comes."

"Well, they dropped two of the robbery charges so you're looking at fifteen years now, which is a lot better than the previous thirty."

"You're right about that."

"I have one more bit of information. The D.A. has put a deal for ten years on the table."

"I'll have to say no to that right now. Let's extend one more month so I can weigh my options."

"All right, we'll be going in the courtroom in twenty minutes to get an extension for a month."

"Tapp, your jury has come back in." Bone-Tone entered the courtroom looking at the jury skeptically before sitting down besides his lawyer.

"We got this one beat," his lawyer whispered in his ear. Bone-Tone rubbed his sweaty palms together as the judge took his seat and the proceedings began.

"We the jury find Johnny Tapp not guilty of first degree murder. On count two of armed robbery we find the defendant not guilty." By this time Bone-Tone was feeling like Uzi. "On the last count of first degree attempted murder we find the defendant guilty."

"Thank you for your service," the judge told the jury panel. "Mr. Tapp you will be coming back next month for sentencing." Bone-Tone's shoulders slumped as his six foot two inch slim frame was escorted back to the holding tank.

A hustler by nature, Bone-Tone had made a decent living selling dope. By twenty-five he was playing with eighteen birds. He had become accustomed to the life style of parties, women, and all the chronic he could inhale. He got his name from his slim build and light tone. At thirty, he was looking at fifteen years or worse, life in prison. All the years of grinding seemed to be going down the drain with him not ready to get out the tub of life. Everybody was chilling on the benches waiting to go back to there temporary housing except Uzi.

"Well my loks, I'll hit you'll up when I touchdown in the turf. Big M-Dogg, how's that ten years you just took feel?" Uzi asked.

"I can handle it, twenty five now, I'll be thirty five when I touchdown." Calvin "M-Dogg" Scott was built like a beast, six-foot-four and solid. His extremely dark complexion gave his face a grimy look that never went away. He was known for being a bully who took what he wanted from whoever.

"Everybody's who's going to Wayside get ready to get on the bus. K-Stone I'll catch you next month," Bone-Tone said while getting shackled.

Before leaving they all embraced each other. On their way out their tank G-Liz, M-Dogg, and Bone-Tone threw up their hand signals to give a final good bye before fading out of the sight of Uzi and K-Stone.

"Uzi, what you got planned for when you get out?"

"First on the agenda is some pussy. Then I'm going to scope out something to rob to get some money to flip a dope sac. Basically, the same program cuzz. Kill some enemies, get drunk, and hold the turf down until you come home."

"Well my bus is here. Be careful out their cuzz; make sure you pop one of those K4's for me."

"You gots that Killa Stone," Uzi replied with a sick grin across his dark child-like face.

On back of the bus, K-Stone slouched down into the hard seat looking out the window into the outside world he hadn't been apart of for ten months. Rather, all his life being he never seemed to fit in until he joined Ransom. He tried to work before but couldn't relate to normal people, normal being people and ideologies outside his community. He laughed in mid thought at the thought of normal people. Never could he view the society he grew up in as normal nor the people that embraced it with all the pain, violence, and neglect he had seen as well as participated in during his life.

Before the gang, he was an outcast lacking confidence. All that changed once he started banging full time. At first he was a simple pawn taking orders from older homies. Fighting his peers to gain respect became a daily task. It was a grueling struggle adjusting to the gang lifestyle.

He went on mission after mission, even after certain homies advised him to kickback. Having nothing to lose fueled him to take on tasks that others only talked about when intoxicated and lied about when no one was around to dispute their war stories.

Years passed and he became the man he always glamorized on the streets as a child. Even his older brother gave him props. His confidence was extremely high. Money was no longer a problem. He had plenty. He went from a Cutlass on eighteen inch rims to a Tahoe fresh off the lot, with twenty-four inch rims. Cash flow motivated him to get his own apartment which had a closet packed with name brand clothes and shoes. To put icing on the cake, he purchased a twenty-thousand dollar gold and platinum incrusted Ransom chain which hung to the middle of his chest, hypnotizing every female he encountered.

Still with all his goals accomplished, late at night when he laid alone, he always felt a constant void. No matter how much he thought about it, he couldn't put his finger on the exact cause. Or maybe he could, but it was too deep in his heart to touch. Even though he was at the pinnacle of what most young Blacks considered the life, none of it made him feel complete and this fact confused him. Drunkenness often intensified these personal thoughts he harbored on the streets, leaving him to ask the question, what else is there to gain that would fill his void? A question he still asked himself.

"Look at me now," he said aloud on the bus,

before realizing how loud he actually said it, causing the other inmates to look at him strangely. All the reputation, all the money, meant nothing in the real world. K-Stone had no significance at all to people in the real world. To them he was just another crazy gang-banging nigga. The thought angered and sickened him, so he leaned back in his seat the rest of the ride. Against his face, the warm touch of the sun seemed to be making payments for all the previously denied days. He stared blankly into the sun light knowing that he would be denied its light another thirty days.

*   *   *   *   *   *   *   *   *   *   *

"Blood, what the hell happened to you?" Bazooka asked Taco angrily.

"Those punk ass Ransacks jumped me after I socked one of their homies."

"Is that right?"

"Yeah, Blood I was beating him down when one of his homies blindsided me from the back."

"Blood, they sure fucked you up."

"I'm not tripping, same thing make a nigga laugh, make a nigga cry."

"So how much time did you get?"

"Three years with half."

"That's straight! They gave me twenty five to life."

Standing six-foot-two two-hundred ten pounds all muscle, Timothy "Bazooka" Hayes was known to be a violent member of Kill 4 Cash Bloods. At twenty-five, he was facing twenty-five to life for killing a Ransom. He'd been beefing with the Ransoms since he was a kid. In fact, it had been so long he could barely remember what the beef started over. One thing he knew for sure was that he killed a lot of them. He was at the point where there was no turning back. Rehabilitation didn't exist in his world.

Chapter 2

A Mother's Tears

Since the death of his older brother, K-Stone's mother hadn't been the same. The closed casket and all his homies at the funeral with his brother's picture enlarged on the back of their shirts didn't add to the healing process one bit. He didn't even cry in fact he hadn't shed a tear since his youth. He just held her in his arms rocking her gently as she cried uncontrollably. Not one word came from his mouth the entire day. There was nothing to say, he had just lost his older brother who he admired and loved dearly. Even though he deemed the K4 responsible for taking his brothers life, it didn't change the fact that his brother was dead. As he dropped the blue rag on the casket while it was lowered, he thought about all the lives he took. This is how I must have made them feel, he thought to himself.

The only memory he carried of his brother was a portrait of him on his neck with C.I.P. Jamal "K-Slim" Pink above it. All the stress he was putting on his mother hurt him. It had barely been a year since the death of his brother and he was sitting in jail, putting her through some more grief. But it would never equal the pain she permanently placed within him.

As a child he had experienced an emotion far greater than love. When his mother would cradle him in her arms he could feel it seeping off her. Such a wonderful feeling he bathed in it. Oh, how he loved his mother. When she beat him at the age five the first time for misplacing the remote, it shattered him. He had realized reality in its rawest form. The look in her eyes was those of a violent stranger void of all feelings. Her beatings still haunted him in his dreams. His first and only love had betrayed his trust. That first beating was the catalyst for all his anger. Unable to harm her, he harmed others whenever he was abused be it verbally or physically. Though she snatched the virginity of his childhood innocence, he knew in his heart she loved him. This is what he reminded himself of daily. The realization that life was often cold made him strong during times of uncertainty such as he faced now. These were thoughts that raced through his mind as he picked the phone up in his cell to dial his mother.

"Hello."

"It's Kevin, how are you doing?"

"A lot better now that you've called. I was just watering the front yard."

"It's good to hear you're getting some air. I went to court today, they offered me ten years."

"You didn't take it, did you?"

"No, I'm going to go back next month and talk them down to five years."

"I don't know about that. You have to explain what you mean? Kevin I don't want you to take anything."

"Now that's not thinking in perspective, I'm going to have to take something. Wouldn't you rather it be a single digit?"

"I rather it be nothing, but you seem to always know what you're doing. Do you want me to come see you this weekend?"

"No, I don't like you sitting in that long line to only see me for fifteen minutes."

"I don't mind waiting."

"But I do, so don't bother. I am about to eat so I'll call you next week."

"Okay, be careful in there."

"I will. I love you."

"I love you too. Talk to you later." Hanging up the phone, he could hear the sadness in her voice.

"What you up in there doing cuzz?" X-Ray asked peeking in between the bars.

"Eating some grub," K-Stone responded wiping his mouth.

"Want to go have some fun Killastone?"

"What kind of fun?"

"You have to come see for yourself little buddy."

"Get my cell racked."

"All ready in progress."

"You got juice like that?"

"I've been in here two years fighting three hot ones and a carjacking, I better have something."

"Just get the cell racked."

"Rack baker three!" X-Ray yelled to the officer operating the front controls.

"So what have you got to show me?"

"You'll see," X-Ray said with a sickly grin on his face. When they got to cell eight, K-Stone looked inside to find Flat and M-Rat on top of somebody wrapped in a blood-drenched sheet, wiggling and screaming.

"Let me go!" That was the only sound you could hear over the laughing and, "Shut up punk!" while Flat was smashing the heel of his shoe in the victims neck. M-Rat was sitting on top of him taking his time and punching him hard in the rib cage, but mostly in the face with some jail-made brass knuckles. They were made from the iron off the beds, with the end of a screw embedded where the knuckles should be and the stuffing from the plastic mattress provided protection for the user.

"I bet you want your mommy," M-Rat joked. "But you can't have her; she's tied up in the next cell."

"You want to get in on some of this K-Stone?" Flat asked pressing his heel even further into the victim's sweaty neck.

"Who do you have in there with you?" K-Stone asked approaching the body.

Pulling the sheet back, he could see it was Taco. Taco, realizing it was K-Stone, pleaded with him to tell his homies to let him go.

"You know dude?" Flat asked.

"Yep, the homies and I beat him down this morning at court. M-Rat and I caught the little busta whacking the turf out on the wall next door."

"Let me go, this shit isn't funny!"

"Shut up punk!" M-Rat said socking him in the nose which was already bleeding.

"Please let...," before Taco could finish his plea, K-Stone kicked him in the mouth busting his lip.

"The homie said shut up."

Taco knew he was doomed. His only hope had just kicked him in the mouth.

"Let me get a smoke X-Ray?" Inhaling the stale smoke, K-Stone looked down at Taco, who was obviously scared. "So how long are you going to keep this K-Fort?"

At the hint of being released, Taco started to regain some of his toughness. "Never thought about it," Flat said releasing his foot off Taco's neck. "You almost finished with that smoke?"

"Yeah, you want to kill it?" Passing the cigarette, Flat took a final pull before putting it out on Taco's cheek.

Burnt flesh engulfed the already musky cell, causing all inside to cough. Taco clinched the inside of his cheek to absorb the pain. Thinking they were about to release him, he wanted to keep some of his gangsterism intact.

"We got us a real tough guy right here," Flat said noticing Taco didn't react to the burn.

"K-Stone, who did you see at court today?" M-Rat inquired.

"I saw M-Dogg, Bone-Tone, G-Liz, and Uzi."

"Anybody catch time?"

"G-Liz took twenty, M-Dogg took ten, and Uzi went home."

"Again damn that's like the third hot one he beat! What about Bone-Tone?"

"Cuzz got found guilty of attempted murder. We both go back to court next month."

"Now that you boys are through playing, it's time for the men to take charge," X-Ray said placing his glasses on the bunk. "We still got grease in here Flat?"

"Sure do," Flat replied rubbing his chin hairs.

Cracking his knuckles, X-Ray let out a long exaggerating "Oh yeah!" All right, K-Stone we'll holla at you tomorrow. We going to punch this K-Fort up a little more, then untie him."

"You better if you know what's good for you!" Taco yelled out.

"In the morning," K-Stone said exiting the cell.

"When I get the feeling, I need sexual healing. Sexual..." X-Ray sang while untying Taco, putting emphasis on sexual.

K-Stone knew some immoral behavior was going to take place after the guard did his last count of the night. A menacing five-foot-six, one-hundred and eighty-five pounds of muscle, Mike "X-Ray" Hambrick had been doing time since he came out the womb. Born to Brenda Hambrick in prison, he developed a liking for the male physique in youth authority, where before leaving he had raped three male inmates. To make matters worse, every time he paroled from jail, he would sleep with all the females in the community. With them being ignorant to his behavior behind the walls, they performed willingly and unprotected. Twenty-nine with three strikes, this was going to be his life. X-Ray had taken a liking to the jail life style. This was his first home, the only place he could be himself, a homo gangsta. He didn't think he was gay, it was the ones he rapped that were gay.

"Here you go," X-Ray said handing Taco a damp towel. "Clean yourself up. We can't have you walking around like that."

Taco snatched the towel wiping the blood from his face.

"Now there's one more thing for you to do before we let you go."

"What the fuck you talking about?" Taco asked, hearing X-Rays voice drop down to a smooth lascivious tone. A voice that was similar to when he was mackin' on a female.

"Look here, there's no need to get feisty."

Taco had heard the stories about men getting rapped in jail. Never in his deepest thoughts did he think he would fall victim. He always told himself, that shit would never happen to him. "Wish a nigga would!" He used to tell his homies whenever the subject came up. "Keep the gay activities to yourself."

"Gay! Who's gay? I just want to satisfy myself that's all." Taking off his shirt, X-Ray revealed numerous tattoos over his chiseled frame.

"Pak!" Was the sound of the punch that landed on X-Ray's chin followed by a couple more. All were met with laughter.

"That's all you got?" X-Ray asked laughing.

Pulling out his back pocket, a six inch rusty knife made from an old pipe, he rushed in close to grab Taco, easily over-powering him. Placing the knife against Taco's sweaty neck, he felt the blood, mixed with pure fear, pumping through his exhausted body.

"Taco is that what your homies call you?" X-Ray asked with his hot breath against his face. Taco gave no response. "Your new name is Tasha" X-Ray said, ripping Taco's boxers off with his free hand.

The ardor in his pants reached its peak, fully erect, he was ready for penetration. "Now you're going to knock him down," X-Ray said pointing to his penis.

"Okay, okay!" Taco said as X-Ray entered his anal cavity. Every time he awoke he would be put back to sleep, as X-Ray and Flat took turns pleasing themselves.

K-Stone could hear the soft sickening rhythmic grunts throughout the night as he lay in his bunk. The whole tier had quieted down to an eerie stillness allowing Taco's rape to be heard in each cell. The behavior that took place that night was not glorified and was actually frowned upon. A part of him wanted to intervene, but heroes were only in the movies. In jail it was everyone for them self. Either you were the victim or the victimizer, doing hole time or hospital time. These were the only options and he followed them. After being in jail ten months, K-stone still found it surprising he was in jail, even though he knew that he would end up in jail if he kept living the gangsta lifestyle. Platitudes his mother use to constantly nag him with, still plagued his mind, especially her favorite:

"You're going to either end up in jail or dead."

It seemed to ring true, his brother was dead and he was in jail. Time and again, he would lie in his bunk, eyes wide open, waiting for the cold breakfast to come to the six man cell he currently lived in.

As he was awakened by the rhythmic snoring of Cesar, his Mexican celly right above him, he recounted the strangers he was forced to live with. Chicago and Butch, two Blacks in their late forties occupied the two upper front bunks. All too often, he was awakened by a silent assault of gas knowing that it came from them. Over to his left, on the lower front bunks were two Whites, Ted and James, both in their early thirties both, meth-heads. They were two cousins from Long Beach. Both of them talked in their sleep. Overall, K-Stone thought his celly's were straight. Once the breakfast got to the cell, everybody started to awaken except Cesar, he never ate breakfast.

"What's on the menu today?" Butch asked in a rugged tone.

"The same thing they have every Friday," Chicago answered in his smooth voice, "cream beef with a flour biscuit."

"You can have mine bro," Ted and James said before rolling back over to sleep. Forcing the food down, K-Stone went on to his daily routine: brushing his teeth, washing his face, and going back to sleep. He usually woke back up when the porters passed out the lunches. Seeing him awake, Butch decided to toss him a lunch bag.

"Finally decided to get up youngsta?" Chicago said reshuffling the cards for another game of spades.

Getting out the bed, K-Stone walked to the sink to splash water on his face, then he headed towards the bars.

"So what are you going to do when you get out youngsta?"

"Where did that come from?"

"I was just making conversation."

"You need to be paying attention to this card game," Butch said scooping up the cards.

"Don't you see me and youngsta is having a conversation."

"I'm more concerned about how I'm going to do this time I'll be getting next month."

"How much time you looking at?"

"Probably five years when I talk them down."

"Oh, you can work with that, you're still young. You just need to get a plan together for when you touchdown, so you want be in here like us old folk."

"I got a plan. I'm going to get sixteen ounces of Sherm, go back to Las Vegas, and double up. That's what I was doing before I got cracked up for these robberies."

"So that's your plan?" Butch asked.

"Sounds like a solid plan to me," Chicago said quickly. "Before I came to jail on this county lid, I was doing the same thing. Been in the game a long time had me a stable along with an older White broad who lived in Hollywood, a real nice area. Selling heroin here and there, I had it sewed up. See, when I get out, I got me a white pearl Bentley waiting on me with a hundred-thousand to spend at my leisure and five bad broads.

"So if you have all this and that, why is it you haven't gone to canteen once, or received one piece of mail?" Butch asked.

"Well you see, my broads don't know where Daddy at."

"What the hell you mean they don't know where you at?"

"They don't. For all they know I was kidnapped by a hater like you."

"Chicago, you full of shit!" Butch said laughing.

"First off, I wasn't even talking to you. I was talking to the youngsta. Now like I was saying KS, I was doing my thing."

"You must have kept a truck load of Viagra for all those broads you were entertaining," K-Stone said laughing.

"Viagra, I don't need any damn pills to get my Johnson up. I'm a pure Black man. I stand tall through it all!"

"All right O.G., while you're standing tall won't you hook me up with a haircut?"

"Can do, pop a razor and wet your hair a little. K-Stone you are an all-right youngsta. So who are you getting all hooked up for?"

"One of my broads is coming up."

"You better marry one of them while you have the time and they are still staying down."

"I'm not really feeling that marriage situation."

"You mean to tell me you're going to do all that time without any snatch box?"

"Never thought about it like that."

"Better start, you going to need somebody to run for you."

"Sew one of those broads up if you want to survive in the pen like a normal human being."

"You got a good point there, Chicago."

"All done, check it out." Chicago passed him a jail house mirror made from the inside of a chip bag that had been cleaned out.

"As always, it's on point. Now it's time to arrange a visit."

Sitting next to the phone by his bed, K-Stone pulled out his phone book from his property bag and started dialing.

"Hello?" A young female voice answered.

"Is Vivica there?"

"She's in the back room. Who is calling?"

"It's Kay."

"Hold on."

"Kay, how are you baby?"

"Cool, just sitting here chilling wondering if I'm going to get a chance to see that beautiful face this weekend?"

"Of course you are baby."

"So what you been up to lately?"

"Just trying to find another job so that I can finish making payments on my new car. Besides that I just started my second semester at USC. How is everything going with your case?"

"I go back next month to try to get them down to a five year deal." Vivica sighed deeply hearing the time K-Stone was facing. "Vivica, are you still there?"

"Yes, that's a long time, Kay."

"Is it too long for you?"

"No, but..."

"At this point in my life, buts are not going to work. Either your going to stay down like a ton or leave."

"Kay, I love you, but I cannot wait five years while you sit in prison. It is wearing me down now, coming every other week."

"Get on then bitch."

"Kay wait!" before she could finish, he had slammed the phone down.

"Stupid bitch!" he said pacing the cell. Seeing K-Stone upset, Chicago tried to calm him down.

"Punk bitch talking about that's too long for her to wait." He kept repeating while pacing.

"She said what?" Chicago asked.

"Bitch said five years was too long for her to wait, when I told her the time I was facing."

"The nerve It's her loss KS. Don't trip off that broad, there will be plenty more coming your way."

After calming down, K-Stone went back through his phone book. Flipping back and forth through the pages he came across the number he was looking for.

"Is this Ivie?"

"This is her. How are you doing Kay?"

"I'm cool. How are you?"

"Good, just getting ready for the movies tonight." "So I'm sitting here doing my nails."

"What movie are you going to go see?"

"Some movie my homegirls picked out."

"Sounds like a plan. Are you going to be available this weekend?"

"Not really, how about I come next week?"

"Next week is cool. I'm going to let you get back to your nails."

"Okay, I love you Kay."

"All right talk to you later."

Not looking too good he thought to himself, "looks like I'll be stuck with you cats for the weekend." Lying back on his bunk, K-Stone reminisced on when he first met Vivica True. Looking slightly nervous, she was in a hurry coming out of McDonalds on Florence and Crenshaw when he spotted her caramel brown five-foot-four curvaceous figure, headed towards her Lexus. Wasting no time, he swerved right next to her car in his Tahoe, jumping out before actually putting his truck in park. For a minute she was startled as she fumbled with her keys. Put off by his boldness, she was reluctant to even speak to him. With a little charm, he ended up leaving with her number that day. A couple of days went by before he actually called her up. When he finally called, they set up a breakfast date at Roscoe's. Picking her up that morning, he had forgotten how good looking she was. H dubbed her Stacy Dash Two. During the date it didn't take long for them to click. Vivica had a good head on her shoulders and came from a good family with both parents at home. That was unheard of in his part of town. That one date led too many more. He ended up spending a lot of time with her, going to all kinds of different places he never thought of. All of this was new for him, most of females he met he would dick down and shake. Vivica was different; she challenged him, causing him to think about what direction his life was going. Conflict arose one night when her condescending mother and father had him over for dinner. While finishing the canapé and waiting on the casserole, her parents started to bombard him with questions about where he worked and grew up, even though they knew he was a hustler. They didn't figure he was a gang member until they saw all his tattoos at a pool party Vivica threw.

He took his gun everywhere he went and the pool party was no exception. Conflict occurred when his glock forty-five fell on the grass while he was undressing for the pool. Quickly noticing the dropped gun, he scooped it up, but not before her mother saw it. Vivica politely asked him and his homies to leave the party. He left, but it didn't register to him what went wrong. Carrying a gun was normal behavior for him. In his part of town, a gun was as common as a pack of cigarettes.

Despite her parents objections they still saw each other. Good times were plentiful, especially when they went to Santa Monica Beach late at night and chilled. Listening to Al Green always made her melt in between her legs and into his arms. He could still imagine the feeling of the breeze of the cold night up against his bare back. It was fun while it lasted, he whispered to himself, pulling the blanket over his face.

"Why you crying baby?" Mrs. True asked sitting down on the bed rubbing her daughter's back. "Now take your head out the pillow and tell me why you are crying?"

"It's nothing," Vivica said wiping her tears away.

"Your sister told me that boy called today. Is that why you're crying baby?"

"He called me a bitch."

"That boy is no good, I've told you numerous times, but don't worry baby, he's in jail now, where he belongs. Move on with your life, losers like that don't deserve you."

"I love him!"

"Let me tell you something, that boy, what's his name?"

"K-Stone."

"He doesn't want anything out of life; if he did he would be using his God given name, not an alias. He's living in a fantasy world. We are not living in the nineteen-twenties, the days of Scarface, Capone, and Bumby Face Nelson. It's the twenty-first century, trash like him is doomed and whoever is involved with them will follow the same path. Your father and I didn't work this hard for you to become some gang-bangers bitch or baby momma. You're better than that can't you see? Kaysto, or whatever he calls himself is no good. All those hooligans from South Central, Compton, and Watts are low-life ghetto scum. They're all an embarrassment to the African American race. For a minute I thought you were going through some type of phase wanting some type of gangster for fun. Hopefully you will see he's no good to you or himself," with that said, her mother walked out her room.

Vivica walked to the back porch to think about what her mother had said. After the incident at the pool party when her parents forbid her from socializing with Kay she tried to argue with them, but the arguments always ended quickly with them wanting to know why he had to carry a gun. No matter how much sense her parents made she couldn't stay away from Kay. He was exciting, fun to be with, and very handsome. Furthermore, he had his own money, a very rare commodity to find. Being with K-Stone made her realize that all the guys before him were just fake gangstas. They never went to their neighborhoods that they claimed. Her second boyfriend had her fooled into thinking he was the real McCoy, telling her how he didn't take anything from anybody. The truth came out when he got beat up and his chain snatched at the Fox Hills Mall by a guy smaller than him. K-Stone had respect everywhere he went, without extras. His confidence was something she had never experienced before. She was getting wet just thinking about how he used to wrap his hand around her long brown hair while pounding her from the back. She even went and got his name tattooed under her navel which displayed "175% K-Stone" to show how much she loved him. At that point, she decided to go see him the next day.

"Pink you have a visit!" the officer yelled down the tier.

"I wonder who this is," K-Stone said to Chicago while putting on his visiting blues.

"Probably one of your little broads, take it easy on her out there."

"I look cool?" K-Stoned asked fully clothed and creased up.

"All the time youngsta." On his way down the tier to the visiting room he wondered who it could be. No matter who it was, it was good to get out of the cell.

Waiting for him to come, Vivica tried to control the butterflies in her stomach. Walking to the window, he saw that it was Vivica, and instantly thought, "This bitch."

Picking up the phone, Vivica started to talk, "Sorry Kay."

"Sorry for what, Miss that's too long?"

"I'm sorry for not responding the way I should have. Don't you have something to say to me?"

"Something! Like what? I know you not talking about when I called you a bitch?"

"Yes!"

"Why apologize for saying something I meant? Why, you looking like you about to cry?"

"I am! You don't respect me. You don't love me. You just love yourself and that stupid gang."

"Hold up now, the turf didn't do anything to you. No need to disrespect the turf. We should get married if you love me."

"You're in jail, how are we suppose to do that?" as he continued to talk she slowly realized her mother was right, he was out only for himself.

"Do you love me?"

"No, I care for you. If we get married I could grow to love you."

"I'm not going to marry you K-Stone."

"What role do you plan on playing in my life Vivica?"

"I'll write you."

"I can't eat your letters when I get hungry at night or cash your love in at the canteen it's time to step up."

"You want money?"

"I want you to realize I want you in my life."

"You do?"

"Yeah, as my wife, so I can hold you and kiss you like we use to do at the Sea Breeze Hotel. They have contact visits in prison."

"We can hold and kiss in the visiting room when I come to see you."

"We can't have sex in the visiting room."

"Oh you want sex?"

"Of course I want some pussy. I'm not a eunuch."

"I'm not suggesting you are."

"Obviously we're going in circles. If you loved me like you say you do, you wouldn't be putting me through this unnecessary stress."

"K-Stone you're an asshole."

"Am I?"

"My mother was right you're trash," that comment raised K-Stone's eye brow.

"Trash, I'm trash now?"

"You've always been I'm just realizing it now."

Before losing control, K-Stone caught his composure realizing he was bickering like a broad. He immediately hung the phone up and walked away leaving Vivica slouched down with her head in her lap crying. K-Stone left the visiting room highly annoyed, realizing he over played his hand, he could have lied. The only thing preventing him was his refusal to submit in any fashion. Ten months of incarceration had taught him that losses were a certainty in jail. Most lose their pride, respect, dignity, and courage, while others lose their family members, females, and homies. The majority lose their minds and themselves in the process. The most important thing he didn't want to lose was his consciousness to recognize when he was not being himself, besides he had a few more cards to play.

"Well Chicago, I got three more weeks until my big day at court," K-Stone said lazily smoking on a cigarette.

"By the time you go back to court I'll be a week to the house."

"What's the first thing you are going do when you get out?"

"First, I'm going to get fitted in some real nice threads. Then I'm going to go by my broad's house to pick up my two-hundred thousand dollars."

"Oh, it's two-hundred thousand now?" Butch said awakening out of his sleep.

"Weren't you asleep?"

"I thought you had a hundred thousand waiting on you?"

"Excuse you sir, like I was saying before the interruption, I had a hundred thousand when I left. But you see youngsta; it's been over six months so it's only obvious that my broad has flipped my money."

"Right, right," K-Stone responded.

"Once all the essentials are squared away I'll probably take a vacation to Brazil, Paris, or the Cayman Islands. Somewhere real nice so I can soak my toes while getting fed the finest caviar by some of my finest broads. Just the thought got me craving some fresh lobster."

"Negro please, negro please. The only eggs you going to be eating are the ones that come from a chicken," Butch said cutting in. "Brazil, Paris! Negro the closest you getting to an island is one in the middle of an intersection. Furthermore, the closet you'll get to something exotic is a catfish meal."

"This is not a warning, there is a hater amongst us," Chicago said imitating an alarm.

"Hater!" Butch said putting on his pants. "You the hater, sitting down there filling that youngstas head with all them lies."

"Lies? Truth is all I tell. It's all I know. Been a hustla since eighty foe, better watch out before I step on your big toe. It's only obvious fool you don't know. Now step aside zero, as I sprinkle this youngsta with this game that will make his mack hand strong. Back to what I was saying, Chicago's getting older now youngsta. This right here is my third strike. So it's a must that I take it easy. You understand youngsta?" K-Stone shook his head.

"That's why I can't pay no mind to what a fool has to say. My only weakness is the heroin, but no need to worry, that's under complete control. Next time you see me, I might be in Ebony magazine in the exotic vacations section. One place you won't see me again is in a jail cell. I have no more to give them. Enough about me, how did your visit go the other day?"

"Had to fire her. She wasn't trying to comply with the script."

"You did the appropriate thing youngsta. Can't allow your emotions to dictate your choices in life especially when dealing with a broad. Got to keep it short and to the point with the broads. Either they pick and choose or stay confused."

"Chicago you got a cold mouth piece."

"Truth youngsta, that's all it is.

Chapter 3

Wayside Blues

Wayside was always better than the county; Bone-Tone thought to himself while sitting in the dayroom; more room to move around, better food, and less fighting. All the stress he was under lately made it fell like he had a huge mole inside his stomach digging around. Ulcers ran in his family and he knew he had one. Last thing he needed was the extra stress of gang-banging. In fact, he really didn't trip too much off where somebody was from if their money was right. Right now his life was on the line with a lot more to lose than his other homies. He had a house that was paid for, five luxury vehicles, and kids. At least his wife was staying solid, but he didn't know how long that would last if he got life. Maybe until the money ran out, he thought to himself. If he wasn't already on parole he would have bailed out and went on the run. He slightly resented K-Stone, Uzi, and homies of their nature. For him, money came first, everything else second. For them, it was the opposite. They made it hard on homies like him who wanted to ball, constantly keeping the turf hot. That made it hard for him to make a decent profit at his spot, while the police constantly circled all the hot spots. With that type of thinking, Bone-Tone felt it was their fault he was in jail looking at life. The only reason he robbed and shot his supplier was because K-Stone and Uzi were going to rob him if he didn't set them up with a come-up. So he was forced to do it to keep from being killed or killing one of them. When the police first apprehended him, he was tempted to tell on some old murders to get off. Being that the case was weak and he had a paid attorney, he decided not to take that route. He had deep regrets about that decision. He just couldn't understand how the jury found him guilty on one damn charge. Looking around, he knew he couldn't live like this for long. He refused to.

* * * * * * * * * *

"Tasha, hook us up something to eat," X-Ray said sitting on his bunk.

"Okay, as soon as I get through washing your clothes," Taco responded in a feminine voice. "What ya'll want to eat?"

"Some chips, a couple of soups, you know the regular."

"What the hell!" K-Stone said barely holding in his laughter out of complete shock at the sight of Taco in some Daisy Dukes cut out of county blues, with the remainder of the outfit used as a halter top.

"Is that lipstick on his lips, and eye lids?"

"No silly it's cherry Kool-Aid." His new formed voice sent shivers up K-Stone's spine.

"Now that's some ill shit."

"You want to come in?" X-Ray asked.

"I'm cool out here on the tier. What happened to cuzz?"

"Oh Tasha, she just came to realize her true essence. We're about to eat in five minutes, want to stay and eat?"

"I'll have to pass on that offer." Lighting a cigarette K-Stone leaned against the wall on the tier. "Where did M-Rat go?"

"They moved him to the four-thousand floor this morning. He was going to holla at you before he left but they were rushing him out."

"Where were you coming from?"

"From the medical line. I needed to get out the cell for a minute you know how it gets."

"Here you go," Taco said passing X-Ray a bowl of food.

Smack! "Don't you see I'm talking to the homie?" Taco fell to the floor apologizing while picking the food up. K-Stone took a deep pull on his cigarette shaking his head.

"Got to keep the bitches in their place K-Stone, you know?"

"Yeah, I know." Actually he didn't know; he never hit a female he was involved with opting to only put his down verbally. He saw hitting a female as a weakness, even though many of his homies would beat their female, thinking it was cool.

One thing K-Stone did realize about relationships with the opposite sex was that a hoe was going to be a hoe. A female is going to do what she's going to do no matter what her male counterpart does to change her. Through kindness or violence, nothing can change a female behavior but her and vice-versa. A lot of females had tried to change him through the years. Most of it was met with laughter; the thought of him not "Crippin," that's a thought he could never conceive. Imagine him telling a rat to stop ratting, when that's all she knew and believed to be right.

"K-Stone, I'll be going to the pen in another day or two. I got found guilty a month ago. Don't look surprised everybody knew I was going to get washed. When I leave you can have Tasha." Is this nigga serious, K-Stone thought as X-Ray spoke? "I was going to leave her with Flat but he be falling in love."

"Cuzz you know I don't get down like that."

"Come on, you know I know that, but in case you get an itch."

"Cuzz I'm good on Ransom Gangstas."

"Well I'll slide her to Flat, he'll be content."

* * * * * * * * * *

"Bring him in here," Bazooka said to Do-Dirty as he dragged an unconscious body into the cell. "Tie him to the bars." Bazooka said looking for the magic shave in his bag. "Looks like you've been growing your hair a long time, Blood," Bazooka said while rubbing the Magic Shave through out his hair. "Let it marinate in there until it starts to sting, while I get the razors ready."

"For your sake you better kill me!"

"Wishes can be granted, Blood. You on K4CB tier now. It's time to do some tattoo checking," Bazooka said carrying some fresh razor blades. "Strip him down to the boxers. Hmmm what do we have here, K4CB187UM," Bazooka said reading the tattoo on the hostage's forearm. "Got us a real life hard-core Ransom Crip. Cosmetic surgery time, hand me my tools Blood. I'm going to start on your back first. Let me know if it hurts."

Bazooka slowly took the razor across the back of the hostage, slowly slicing the outer sides of the tattoo. This sent excruciating pain down the spine of the hostage, causing him to flop like a stringed up fish. Unable to scream with the wet sock stuffed in his mouth, he let out deep breaths through his nose. Once Bazooka finished slicing around the pattern of the tattoo, he slowly peeled the thin hanging skin off like a fruit roll-up, starting slowly then ripping the remaining skin off fast.

"How about a pat on the back?" Slapping him on his raw back, he told Do-Dirty to turn him back around, as he stretched.

In the dark cell, the hours passed fast, with the hostage slipping in and out of consciousness.

"We got another two hours Bazooka, before the officer walks."

"I'm almost finished. Just give him time to wake up."

As the hostage woke, Bazooka started on his forearm, cutting as deep as possible removing the K4CB187UM. Grabbing the hostage tightly around his jaw, Bazooka whispered into his ear with his breath reeking of pruno and cigarette smoke.

"I could kill you, but I won't. Dead men can't spread legends, Mr. Money Rat, is that your name?" M-Rat was too weary to respond.

"Untie him, Do-Dirty, so we can wrap him up." After wrapping him in a green blanket and placing his fallen out hair in his mouth, they put him at the end of the tier, while their homies distracted the officers.

"Place all mail going out on the bar," the officer said while doing his last count.

When he arrived at the end of the tier, he noticed a body lying wrapped up against the wall and radioed it in.

"We have a man down on the four thousand floor, Denver row!" He screamed into his walkie talkie.

As the medical unit placed M-Rat on the stretcher, the silhouette of his arm dangling with dripping blood could be seen on the wall. The image gave Bazooka a sense of completion; causing mayhem was his number one skill.

"I think I found my calling, Blood. My new name is Dr. Bazooka. Let me hit that smoke." Do-Dirty passed him the cigarette. "Yeah, Blood I'm sure going to miss the streets, hanging in the set, tossing hood-rats, and getting blowed. Come to think about it, I can do all that in prison, minus the hood-rats. Well, looks like we're going to be good friends from here on out," Bazooka said looking at his palm desperately.

Preparing for the shower, K-Stone began to examine his body. Being in jail with grown men and guys his age that had been in Y.A. all their lives, made him fully aware of his skinny stature. In the county you had to be at your best or you could fall victim to a beat-down or worse. Even when inmates were at their best they still got touched. His first month in, K-Stone started doing push-ups and various workouts to build his strength. Usually he had his knife, but due to the metal detectors, and constant strip downs it made it difficult to take it back and fourth to court. He relied heavily on his hand skills; they could make you or break you in this cold perdition.

Shower time was the most vulnerable time; one had to wear shower shoes down the tier. Like wilder beast, inmates would herd to the showers, body against warm body to make it first to the showers. The aroma of fifty different body odors incased by closed doors bombarded ones nostrils.

"It's about time they gave us a shower," Butch said wrapping his towel up. "It's been damn near two weeks since I've taken a proper bath. I'm too big to be constantly taking wash ups in the sink." K-Stone shook his head in agreement. Making their way to the shower K-Stone saw Flat and Taco walking hand in hand to the shower.

"K-Stone hold up!" Flat yelled from down the tier.

K-Stone kept walking, pretending not to hear him calling. When they reached the shower stalls, Flat tried to speak to K-Stone.

"You didn't hear me calling you?"

"Nope, I was concentrating on getting a spot in the shower."

After the shower, K-Stone went back to his cell, drying off so he could relax.

"I know you heard your homie calling you," Butch said putting on his deodorant.

"Sure did, I wasn't trying to holla at him while he had that He-she with him."

"When I first got here Taco was a hard-core gang banger. He use to walk around with his pants hanging down, every other word was Blood and every word that begin with the letter C, or sounded like it, he put a letter B on it. To see him now is unbelievable. I have two sons about your age. I did my best to keep them away from gangs and I succeeded. Both of my sons are in college on athletic scholarships. They're two well-rounded individuals. Eventually K-Stone, you're going to have to stop gang-banging. I've seen many of your homeboys since I've been down. What I see in them I don't see in you. Potential, is what I see in you, to do something else with your life. However your case turns out you have ample time to make a change, K-Stone."

"Change and do what?"

"Anything you put your mind to youngsta."

"At this point in time my mind is on Crippin'. This is what I feel comfortable doing at this point in my life. I feel you but I'm not ready to lay my blue rag down. Crippin' runs too deep for me to just stop."

"Change doesn't come over night that I understand. I'm just suggesting that in the future you think about change."

"For you, I can do that."

"No. Do it for yourself."

"By the way what are you in jail for?"

"For assaulting a youngsta who vandalized my property three times. When I caught him the last time I lost my cool, physically disciplining him, which I had no right to do. In the end the youngsta ended up calling the police on me."

"Naw, you bullshiting?"

"Serious, I took a year county lid. Since it was my first offense in forty-seven years, the judge went easy on me."

"Why didn't they give you probation?"

"Because I refused to apologize to the victim."

"They wanted you to apologize?

"Yes, can you believe that?"

"I feel you Butch," K-Stone said giving Butch dap. "If it had been me he would have been laying in a coffin."

"I have never used a gun; I could never bring myself to take a life, especially a young Black life. What's a life? Do you value life K-Stone?"

"Mine and my families lives."

"Are you sure?"

"Sure about what?"

"Sure you value your life? Because from the way I see it you willing to die for a street you don't even own."

"Heard that line before, is there a special quote book non-affiliates get? What's the difference from what I do and what the Blacks did for America in the Civil War? They fought for something that they weren't accepted in. So what's the big deal if I'm doing what I believe in? It's been about the red and blue since the Medieval Times. America is one of the hardest gangs in the world their gang flag is red, white, and blue and they represent to the fullest. I'm just doing what I'm allowed to do. The world is built on versus and opposites, sun and moon, night and day, land and sea, dark and light, old and young, men and women, Christians vs. Muslims vs. Jews, rich vs. poor, Bloods vs. Crips, Whites vs. Blacks, police vs. criminals, good vs. evil, and Republicans vs. Democrats. Life runs on gangs and who's against who. I'm just following the examples laid down by the world and history. You think I don't know the shit I do is wrong? I know it's not cool, but I play a small part in the scheme of things that go on in the world."

"But you do play a part. Those are some interesting concepts and facts youngsta, you got me really wondering, why you gang-bang?"

"Look Butch where going to have to finish this conversation later. I'm about to lay it out."

One thing K-stone noticed was the days and nights were never the same in how they played out. Some went by fast while others passed slowly. It had seemed like he just put his head to the pillow now it was noon into another day. It had just dawned on him that he had to go talk to Flat today. Wanting to get that part of his day out the way he prepared to get his cell racked to go down the tier.

"Flat, is it safe to come down there?"

"What do you mean is it safe?"

"You might have been busy with your He-she."

"Ha, ha. You stay with some jokes don't you? How did you get out of your cell anyway?"

"Why? You the police now?"

"Feeling good today aren't you? So, you go to court next week?"

"Yeah, me and Bone-Tone."

"You think their going to wash the homie?"

"To keep it real, yeah."

"Those judges in CCB not playing, I wouldn't put my life in the hands of people I don't know, let alone twelve. Paid attorney or not, especially if I know I did it. Humans' natural response to crime is to sympathize with the victim. Humans are bread that way; you think movies and television are just for entertainment? Movies implant the seed that heroes are to be cheered and the bad guys are to be hated without thought. Think about when you were a kid watching a cop movie, who were you cheering for?"

"The cop."

"Now you see my point about the good guys. When I used to watch America's Most Wanted I wanted the criminal to get caught and I'm a criminal. Knowing that, you'd think I would put my life in the hands of people who probably don't even think for themselves."

"I never looked at it like that cuzz. Wish you would have told me this before I took it twelve in a box."

"When the judge sentenced me it felt like my soul was ripped out of my body. Twenty-eight years old and my life is through. When the judge slammed his gavel, it mentally broke me. Look at me. I'm fucking a man and calling him Tasha. There's no turning back from this. I have no appeals issues. I'm stuck, fifty-five to life. I should be catching the chain right after you take your time. I struck M-Rat a kite but I haven't gotten a response yet."

"Ah still here," K-Stone said wiping the sleep from his eyes.

"K-Stone you up?" Butch whispered across the cell.

"Barely," K-Stone said in a discordant voice.

"I want to finish that conversation we were having yesterday."

"It's too early; we'll chop it up in the afternoon."

"That'll work youngsta."

*   *   *   *   *   *   *   *   *   *

Panoramas of his life flashed before his eyes, as each day drew him nearer to the decision that would dictate how he would live out the remainder of his life. Bone-Tone lay in his bed unable to sleep from the stress he had been under, not even sleeping pills worked. All that kept replaying in his mind was what to do, but in the end, he knew there was no way out. All he could do at this point was appeal whatever sentence the judge handed down.

"Nigga, you better stop stressing up on that bunk, looking all sad and shit," M-Dogg said while making something to eat.

"Let me get some chips out your bag."

"Go ahead cuzz."

"You up there crying?"

"What you say to me?" Bone-Tone responded.

"Nobody cares you facing life, you better man up. Around here, moping, that's not going to solve your problem. Next time you get snappy with me, I'll give your face a legitimate reason to be twisted up," M-Dogg said cracking his knuckles.

Bone-Tone did what he always did when confronted by an aggressive homie; he bowed down.

"Your right M-Dogg, I've been letting the time control me." Vultures like M-Dogg are one of the reasons he dreaded going to prison, Bone-Tone thought to himself as he hopped off his bunk to brush his teeth.

On the streets he could avoid them as he drove by in his Escalade. Hidden behind his tinted windows, he would laugh at their envious gazes. Envy combined with hate is what he felt for them. He wished he had the heart like them, to step up to the tasks required to gain stripes and respect that came with it, real respect. The only respect he received was for his money and cars. Too much patience caused him to become a coward throughout the years. With the money came weakness, the more money he gained, the less he was willing to do things that would jeopardize his new lifestyle he'd grown accustomed to.

Prison is a closed community. It's filled with society's failures who feed on "his kind." "His kind," being those who succeeded in life. He would be hated for just having glanced at the mysterious joy of life from which the glorious nectar flowed. For a sip, men have killed, robbed, denied their families, and communities to prosper to gain a small taste. For just being laced with the game to get rich made, others envious. He often wondered what they were missing; what stopped them from having it? It was as if they blamed him and those of "his kind" for their failures. They were always wanting, expecting, and demanding a hand-out, he didn't have, for another grown man.

"Hurry up over there. How long you going to brush your teeth?" M-Dogg said Damn, he's getting on my nerves, Bone-Tone said to himself. It was definite that he had to find a way to get out of the dorm with him. Everyday he was asking for something.

"I'm almost finished. What did you want?"

"I wanted to slap some bones."

"Set them up, I'll be in the dayroom in ten minutes."
"What's going on Butch?" K-Stone said lighting a cigarette up.
"You said you wanted to holla this morning?"

"Yes, I was thinking about our conversation and wanted to know how you felt about your dead friends? That's if it's not a touchy issue with you."

"It's not a touchy issue for me. I was raised around death. So what exactly do you want to know?"

"How you feel inside when it happens?"

"The same way I feel when I watch T.V. and see someone who has died who lives on the other side of the world."

"And how is that?"

"I feel nothing, I knew death was a part of the contract when I signed up; cut my emotions off a long time ago. I couldn't shed a tear if I wanted to. All I can do when one of my homies gets picked off, is go put in work; that's how I mourn. The tears I shed are lead. The frustration I feel from knowing I'll never see my homies again screams out the mouth of my pistol. You can find my emotions inside the shell casings at the scene of a crime."

"So when one of your family members die how do you react?"

"The same way minus the gun play."

"Are you listening to what you are saying?"

"Yes, what's wrong with it?"

"It just seems so cold hearted."

"Cold hearted. What's so cold about it?"

"You seem to kill with no regard for human life. K-Stone, you seem heartless."

"I have a heart, what I'm telling you is my reality. I live in a war zone. I'm just adapting to my environment. What else do you expect me to do? Instead of sheep, I counted gun shots at night. Every night is New Years Eve in my neighborhood. Honestly, you expect me to be emotionally stable? Instead of manicured lawns on the block, I stayed down the street from a crack house. Instead of soccer moms, I saw my homie's moms selling their bodies on Figueroa. Sex was introduced to me by "strawberries" asking me if they could suck my dick in the alley for my lunch money before school. I've lived like this without shedding a single tear or complaint. How could I? This is life in the ghetto."

"Sorry to hear all that K-Stone."

"Don't be sorry, unless you had a hand in my community's destruction. I don't need pity or pats on the back. None of that will bring my natural human emotions back. Besides, I don't want them back. I have no need for them. Not having them makes me a better gang banger. Having no emotions, I don't think twice about committing violence or putting my gangsta hand down in any situation. You think the judge had feelings when he sentenced you?"

"That's a different situation."

"What's the difference? He knew that you were protecting your property and if he didn't know all he had to do was look into your file. But he didn't, because he didn't care about your life. All he saw was another nigga sitting in his courtroom. And you call me heartless. He sentenced you to a year in a place where you could be killed, a hard working, and tax paying citizen."

"You kind of got a point there youngsta."

"I only state the facts as I see them. We live in a world that has an obvious corrupt and racist legal system which religiously practices rail-roading minorities. They're playing with peoples' lives daily, year-round, and you call me heartless?"

"K-Stone I didn't mean to offend you."

"I'm not offended. I just get worked up when I get to thinking about how powerless I am under these circumstances."

"We'll pick the conversation up later."

"All right, I need to wash anyway. I'm going to need another hair cut for tomorrow, Chicago."

"As soon as you get finished washing, I'll hook you up."

"That'll work."

"So you are getting ready for another visit? You sure got a stable of broads for a youngsta."

"Somebody got to do it."

"Kind of remind me of myself, youngsta. I'm ready when you are," said Chicago gathering his tools to trim-up K-Stone.

"As always you've done an impeccable job. Good looking out. How much for the damage?"

"It's on the house. So which one is coming to see you this weekend?

"My slim goodie, Ivie. Here, check the picture out."

"That's a nice one there, she kind of favor that actress broad. What's her name??? It's coming to me...Megan Good."

"Ivie!" K-Stone said to himself as he sat on his bunk.

It was crazy how they met. He was driving down Hoover on the way to the turf when a crash unit pulled him over. Across the street in the Jack-N-The-Box parking lot he could see her smiling at him. While the pestering cop was writing him a ticket for loud music, he was making noticeable eye contact with her. He even yelled across the street for her to hold up when the cop went into lecture mode. After the cop left, he swerved into the parking lot to finish hollering at her. Later on that week he called her up to come hang out with him. The only problem was that she stayed in the center of his enemy's turf. So he did what he always did when faced with a dilemma of that nature. He rented a low-key, smoker car for a couple of hours. He substituted his Glock 45 for his Mack-11Uzi just in case she tried to set him up. One warning he gave to every female he encountered, was if they ever tried to set him up, he would kill them first. Sometimes he would wish for them to try something so he could trip, but it never happened. There were no confrontations when he picked her up. They smoked on some "chronic" that night and had sweaty sex. He knew that night she was a "keeper." She didn't talk too much, she was cool to hang with, and she had good snatch.

With so many ballers in L.A., it was hard to run across a female with some decent, let alone, good snatch. It was the main reason he kept her around. Problems started to occur when she would whine about why he never took her out. She felt like he was using her for sex, which he was but he couldn't help it, she gave in so easily. What was the point in going out when he knew what it was going to lead to anyway. Might as well cut to the chase, he would say to himself. He gave in a couple of times to stop her nagging, but what she failed to realize, was it was a privilege to be in his presence. The majority of females he had sex with were just one night stands. Even though Ivie wasn't a "hood-rat," the rules still applied to her too. It was an unwritten rule not to lay up with "hood-rats" even though many did. He didn't indulge, he refused to fall victim to the "hood-rats" bag of tricks. Bitches had tactics and if you were a tender dick, you would become a victim quickly.

Being aware of these types of strategies gave him an extreme advantage. Every scam females used with their snatch he would use with his dick. When they withheld, he withheld. He observed their behavior, never getting caught up in the mind frame that he was a man and the female-can't-play-me trap. He had seen the hardest of his homies fall victim to "hood-rat" tactics. Next time he saw them at a function they would be wearing his and her outfits, with his homies openly knowing that their new interest had been tossed by multiple homies. A month or two passes by and he has her name on his chest or neck, talking about she's having his baby. He refused to ever go out like that; thinking about it gave him shivers. The main plan now was to convince Ivie to marry him. The thing that would make it difficult was that they were never an official couple, at least in his eyes. He figured he would play it by ear, read her body language, and then act on it from there. With those thoughts, he lit up a cigarette and hopped on the phone.

"Who is this?"

"K-Stone, little homie."

"What's up cuzz?"

"Same old shit, let me holla at Uzi."

"He's in the front right now, hold on," he said. "Give him five minutes he's talking to a pound-cake."

"Is that right?"

"Yeah it looks like one of your old females."

"I see you stay with the jokes. What's been going on in the turf?"

"Same shit when you were out here. Making money, killing K4's, tossing "hood-rats," you know the program cuzz. K-Stone you heard about M-Rat?"

"Nope, what was I suppose to hear?"

"That K-Fort Bazooka cut the homies tattoos off."

"Hell naw, I haven't heard that, you sure?"

"Uzi told me the other day he was in the infirmary. Anyways, here comes Uzi he'll tell you. Holla at you later, Crip."

"What it do cuzz?" Uzi yelled into the phone excited.

"You know how it is in here."

"That I do know you get those green-backs I shot you?"

"Yeah, that was good looking-out; that will hold me until I catch the chain and beyond."

"When you get to the pen, I'm going to shoot you some more loot and some flicks of the homies."

"That would be the business."

"Don't trip. It's a small thing to a giant. When you touch down I'm going to be all the way right. K-Stone you don't have to worry about nothing, and that's on Ransom."

"I can feel that."

"I hope so cuzz, I mean it; you know you my lok. We grew up together, I knew you before I turned the turf, feel me?"

"I feel you, but kill the sentimental crap."

"So you are going to be going back to court Monday to hear that deal? Make sure you hit me up and let me know what they served you with."

"Why didn't you tell me about M-Rat in the letter?"

"I had just found out after I sent it off. Besides, ain't anything you can do, I already checked on the K-Fort that did it and he caught the chain to Delano. We'll holla about that later though, I'm about to smash out so hit me later."

"Later then."

It was always good to holla at a homie, but at the same time it reminded him of what he was missing while being in jail.

"Damn!" K-Stone yelled, punching the wall.

Friday night and he was locked down unable to do anything but be mad and punch the walls of an old cell. His hands had become immune to punching the walls throughout the ten months of disappointments that had come regular. It was times like these that it would dawn on him that he was really locked down. He was still in denial with the reality of his situation. Since being incarcerated he hadn't seen a T.V. and the only time he heard music was when the officers would be cool and play it on the loud speaker. Besides that, he would hear some on the bus back and forth to court, but the majority of the time the bus driver would play everything but rap. It would have soothed his mind after a long day at court. The only music he listened to on the streets was hard-core-kill-your-momma, bury-you, dig-you-back-up-so-I-can-kill-you-again raps. He had to admit that some of the new music didn't sound too bad. Or, maybe ten months confined to a concrete box was taking effect. Either way, it was time for a drastic change of scenery. Putting out his cigarette

in the toilet he could hear it sizzle and thought to himself, that
that was exactly how his life felt at the moment, sizzling out
slowly.

It was five-thirty a.m. when Ivie woke up, getting ready to
go see K-Stone. "Damn I don't feel like standing in this long line
this morning," Ivie said to her sister while reaching for her car keys.

"Then why you doing it?"

"Because I love him so much."

"He doesn't love you, and if he tells you he does it's only
because he's in jail."

"You just don't like him that's all," Ivie said going out the
door.

Actually, Gina did like K-Stone until he started seeing Ivie
regularly. She always got stuck with the good looking-broke ones or
the balling-ugly ones, never the two combined. To see her younger
sister find the right one before her made her boil to the bone.
Especially when K-Stone would completely ignore her advances.
The few times K-Stone did come in the house to hang out, which
was rare, he would barely say two words to her. She wanted to ride
in his Tahoe as much as she wanted to ride his dick. She prepared a
plan to lure him from her sister. She could remember the day
clearly.

It was a hot summer day. She and a couple of her homegirls
had gone shopping at the Slauson Swap-meet for some new outfits.
She purchased some skin tight Apple Bottom pants to complement
her shapely lower body and a matching shirt to complement her big
breast. After leaving the Slauson Swap-meet, she walked to her
friend's house to take a shower and change into her new outfit,
proceeding to claim what was supposed to be hers in the first place.
Stepping off the bus car horns immediately started honking. She had
turned down three guys on the bus that were trying to get her
number. As she turned the corner where she knew K-Stone would
be hanging out, she quickly noticed his beige Tahoe sitting on
twenty-fours sparkling from the reflection of the sun.

"Slow down girl!" Gina told her home girl before they made
it half-way down the street. K-Stone's pound-cake alarm went off
as he focused his sights on the "two-pound" cakes walking down the
street. One looked strangely familiar he thought to himself, but they
were too far away to tell.

"Check it out G-Liz, we have two pound-cakes we might be
able to toss tonight."

"Which one you want K-Stone?"

"The short thick one on the right, you can get the tall one."

"Wait, I know who that is!" his excitement leaving immediately.

"Who is it?"

"Ivies hood-rat sister Gina. Wonder what the hell she doing over here."

"What's up K-Stone?"

"Where's your sister at?"

"Do I look like her shadow?"

"What you doing over here?"

"I came to see you baby," she said reaching to touch his chest. He quickly moved away, lighting a Camel he had in his ear.

"Seriously, what are you doing over here?"

"I am serious, why you acting like that?"

"You're a scandalous little hoe." She wasn't expecting this type of reaction. "From what it looks like you came over here to give me some of your nasty snatch."

By that time, G-Liz was laughing uncontrollably and saying, "You crazy cuzz!" repeatedly as her friend stood by looking embarrassed. This was the first time that a guy had ever clowned her and she didn't know how to react. She was speechless. K-Stone took slow pulls on his hump as he observed her curvaceous form. Gina was not bad looking; in fact, she was very attractive. He just despised her kind because she was only chasing the money.

"Look Gina I was just clowning with you let me holla at you in the truck." At the sound of that she quickly snapped back into her natural bold self.

"What about my home girl?"

"G-Liz will keep her company."

"You cool out here with him girl?"

"Yeah, she cool. You acting like I'm a rapist or something."

"I'm cool girl, go do your thing."

K-Stone purposely let Gina walk in front of him so he could admire the tightness of her Apple Bottom Jeans.

"Is there anymore room for me in those jeans?"

"Might be," Gina said stepping inside the truck.

As he inhaled the "chronic," he passed her the "Chocolate Philly Blunt." Inhaling the weed deeply, she started coughing uncontrollably. She wasn't use to smoking "chronic." The guys she usually messed with could barely afford a car, let alone enough "chronic" to fill a blunt. Once the "chronic" took effect, K-Stone was ready for some oral comfort.

"So what's up?" K-Stone said grabbing the remote control for his radio.

"What do you mean what's up?"

Unzipping his pants and not trying to hide his intentions he asked for a sample of "dome." Gina could plainly see the bulge in his boxers and the look in his frigid eyes that he wasn't asking, he was telling her, and she liked it.

"You think I'm going to just do..." Before she could finish her sentence he had palmed the back of her head pulling her down slowly but steadily towards his pulsating erection. She quickly wrapped her glossy juicy lips around the head of his penis, slowly bobbing up and down as he leaned back watching. He could tell she was a well experienced "head doctor." Euphoria over came him as he erupted in her mouth. After the oral episode was complete, he immediately unbuttoned her jeans pulling them to her knees. Turning her around, he could see she looked even better naked instantly getting him rocked up again. Placing the Magnum condom on, he slowly entered her from the back. He could feel her moist warm vagina lips slowly enwrapping his penis. This made him pound even harder as he placed her head in between the cushion of the seat like an ostrich. This scenario played out in his mind as he put his blunt out in the ashtray.

"K-Stone are you ready?"

"Ready for what?" he said turning in her direction to find her top off, breast exposed.

"I'll catch you later; I got something else to do."

"Something better than this?" she said cupping her breast.

"Put your clothes on and get out my truck."

"At least you can take me home."

"Get home the way you came."

"That's how you going to do me K-Stone?"

"How am I doing you?"

"You going to make me catch the bus home?"

"That's how you been getting around. Besides there are nice people on the bus you can meet."

"Not funny! You really not going to take me home?"

"Oh, you thought I was playing. Get yourself together and step out the vehicle. I got business to handle and you are making me late with this nonsense." Seeing that she wasn't going to take "no" for an answer, he quickly switched to plan B.

"Check it out Gina, wait here with G-Liz. I'll be back in twenty minutes to come get you." He said looking at his watch. "We'll go see a movie, then get a room."

"A movie and room?"

"Yeah, whatever you want to see, just chill here till I get back."

"You're not going to come back to get me."

"Yeah, I am," he said, barely holding back his laughter.

"Put that on Ransom, you're coming back to get me."

"The turf isn't a credit card; I said I was coming back." With that she stepped out the truck. K-Stone threw his truck in reverse to holla at G-Liz.

"Cuzz, I'm gone catch you in the morning."

"What about the pound-cakes?"

"Do what you do, toss them," K-Stone said smashing off.

Gina waited for hours but he never came back. She felt so humiliated; she spent all her money on her outfit and didn't have a way home. She begged G-Liz to take her home but he wouldn't, unless she gave him some. After degrading herself some more, he finally dropped her off at home. Now it was payback time, she would do whatever it took to make her sister leave him so he could suffer alone.

Chapter 4

More Drama

"Well Chicago it's time to go put this verbal to use."

"Don't hurt her youngsta."

K-Stone felt great as he strolled to the visiting room. Ivie was a cool female and he would be able to go out and chill today. He had seen her smiling as he approached the plastic window engraved with graffiti. He quickly sat down, picking up the phone.

"How you doing Ivie?"

"Much better now that you're here."

"You look tired."

"I am I've been standing in line since six o'clock."

"I appreciate you taking the time to do so."

"It's okay. You don't have to say all that. I wanted to come see you."

"There's a question I need to ask you."

"Go ahead."

"If I take five years Monday, will that be too much time for you to handle?"

"No, I can deal with that."

"The reason I asked is because I rather you leave now, then when I get to prison."

"I would never leave you K-Stone, I love you."

"Don't cry I just needed to know where you stood."

"Your letter came to the house the other day, it was nice."

"Glad you liked it, I meant every word."

"How are things going with your living conditions?"

"They're much better now. Gina and I got a place together off of Vermont. It's a quiet area."

"That's cool, so how am I going to get in contact with you?"

"The calls from my mother's house are being forwarded to my new place."

"What do you think about getting married?"

"We could get married if you really want to."

"I wouldn't be asking if I wasn't serious."

"When do you want to get married?"

"As soon as I get to prison."

"Have you been staying out of trouble lately?"

"Of course, I always stay out of trouble, you know me."

"That's why I asked."

"I've been behaving myself lately."

"Well that's good to know, because there's going to come a time when you're going to have to stop gang-banging."

"Where did that come from?"

"It's the truth Kay, I won't be coming to see you if you come back to jail again."

"That's understandable, I'll be more careful next time."

"More careful? You're going to have to stop completely eventually. Kay you're going to have to grow up!"

"Grow up! That sounds like your punk sister talking, not you! I've been grown since the womb."

"You're taking it the wrong way. I just mean you need to make an honest living." "What's dishonest about what I do?" You don't even know what I do."

"I know enough to know it's not honest. Honesty doesn't put people in jail."

"Relax little lady I feel you. With your support I'll be able to make some changes in the future."

"That's all I wanted to hear Kay, that you'll make an attempt."

"One minute left!" the officer yelled down the aisle.

"I don't want to leave baby."

"I don't want you to leave either, but this is how it works."

"I love you K-Stone."

"I love you too." It was the first time he had told a female outside of his family that he loved them.

He felt his under arms become moist as the unfamiliar words left his mouth. It was an awkward feeling that had over-taken his insides, but he doubted its authenticity. Many thoughts traveled through his mind most of them good, but one in particular thought stood out. Was he serious when he said he loved her? If he had to think about it maybe he didn't mean it. Then again, since he was thinking about it maybe he did mean it. Mostly he said it out of necessity; working with the cards he was dealt. His situation was starting to look a little brighter as he inhaled slowly on a cigarette, leaning against the wall in his cell, enjoying the effects of the nicotine traveling through his blood stream. For a brief moment he had left his body drifting mentally away to the streets.

"Wake up!" Chicago said slapping his hands together a few inches away from K-Stone's face.

"Huh?" K-Stone said coming out of his trance."

"That visit must have been mighty nice. Look at him Butch. What that look like to you?"

"L.O.V.E.!" Butch replied putting an emphasis on each letter. "The youngsta has been sprinkled."

"Sprinkled with what?" K-Stone inquired.

"With love dust youngsta."

"Both of you are mistaken, this is a look of completion. I just laid my mack-hand down and right now I am just soaking in the essences of my triumph."

"How long you think I've been doing this youngsta?" Chicago said peering down on him.

"From the wrinkles on your bald head, too damn long."

"Joke if you want, but I can tell you harbor some feeling for the broad. There's nothing wrong with it, its normal behavior. Just don't let it cloud your judgment. Being in love while incarcerated can damage your mack-game severely. You want to keep your foot on her neck at all times. Make sure you keep that state boot directly centered in on her pressure point. As soon as you let up a little, the game will change on you so fast you won't know what hit you youngsta. Take heed, stay stomp-down it doesn't matter you're in jail. Stay stomp and she'll stay get sweet and watch her flee. Believe what I say I've been doing time my whole life, youngsta. If there was a degree I'd make a doctorate in this here player-game."

"What makes you think I haven't been staying stomp?"

"You have, I'm not refuting that. But the way you strolled in here twenty minutes ago, it looked like you were ready to sell all your worldly possessions, buy a ring, and tuck the rag in and start anew."

"Whatever, nothing going to stop my Crippin, I'm not selling nothing but a dope sack."

"That's right youngsta."

"In fact I'm about to call and check on my investment right now."

"Hello. Is Ivie there?"

"No nigga, she not here!" Gina said hanging up the phone.

"Who was that Gina?"

"Somebody making a prank call."

"How long you going to be on the phone?"

"Why?"

"K-Stone is going to call me."

"That loser got's nothing else to do, he can wait."

"Don't talk about my baby like that!"

"Your baby! That nigga don't love you!"

"Yes he does, he told me today." Hardly holding in her jealousy, Gina spit back, "The only reason he told you that is because he's in jail."

"That's not true Gina."

"Then ask him when he calls why is he just now telling you he loves you? You're his last resort that's why he's being so nice. You are the only silly female still hanging on after ten months. You really think he wants you?"

"Why do you say these things?"

"Because I don't want to see your life ruined by someone like him."

"But you don't even know him like that. Why all of a sudden do you hate him?"

"I've always felt he was a loser, I never mentioned it because I thought it wouldn't last long."

"Just mind your own business Gina."

"Okay, don't say I didn't warn you." Seeing the conversation slipping from her grasp, Gina quickly revamped the direction of the tension. "I know you love him, just make sure he really feels the same way. Will you do that for me?"

"Yes."

"Now give your big sister a big hug." While embracing each other, Gina could barely erase the sinister grin on her face. "We should go see a movie."

"Just you and me?"

"Me, you, and a couple of male friends of mine."

"I don't know about that Gina."

"What don't you know? You can't stay cooped up in the house like you are in jail too. You got to live; anyway it's just a friendly date, nothing serious. Unless K-Stone got your mind that far gone that he's controlling you from jail."

"I run my own program; I can go if I choose to."

"Could of fooled me, you still haven't said if he gave his okay." With that comment Ivie wanted to know what time she needed to be dressed. "We'll be leaving at eight-thirty tonight," as the phone started ringing, Gina quickly blurted out "that might be your controller right there."

"Hello. Calm down K-Stone it was an accident."

"It wasn't no damn accident. I heard you in the background when she hung the phone up. It's the only reason I called you back. You need to check your sister!" After reassuring him it wouldn't happen again he calmed down a bit.

"That's more like it; she's starting to get besides herself with that childishness."

"What do you mean, by that's more like it?' Surprised that Ivie questioned him, he scrambled to deliver a response.

"It's been past due that your sister needed a decent checking. Why you getting all emotional?"

"When you said that's more like it, it sounded like you were giving me an order."

"Why would you think that? I've never tried to control you."

"I know that, I just have a lot on my mind."

"That's understandable; what's been on your mind?"

"All kinds of stuff, it's hard to explain."

"Take your time I don't have anywhere to go."

"Don't get mad K-Stone. I need to ask you a question. When you said you loved me, did you mean it?"

"Of course I meant it, I wouldn't of said it if I didn't."

"The reason I asked is because you never told me on the streets."

"The reason I never told you on the streets was because I didn't know how to express these types of feelings."

"So how can you express yourself so well now?"

"Because I have a new perspective when it comes to our relationship. Any day can be my last day in here so I want you to know how I feel in case something should happen to me."

"It just seems that all we did on the streets when you were out was have sex."

Damn! Where was all this coming from, K-Stone thought to himself? Her punk-ass sister was behind this, he knew it. Realizing what was taking place he would have to launch a counter attack against her sister's plot.

"We went on dates, when I was out there."

"The only reason you took me places was because I kept asking you."

"But I took you when you asked so that's all that matters. How did you go from feeling good this morning, to dwelling on negative past events?"

"They're not negative, they're real events that took place in our relationship, and I need to remind myself of them."

"Look Ivie, we're moving forward with this relationship. What took place on the streets stays on the streets. I can't reach back in the past and change my behavior. It's frivolous to sit here bickering back and forth, shifting the blame when the only outcome will be negative. That will hurt both of us in the end. Unless you disagree with that decree, let's talk about something else."

"Your right Kay, if I didn't complain then I shouldn't make an issue now."

"So what you got planned for the night?"

"My sister and I are going to the movies."

"Just you two are going?"

"No. Me, her, and two of her male friends." An awkward silence fell between the two of them for a minute.

As K-Stone absorbed what she said, she waited on a response. "Kay, did you hear me?"

"Yeah, just be careful and enjoy yourself."

"Are you sure? I thought you were going to be mad."

"For what? I trust you. I realize you have to have fun too. You can't become a loner because I'm locked away. Why are you crying?"

"I just miss you so much that's all. I can't wait to touch you again baby."

"The feeling is mutual. We'll be together soon. Lunch just came, so I'll holla at you tomorrow."

"Okay, I love you Kay."

"I love you too," he said while shivers ran down his spine.

It still felt strange saying those words. K-Stone wasn't feeling the little double date Gina had concocted. The only reason he didn't disclose his true feelings was because it would have fed into Gina's plan that he was trying to control Ivie. Gina's games could be seen through, like cellophane. Although covert to Ivie, they were clear and elementary in his eyes. He knew his calm response would deflate Gina's controlling strategy. Now all he had to do was figure out what schemes she would use next. "Tomorrow's your last day in this cement cave, Chicago."

"Yeah, I'll send you a postcard from my island vacation, youngsta."

"That'll work; just make sure you include one of those pound-cake hook-ups you going to be surrounded by."

"That can be arranged youngsta. Something sure smells mighty right over there."

"Just hooking up a going home spread for you."

"What do the ingredients consist of?"

"Cheetos, beans, rice, tuna, and some Ramen."

"Sounds like the closest were going to get to a gourmet meal."

"Are you going to share some of that extra cash your broads made for you out there?"

"Hell no! I don't give a broad nothing. I wouldn't give a broad a tear to cry and that's no lie. The only thing I'm going to give her is permission to make more money. This is delicious you have a cool cooking hand on you youngsta. I hope everything goes all right for you on Monday."

"Don't trip, I'll be cool. All that matters is it's going to be over."

"You'll like the pen a whole lot better than this dump. You can spend one-hundred and eighty at the canteen, plus you get your own T.V., radio, and tapes. They have food sales, two men cells, and you get night yard. Your time will really start to fly once you hit the pen. Compared to this it is the Hilton; a lot more room to move around.

"I can't wait to get there!" K-Stone said, gulping his Kool-Aide down in one swallow. "All that food and thinking got me tired," K-Stone said lazily lying on his bunk, smoking a cigarette, which had become a ritual after every meal.

He was thinking about what Chicago had told him about the pen. His time so far was moving all right, but he was ready for it to zoom by. He was feeling a two man cell, his own T.V., and radio to control as he pleased. Just the thought of controlling something made him feel partly human again. At this point, he wasn't controlling anything, not even his own mouth. To a certain degree he had to dilute much of what he had to say to everybody. Just ten months ago he was giving orders to dope fiends sending them on errands at his leisure. Now he was like the dope fiend. Taking baths out of the sink, going to his cell on command, and receiving strip downs. Taking orders like open your mouth, and bend-over-and-cough on a regular basis. It seemed like only yesterday he was laying in his king size bed flipping channels on his Sony with a proper naked pound cake at his side. Now he was lying on a thin plastic matt, fluffing a stiff pillow, filled with miscellaneous garments watching the Waltins. All that really mattered was how many years he would have to endure this punishment he had put on himself, and would he be doing it alone or with a companion? Either way it went, in the end, he would have to do the time.

* * * * * * * * * *

"Three bitches in the back with Ransom hats on!" M-Dogg said, slamming the domino down on the table.

He and Bone-Tone had been playing all morning, killing the remaining hours of the day. The last couple of weeks had been strenuous. As usual, M-Dogg was working his last nerve with constant mood swings and demands for food. Bone-Tone had been waiting patiently for his doctor's slip to process so he could go to the medical dorm.

"You better not be working me on that score, cuzz," M-Dogg said slamming another domino on the table.

"That's game!" Bone-Tone said winning the game with a fifteen point play. "That's three in a row."

"You trying to clown cuzz?" M-Dogg said shaking the dominos on the table for a new game.

"Clowning you on these bones."

"Is that right? How bout I clown with your canteen bag?" Bone-Tone was ready to respond when an officer called his name to pack his property.

Bone-Tone made his way up the stairs relieved and not trying to conceal it. M-Dogg, realizing Bone-Tone was leaving, ran up the stairs behind him.

"So you are going to the medical dorm? There's nothing wrong with you unless stressing and acting like a bitch is an illness now. You were just going to creep out of here without telling me?"

"Nigga, I don't have to tell you nothing."

"Oh, you're a tough guy now?" M-Dogg said bawling up his fist pressing up against his side.

Noticing M-Dogg's demeanor, Bone-Tone knew he was going to have to fight him today.

"Leave your canteen bag here when you leave. You go to the canteen every week you won't miss it." Bone-Tone bawled up his fist tightly as he peered up from his slouched position.

"As a matter of fact..." before M-Dogg could finish his sentence, Bone-Tone landed five quick blows to his already distorted face, splitting his lip in the process.

Quickly side stepping, M-Dogg avoided the rest of the surprise attack. Regaining his balance, he landed two blows to the side of Bone-Tone's head causing him to stumble backwards into the double bunks. Bouncing off the impact, Bone-Tone rushed M-Dogg with a barrage of punches which M-Dogg barely avoided as he backed up aiming for Bone-Tone's chin. Once he found his opening, he fired off two quick solid blows that found their target, dropping Bone-Tone instantly in mid flight. Seeing that Bone-Tone was dazed, he quickly moved in, grabbed him by his shirt collar, pulled him off the ground, and placed him on the bottom bunk. Turning his back to Bone-Tone, he walked towards the bathroom to tend to his bleeding lip.

Gaining full consciousness, Bone-Tone stood to his feet as M-Dogg approached him holding a bloody piece of tissue on his lip. Bawling up his fist stiffly, Bone-Tone was ready to attack. Instead of approaching in an aggressive manner, M-Dogg extended his arms towards Bone-Tones hand. Bone-Tone looked at him ready to attack, but didn't being he was confused by M-Dogg's actions.

"You are going to leave me hanging?" The question and gesture completely threw Bone-Tone out of his attack mode. He gave him dap not knowing what else to do. "I can respect that cuzz," M-Dogg said, gathering the rest of Bone-Tone's property for him.

As they walked down the stairs M-Dogg returned back to the table and Bone-Tone went out of the dorm to the eight-hundredth floor. Bone-Tone thought to himself as he left, if that was all he had to do to get him to leave him alone, he would have been punched him in the mouth. All this time that's all he wanted was a punch in the mouth.

When Bone-Tone got to his new dorm, he went straight to sleep. It was a huge relief to get away from the added stress of M-Dogg. Even though there was a high ratio of weirdoes in his new dorm, it beat being in a dorm with a vulture.

The next morning while he was getting his toothbrush out of his property someone called his name.

"Over here Bone-Tone!" the sickly voice said.

Following the voice he found M-Rat lying in the bed.

"What happened to your hair?"

"Some K4's caught me slipping in the county and tortured me."

Bone-Tone looked at him in disbelief until he removed the covers to reveal his mutilated back and forearm. At the sight of his mutilated homie, he forgot about all his problems.

"How are you holding up?"

"Not too well, the extended exposure to that filthy cell on my open wounds gave me an infection. The infection is eating away at my skin. The doctor said I might die if it continues to spread."

"Why did they move you to Way Side?"

"The deputy said they received a kite that they were going to finish me off."

"You think you going to pull through?"

"I have no choice somebody has to pay for this. It's the only thing that fuels me everyday. When I get to the pen every K-Fort I run into, I'm going to stab young to old. Enough about that, it's starting to get me heated. So you and Killa Stone going to court in the morning?"

"Yeah, it's the reckoning day."

"You'll come out all right."

"I hope so, believe me, I hope so."

"I need to get some rest; I'll holla at you later tonight," M-Rat said pulling the blanket over his head.

"It was a pleasure doing time with you youngsta. To the haters, you know who you are. Stop hating," Chicago said, looking at Butch from the opposite side of the cell. Extending his hand through the bars Butch shook his hand. Walking down the tier Chicago yelled back to Butch to look him up when he got out, he'd give him a job.

"Sure you will. That guy is crazy. The only island he's going to be on is the one selling roses in the middle of the street."

"Why you talking about my old school partner like that?"

"I didn't mean it in a mean way. Chicago is an all right brother. He just needs to get himself together and start living in reality. Butch we'll have to holla later. I have to get on the phone."

"Did you enjoy your hot date last night movie girl?"

"It wasn't even like that."

"I'm just messing with you. Did you have a good time?"

"It was all right, nothing special. We got back around midnight."

"Who are you talking to?" A male voice said in the background.

"Get out of my room!"

"Who was that?"

"Nobody, Gina had her boyfriend and his friend stay the night after the movies."

"Is that right? I wonder where Gina's boyfriend's homie slept last night."

"What's that supposed to mean?"

"Exactly, what it sounded like."

"He slept on the couch."

"Then why is he asking who you're on the phone with?"

"Your guess is as good as mine. I told him last night I had a man."

"Obviously he didn't spend the night over at a female's house without hitting or getting some type of satisfaction. Unless he's just a real sucka."

"Everybody doesn't think like you K-Stone. That's one of your problems you think everybody thinks and acts like you."

"My mistake, the perfect gentleman who took you out last night would never try such a thing. He may have busted into your room a minute ago asking you, a female that told him that she was already taken, who she was talking to on the phone. But it would go against his moral code to try to make a pass at you last night while his homeboy was pounding on your hood rat sister in the next room."

"Don't disrespect my sister, Kay."

"What? You know as well as I know that your sister is a hood rat." Ivie paused for a minute thinking of a response. She knew in her heart that her sister was a hoe it just hurt to admit it.

"Just don't say those things about my sister." As Ivie continued to talk she didn't notice the silhouette of her sister's feet at the foot of the door listening to every word. Gina sat stewing by the doorway over the comments K-Stone was making about her. She was going to really vilify him once her sister got off the phone. Hood rat she repeated to herself. How was a loser going to call her a hood rat? At least her plan worked last night. She had convinced her sister to get lose and have fun.

After the movies they all came back to the apartment and smoked some weed, drunk some E & J, and popped some E pills, while R. Kelly was playing on the stereo. Ivie didn't do drugs regularly, so when she took them she was kind of out of it. As the night went on, Ron, Gina's boyfriend's homie couldn't keep his hands to himself. He tried all night to sneak a feel in, until she screamed for him to stop. She had promised herself that she wouldn't cheat on K-Stone because he was in jail. But Ron was offering to perform a pleasure that she so desperately desired and longed for. A delightful pleasure K-Stone refused to do. Even though Ivie did him with no hesitation, he would never lick her between her thighs. Since meeting K-Stone, she learned that he lived by a set of silly rules. One of those rules that he made absolutely clear when it came to sex was he didn't do oral, but he loved to receive it and she didn't mind. The sex more than made up for the lack of oral. She could hardly resist the proposition that Ron made to her last night. All he wanted to do was eat it; no penetration.

A couple more sips of E & J and she gave in. Being she had a skirt on she easily slid her g-string panties off, placing the damp garment on the arm of the couch. While slowly positioning her body against the back of the couch, she opened her legs placing her feet at the edge of the couch. Ron then quickly dropped to his knees to perform his specialty. The orgasm quickly sobered her up, making her feel guilty in the process. Realizing what she had just done, she took off running inside the bathroom to clean herself leaving greasy mouth Ron still sitting on his knees wondering what went wrong.

Early that morning she told Ron that last night was a mistake. It was the drugs and alcohol that made her give in. He didn't seem to understand she didn't want to be with him. That's the reason he pulled the phone stunt that morning. K-Stone would leave her if he found out. Her conscience was telling her that he already knew. K-Stone was far from naïve. Hearing Gina's company leave, she took deep breath of relief.

"Sounds like the release of stress."

"I'm not stressing."

"Believe me; I know your new boyfriend helped relieve that last night."

"K-Stone, that's not funny."

"Who said I was being funny?"

"Seriously I don't need this today Kay. Call me back later."

"I'll holla when I get back from court tomorrow."

Hearing Ivie's door unlock, Gina placed her third installment of her plan to work. "Had fun last night sis?"

"So, so," Ivie gestured with her hand.

"Why you say so, so?"

"Because I felt like I was cheating."

"You have a lot to learn, girl. He wasn't concerned about cheating when he was out free chasing all those other females while you were at work."

"How do you know he was cheating?"

"Will you wake up out of dreamland, girl? Everybody knows K-Stone was sexing females from Westchester to Watts, but you. A couple of my home girls even slept with him."

"Stop lying Gina!"

"I would tell you to ask him yourself, but what's the point, he'll just deny the whole thing and you like his little puppy will believe him. I bet he's still telling you he loves you? How can he love you and disrespect your sister? Huh? Can't answer that, I can because he don't really love you. That's why he makes you set an appointment before coming to see him. So you won't bump heads with his other females."

"Worry about your own man Gina."

"Don't get mad at me, I'm just trying to help you out with the problem you have."

Ivie wondered if what her sister was saying was true. She felt so guilty about what happened last night. It wouldn't be right to question him about his infidelity. Plus she didn't want to dwell on the past she couldn't change. Gina noticed that her plan did not have the desired affect she thought it would. She would have to figure out a way to get some information on him that only Ivie would know something really personal.

K-Stone lit up a cigarette, savoring the bitter taste of burnt tobacco on his tongue. Blowing the smoke out his nostrils slowly, he could visualize Ivie's face in the cloud of smoke. He pictured them chilling under a tree on a rainy day at the park they frequented. Minus the mental warfare taking place in their relationship currently, K-Stone missed hanging with Ivie. She was starting to pick up bad habits that were causing conflict. If they persisted it would be their undoing. Ivie needed to start doing her own thinking and stop letting others influence her thoughts.

The officer finally did his last count which meant it was around seven in the evening. Everybody else in the cell was preparing for sleep. He wasn't even going to try to go to sleep the night before his last court date. K-Stone had five cigarettes twisted up on the edge of his bunk ready for the long night ahead.

* * * * * * * * * *

"M-Rat, I don't know how you dealing with that life sentence."

"Don't have any choice, what am I going to do, cry?"

"No, but you seem content with it."

"To be real, I was in the way out there on the street. In thirty-one years, I've only spent sixteen on the streets. My baby mommas won't let me see my kids. Even if they did, my kids don't know me. There are a couple of raggedy bitches on my team. Besides that I don't have anything on the streets waiting on me. So it doesn't really matter if I have life. My mind had a life sentence since I was an adolescent. In your case, life in prison will hurt and we both know that. Luckily, you got that high priced lawyer. He should be able to pull something out of his hat before sentencing. The most I see you getting is ten years. All you can do is hope for the best and expect the worse at this point."

"That's a hard pill to swallow M-Rat. I'll just remain optimistic until the morning."

"You don't have any choice cuzz."

"Can't argue with that, this is going to be the longest night ever," Bone-Tone replied sipping on a cold cup of coffee.

* * * * * * * * * *

"You know this is a known drug area sir?" the officer said stepping out of his patrol car.

"I wasn't aware of that sir. I was just coming to see my lady friend."

"Do you have identification on you sir?"

"Yes."

"Are you on parole?"

"Yes."

"That means I'm going to have to search you and if you're clean you can go. Put your hands behind your back and spread your legs. Do you have anything in your pockets that will poke me?"

"No sir."

"What do we have here?" the officer said reaching in the suspect's right front pocket. "I'm going to have to handcuff you now sir."

Once the cold steel cuffs were clamped on the suspect, he began to say repeatedly. "This is not happening in a low whisper."

"Oh yes, it's happening. Now where did you buy this dope from?"

"What dope, I have no idea what you are talking about."

"Have it your way," the officer said slamming the door behind the suspect. While inside the police car the officers looked over the evidence, and then read the suspect his Miranda Rights.

"There's barely enough here to get high with," the arresting officer's partner said, looking at the dope.

As they began to drive off from the scene the suspect began to beg for his freedom. "Just let me go! These pants are old and borrowed. There's no telling how long that dope was in the pocket."

"Shut your mouth," the arresting officer's partner said.

"This will be my fourth strike. They'll give me life for this."

"Tell it to the judge loser," the officers said simultaneously while entering the garage of Seventy-seventh Division Police Station.

The suspect fought to keep his head erect as the tears flowed down his face like a broken faucet. He had sold his life for a dime piece of dope. There would be no deals to be made this time. He would have to go twelve in a box and hope for the best and expect the worse. The old jail platitude had become a staple in his life. Forty-three years of living had brought him to the point of no return. With none of his goals accomplished, thoughts of hanging himself crossed his mind as they turned the key to lock him in his cell. After further thought, he reconsidered, it would be best to wait until after the trial. He would represent himself and drain all the available resources the court would provide.

*   *   *   *   *   *   *   *   *   *

The officer was startled to find K-Stone fully dressed standing at the bars with a foam cup in his hand. He was looking forward to banging his flashlight against the bars and to flash the light in his face as he awoke, being unable to do this clearly pissed him off.

"You're going to court this morning Pink."

"Don't you think I know that?"

At Wayside Bone-Tone was repeatedly pushing the hot button at the sink trying to get the water as hot as possible for some motor oil coffee? He was feeling better than he had expected. Taking a deep breath he walked back to his bunk to lotion-up and throws his blues on. Today is the day, he thought to himself as he walked down the dim lit stairs to leave the dorm. His wife, kids, and mother were coming to court today to support him. A decision he was against, his mother insisted that the family be there. Who was he to argue with the women of his life?

For some strange reason, it always smelled like fresh cut grass mixed with burnt oil when he stepped outside to board the bus.

So far the morning transition to court was going along smooth. He had landed on Mr. Holmes's bus. He was an older Black man in his early fifties that acted like he was in his early twenties. He recited a rap quote every other sentence. It sounded foolish spewing out of the mouth of an uncomfortably built older man. But no one ever complained or clowned him because he played the rap station faithfully. This particular morning the radio station seemed to play all the songs he listened to on the streets that brought in a flood of memories, and the coffee's caffeine was the closes he was going to get to a high.

Five minutes away from the court building, the morning sun, which had barely come out was consumed by a dark head of clouds that brought darkness upon the bus. Along with this change in weather came a change in his mood. Bone-Tone went from being calm and collected to overt panic. The whole morning he had psyched himself into believing he was mentally ready to stand before a judge. As the bus entered the mouth of the court building he could feel his underarms begin to perspire uncontrollably.

Pacing back and forth bobbing his head to a rap verse he couldn't get out his head, K-Stone was buzzing off the second cup of coffee when he got to court. Though there wasn't a clock in the tank, he knew he'd been in the tank about thirty minutes and the Wayside bus would be on its way any minute. Today he could relax in the tank. It seemed from the looks of things that they scheduled all the dope fiends, elderly, and non-affiliates to come to court today. There were a couple of gang members but they weren't immediate enemies that he needed to trip on.

K-Stone rated enemies on a hate degree level, and K4CB were at the top of the totem pole. This meant they got smashed on sight with no hesitation. The other miscellaneous gangs they beefed with were at the bottom, meaning it was at the discretion of the homies that ran into them what actions should be taken. When it came down to gun play and fighting they would bow it down after a few casualties. It made his day to catch an enemy who thought he was hard, and break him down viciously with his hands. K-Stone had one match and two cigarettes on him that were for him and Bone-Tone at the end of the day. They would need them, he was sure of that.

From the look of Bone-Tone's demeanor as he walked into the tank, K-Stone could tell he had been going through a lot. He wasn't even trying to conceal it either.

"I would ask how you were doing, but I can clearly see. I won't bother giving you the "it's going to be all right speech." We both know that's bullshit." Bone-Tone sadly nodded his head in agreement with the comment.

Though Bone-Tone didn't feel like talking, he knew he had to in order to clear his mind of what he was facing.

"M-Rat told me to tell you what's up?"

"Where you see M-Rat at?"

"We in the same dorm together."

"So it must be misinformation about what happened to him. If he's in a regular dorm with you and M-Dogg."

"It's true, we're in the medical dorm. I moved out the dorm with M-Dogg."

"Why? What's wrong with you?"

"Ulcer."

"That comes from stressing, doesn't it?"

"Unbelievable stress."

"What happened to your eye?" K-Stone asked noticing a mild swelling over his left eye.

"M-Dogg and I got down."

"Is that right." K-Stone loved to hear about violence.

He didn't care for homies fighting each other when there were numerous enemies they could be fighting instead, but he had come to accept the practice. Experience had taught him that all homies weren't homies just because they claimed the same turf.

Knowing how M-Dogg was, he already knew the reason they got down. Bone-Tone wasn't a major factor on the turf. Homies would always push up on him with fake beefs, knowing he would give up some dope or money to wiggle out of a conflict. K-Stone, being K-Stone, still asked for the sake of entertaining himself. As Bone-Tone explained what had happened, the story was sounding on point until he got to the part where he struck M-Dogg in the mouth. K-Stone immediately interrupted Bone-Tone to ask more detailed questions.

"Hold up cuzz, you telling me you socked big M-Dogg in the mouth?"

"Usually I avoid that behavior but you know the type of character he can be." With a smirk on his face, K-Stone shook his head confirming that he knew.

"There's only so much I could take. Everyday he made antagonizing comments to me. When he pushed up on me before I left the dorm, he had worked my last nerve. So I just bawled my fist up and gave it to him."

"That's right!" K-Stone said as he was giving Bone-Tone dap, knowing he wouldn't make up a lie so elaborate just to impress him.

"Pink you're going into the courtroom in five minutes!" the officer yelled into the tank.

Instantly, the news broke their conversation and K-Stone and Bone-Tone said nothing but exchanged looks of understanding mixed with regret.

Leaving the main tank, K-Stone was accompanied to a smaller tank which he was placed alone. He used the opportunity to lie on the bench and gather his troubled thoughts as he stared blankly at the graffiti ceiling. Falling deeper into an empty minded trance, he failed to hear his lawyer approaching.

"Are you awake Mr. Pink?" Startled by the sudden voice, K-Stone jumped to his feet shaking off his daze.

"How you doing today Mr. Pink?"

"Better than most, worse than others."

"Five years, one strike, eighty-five percent."

"Where do I sign?"

"Those procedures will take place in the courtroom. Forgive me; I almost forgot to tell you your mother is in the courtroom. She called me to get your court date last week." The news of his mother in the courtroom took him completely by surprise and could be seen on his face.

"Everything all right Mr. Pink?"

"I'm cool." As he walked into the courtroom, he gave his mother a half wave because his hands and waist were shackled. Sitting in the chair next to his lawyer he "mad-dogged" the D.A. as she informed the judge of the deal. Noticing what he was doing, his lawyer whispered into his ear for him to stop.

Once the papers were signed, the judge gave him a boring speech he was not trying to hear. During the speech, K-Stone whispered to his lawyer and asked him to ask the judge if he could get a hug from his mother before leaving? When he walked out of the courtroom, he walked over to his mother and gave her a brief hug. As they broke away from each other, he told her he loved her. He then turned his back to avoid seeing her tears.

Walking back to the tank he felt totally relieved. It was as if a ton of bricks had been lifted from his back. He snatched his lunch off the table before going into the tank. Reaching in his waist-band,

he pulled out the two cigarettes and a match placing them inside
the empty lunch bag. Peeling his orange, he imagined about how
fun the pen was going to be. He was going to see homies he hadn't
seen in years. In a way it felt exciting; it would be his first time
going. The only part of the judge's lame speech he listened to, was
when he said he would be leaving in one week.

"I know this judge he's pretty lenient," Bone-Tone's lawyer
said placing his arm around his shoulder.

By this time all the nervousness had ceased within him. All
that remained was a feeling of stillness, for an emotion he was
struggling to identify. Once the judge announced the penal codes, he
started to read the sentence.

"Mr. Tapps you have an extensive criminal record for selling
drugs which eventually graduated to attempted murder. This tells
me, Mr. Tapps, that you're a menace to society. It gives me no other
choice but to sentence you to fifty-five to life with possibility of
parole."

Before he could process what he heard, his lawyer quickly
leaned in on his side and informed him that he could appeal. After
the sentence settled in, he tried to faint; hopping that he would
awaken and find it a misunderstanding. Hearing a commotion in
back of him, Bone-Tone looked over his shoulder to find his wife
and mother passed out on the floor with his two daughters crying
uncontrollably. Before he could react, the judge ordered the bailiff
to escort him out of the courtroom.

Dampening a cigarette with his tongue to make it burn
slower, K-Stone proceeded to spark up the cigarette as Bone-Tone
entered the court tank. The look on his face instantly told him that
they had washed him. It was a look of helplessness he had seen
countless times before. As Bone-Tone approached, he passed him
the already lit cigarette. Bone-Tone grabbed it quickly; inhaling so
hard the cigarette was to the butt on one pull and exhaled a large
cloud of smoke he said, "I'll be back on the streets soon. I got good
issues for my appeal."

K-Stone just looked at him skeptically. His words sounded
barely convincing but his face told what his words concealed, utter
defeat. Bone-Tones face and body were trembling like a generator
on its last drink of fuel. He tried, without success, to hold back the
needed tears. Quickly rushing to the toilet area he snatched up some
toilet paper off the floor to wipe the flood of tears and snot streaming
down his distorted face. Trying to control his rapid breathing proved

impossible as each breath made it more difficult to do. He then flushed the toilet afterwards to give off the impression he had taken a leak. He then bent down towards the sink to splash water on his face. Slowly he returned to the bench besides K-Stone, placing his head in his lap as he sat down.

"Everybody going back to the county get ready!" the officer yelled into the tank. "Snap out of it. They can't keep a real Ransom down."

"I'm all right, just got a lot going on inside my head."

"Well, I'm gone cuzz. I'll catch you at Delano", K-Stone said while giving Bone-Tone dap, as he left the tank.

Chapter 5

House of Many Names

One thing that made this bus ride significant was it would be his last time going to court. Each day starting now would be a day closer to the streets. He laughed as the thought of love crept in his mind. How could he love something that didn't love him? Here he was fantasizing about running the streets, but everything concerning the streets wasn't even thinking of his well-being.

From the gate to the bus, it seemed as if Bone-Tone had a ton of bricks attached to each leg, immobilizing his steps. Once on the bus he fell into a seat, staring blankly out the window, measuring each breath as the bus slowly backed out of the court garage. Each car that passed by on the free-way reminded him that he could possibly never sit behind the wheel of a car again. It slowly started to sink in, that he would watch his kids grow up through pictures and weekend visits. As the bus pulled into Wayside, Bone-Tone made a silent vow to himself that he would see the streets again.

"How did everything go at court?" Butch asked as K-Stone entered the cell with the look of relief.

"Five years eighty-five percent."

"Well, at least you got what you were looking for."

"Yeah," K-Stone said, lazily sitting on his bunk.

After lighting a cigarette, he called his mother to see how she was holding up. "You made it back quickly this time?"

"Yeah, I lucked up and caught the second bus going out."

"I won't be able to call you from Delano. It'll probably be a month or more until you hear from me again."

"You're not going to write?"

"As soon as I get pencil and paper I'll write to let you know where I'll be going from Delano."

"How do you know you are going to Delano?"

"Asking around here and there, that's how I found out."

"Where will you go from there?"

"I have no idea. As soon as I know, you will know."

"Kevin, don't get into any trouble up there. I need you to come home to me."

"Don't worry about me. I'll be straight."

"Don't forget to send me a couple of visiting forms."

"What makes you think I want you visiting me?"

"Boy you better stop playing with me!"

"All right, you can come see me."

"I don't need your permission. I'll come see you regardless."

"Let me get settled and make a few calls. I'll call you right before I leave."

"Who you got to call more important than me?"

"Nobody is more important than you. I just got some loose ends I have to get tied together."

"Okay, make sure you call. I love you."

"I love you too." Hanging up the phone, he quickly dialed the spot in the turf hoping to catch Uzi.

After twenty rings, he accepted that no one was there, so he tried to catch Ivie. "Hello."

"What's wrong with you?"

"I just got out of the shower. I had to run to the phone."

"What time is it?"

"Two thirty-six. Why?"

"Just curious why you're taking a shower so late in the day."

"K-Stone you know I like to take showers."

"Yeah, I can see. I'm going to start calling you the little mermaid."

"Funny! How did things go at court?"

"The way I expected. They offered five years and I took it."

"Are you okay with it?"

"I'm good, it's what I wanted. It's a long way from thirty years."

"You miss me Kay?"

"What you think?"

"If I knew I wouldn't be asking."

"Everyday like my freedom. It'll only be a couple more months before I see you face to face anyway. I just look forward to that."

"That's sweet, Kay."

"Come on with all that."

"Don't forget to send the marriage package off."

"That's one thing I won't be forgetting. It's been a long day for me. I haven't had a decent meal all day. So I'll get at you later this week."

"I love you K-Stone."

"I love you too." Hanging up the phone he kicked his feet up on the bunk to relax a minute because the day and the many events finally took its toll.

*   *   *   *   *   *   *   *   *   *

"We'll finish the game up later cuzz," M-Rat said placing the cards on the table.   Walking back to his bunk to make a shot of coffee, he noticed Bone-Tone walking back to the dorm. From the gloominess that entered with him, he knew he had "crapped" out at court. He knew the very look well because he wore it everyday. M-Rat decided that he would let him settle in before approaching for a conversation. Shit! He knew oh so well how he felt after getting "broken off" with life.

Grabbing his shower bag off the bunk, Bone-Tone made his way to the shower. Placing his nozzle on the sprayer, he stepped in the shower. The burst of hot water hit him hard against his face causing him to hold his breath at first. After standing in this position for about seven minutes, the water started to just slide down his face. He then opened his eyes to see his reflection in the aluminum shower. It was as if he drifted to his own world from the shower. Bone-Tone found himself in a daze which he neither was unable to control nor wanted to. M-Rat just stood at a distance watching him go through the motions, he was familiar with himself. He knew if he continued this behavior he would be stuck.

M-Rat thought to himself that it wasn't his place to intervene. This battle would be a battle he would have to fight by himself. Either he would give into the depression or fight for his freedom and sanity.

It was somewhere between two and three a.m. by the quietness of the dorm. Bone-Tone could barely keep his eyes shut for ten minutes at a time. When his blanket fell to the floor he finally snapped out of his forced sleep. The events of the other day wounded him deeply. It almost caused him to throw in the towel and soak in a permanent self-pity. Then he got to seriously thinking about all the accomplishments he had made in his life. By the end of the night, Bone-Tone had concluded that his life would not end incased behind cement and barbed wire fences. With the decision made, he mentally put together an outline as to how he would regain his freedom once he hit the pen.

* * * * * * * * *

If there was a murder or shooting in L.A. County, most
likely he did it. To make matters worse his previous jail experiences
had done nothing but exacerbate Uzi's lethal behavior. It had only
been a month since his release since his last one. Up to this point, all
his plans were falling into place better than expected. His spot was
cracking in a major way, thus affording him the opportunity to
purchase a midnight blue Monte Carlo, fresh off the lot. On his
usual mid-day turf patrol he noticed a proper pound-cake at the
corner on the opposite side of the street. He had to holla at her.
Every time he busted a new female or busted on some enemies,
thoughts of his lok K-Stone came to mind. From the looks of things
she was his type as well as his loks, short and thick.

After maneuvering behind some back streets to get to where
she was walking, he jumped out on her causing her to jump from
surprise.

"Where are you on your way to?"

"Why? Do I know you?"

"You might, stop and find out."

"I'm listening," she said slowing down to notice he had just
jumped out a brand new hooked-up car.

"My name is Uzi, how bout you jot down your number so I
can call you."

"I don't have a pen on me."

"Don't worry, I got one. Just walk over to the car with me
and write it down." As he searched his glove compartment for a pen,
she was observing his tattoos around his neck and down his arms.

The one that stood out the most was the Ransom tattoo
underneath his left eye that she could see clearly when he took off
his shades.

"Here you go, pen and paper. So where are you on your way
to?"

"To my home girl's house to get my hair braided."

"What's wrong with it now?"

"Nothing, braids are just easier to manage."

"That makes sense, I'll call you soon Gina," Uzi said as he
read the barely legible writing.

"I'll be looking forward to it," she said turning around
slowly, making sure she put an extra twist in her walk so Uzi could
notice.

A couple of days passed before he decided to call his new "pound cake." He was going to call last night but his time had become consumed with a lot of work as the spot continued to grow in clientele. He refused to stop what he was doing to pick up some bitch. Money always came before a nut, but it had been a few days since he had sex. Uzi was starting to feel the effects as he watched the B.E.T uncut music videos he had taped the night before. After debating with himself for about an hour, he decided to call her, though it was against his better judgment. He wanted to ask if she wanted to come over to the spot and hangout while he made his money. Doing it this way, he would make money and get cheeks. But the only down-fall would be that she would know how he got his money. Fuck it, he thought to himself, as he whipped out his Next-Tell to dial her number.

Three days had gone by without a phone call and Gina started to wonder if he had lost the number. Being close to getting K-Stone "caught up," had her unable to keep still. The only regret she had was she didn't get his number.

Giving up all hope, Gina started to think of another scheme until the phone rang.

"Hello?"

"Is this Gina speaking?"

"This is her, what's up?"

"Your legs if you act right."

"Who the hell is this?"

"Who do you want it to be?"

"Stop playing on my phone or I'm going to hang up."

"You still didn't answer my question." Stalling for a few seconds, Gina was still unable to catch the voice but then came to the realization that it could only be one person.

"Is this Uzi?"

"Is that who you want it to be?" After a slight hesitation she gave in and said yes.

"It sure took you a while to answer. What you got planned for the night?"

"Nothing that can't be canceled."

"Be ready in an hour. I'll call and get your address before I come." Hanging up the phone, Gina quickly took a bath, unwrapped her hair, and spent the remaining time picking the right outfit for the night.

Thirty minutes had flown by before she decided to wear the tight fitting Baby Phat jeans that were cut low to expose her matching pink g-string. Her breasts seemed to be growing by the month. Her strapless shirt was fitting extra tight causing more cleavage to hang out than she wanted.

Modeling in front of her full-length mirror by her bed, she thought to herself it couldn't hurt; besides it was for a bigger purpose.

On the other side of town, Uzi was organizing his CDs in the back of his trunk while his car heated up. Having obtained the address he was ready to go. Before pulling out of the drive way, he checked his forty glock to make sure one was in the chamber. He then "mashed-out" leaving behind a cloud of smoke.

Arriving at the address ten minutes early, Uzi circled the block for any unusual behavior. Feeling secure with the environment he called to inform Gina that he was in front of the building. A grin spread across his dark childlike face when he saw her step out of the small apartment building all fixed up. He immediately thought to himself that tonight was going to be a good night as he unlocked the door for her to get in.

"So what do you have planned for the night?" Gina asked expecting to go to a restaurant or something nice.

"Basically I got some business to handle at the spot, but I wanted to kick it with you. So I figured we'd rent some videos, order some pizza and chill."

"Sounds like an in house date. It's cool. What's that music you're listening to?"

"C-BO's greatest hits."

"You don't have any R. Kelly or something else?"

"I don't do R & B music."

"Why is that?"

"It's too soft for my lifestyle. Well, here we are," Uzi said pulling into the driveway. "Watch the floor board on the right it's not stable."

Walking through the narrow hall way leading to the spot, Gina tried not to touch the decrepit walls. From the squeaky floor boards and unkept dim lit surroundings, it was very clear Uzi had brought her to a dope spot. When she entered the inside of the spot, she was blown away by the flat screen T.V. It looked like a mini movie screen hanging on the wall. The carpet was a soft ivory white that gave her feet a sinking feeling as she took in all the novelties in the small apartment. Admiring the matching furniture and walls, she completely forgot her true agenda for the night. As her body was consumed by the expensive couch, she found herself relaxing. Although there was knocking every five minutes, Uzi made her feel quite comfortable with his sense of humor and unctuous behavior. It had been some time since she kicked it with someone who made her laugh. It took her mind off of everyone else's business. In a strange way, it felt like Uzi might be the one she was looking for. All the qualities she was looking for he had money, looks, and a "gangsta."

Two purple kush blunts later, Gina was horny as hell. Walking out of the bathroom back to the front, Uzi crept behind her pressing her body up against the wall in the hallway. She could feel the bulge in his pants rising between the crack of her butt. Placing his lips on the back of her neck he licked her slowly up to her ear lobe, sending short violent shivers down her body ending in the south bush. She tried to turn and face him but he pressed her firmly against the wall as one hand caressed her hard nipples while the other hand was unbuttoning her pants. By this time she was glazed and ready to be penetrated. Before penetration, Uzi reached into his pocket for a Magnum then unzipped his pants and rolled the condom on quickly. Tearing her g-string off, he spread her legs and took her right up against the wall. Gina bit her bottom lip desperately trying not to scream his name as he broke through new walls within her.

The ardent sex lasted the rest of the night, ending with her asleep in the back room naked. Awakened by the sun's rays stained upon her face, she glanced around the room looking for Uzi. But Gina only found her clothes on a chair besides an old wooden dresser. Wondering where Uzi was, she couldn't help but think for the first time in her life, she had been satisfied sexually without any oral pleasure.

Freshly dressed, smoking on a joint, Uzi sat on the edge of the bed handing Gina a bathing kit.
"Finally decided to wake up sleeping beauty?" The smells of weed early in the morning made her stomach turn.

The strong odor prevented her from answering and instead she just nodded her head in agreement. Noticing she didn't respond verbally, Uzi felt she was self-conscious about not brushing her teeth.

"Have to hit the grill before you speak? You females are crazy; I'm not trippin on that shit. When you get finished I'll be in the front." While in front of the apartment, Uzi counted the remaining money he had made last night.

He easily cleared three thousand a night, and on a good night five thousand. But it was starting to try his patience with all the time it consumed. Sooner or later he would have to put together a plan to get one large amount. People in the streets rarely saw the struggle involved in "selling work." There are seventy-two hour days and conflicting personalities on a daily basis. Not to mention, when he received bad work and still had to move it. All others saw was the cars, chains, and cash. Like many others, he was on the outside looking in, just seeing the glitz and glimmer having his hand out. In a way, he started to feel Bone-Tone's plight.

Rapping the remaining money in a rubber band, he almost forgot about Gina. It was the first time he had let a female spend the night. Looking at his gun on the table he hoped he wouldn't have to off her. A decision that would get straight approved if any shady characters popped up around his spot.

While she occupied his mind, he noticed his nature begin to rise. Uzi proceeded to the bathroom for another couple rounds of ping pong.

Three weeks had passed and for the first time Gina knew she was in love. Since the first night, she had a feeling it would kind of turn out this way. There were a few doubts however, when he didn't return any of her phone calls for a week after the amazing night of sex. Chopping it up as a one night stand, she was angry that she didn't find out one thing on K-Stone.

When Uzi finally contacted her, they decided to go on a real date. Then he explained to her that he had to go out of town to handle something, which is why he didn't answer his phone. She had been patient up to this point about asking Uzi about his home boys. He wasn't like the other niggas she had been with who were talkative about everything that took place in their lives.

Force was needed to make Uzi talk at times. He would let her run the conversation while he relaxed, getting high. Plus, she didn't want to ruin a good thing by mentioning his homies names, making him even more suspicious than he already was. Being with Uzi was like dating Double-O-Seven. He always kept a gun or two on him at all times everywhere they went. Whenever they went to a hotel he would check underneath the bed, bathroom, and even the refrigerator. On the way there, or anywhere, he would constantly look in the rearview mirror and keep approximately thirty feet behind any car in front of him. Besides his paranoia, he treated her considerably well compared to other men in her past. They went out every week, to wherever she wanted to go.

The only problem now was seeing her sister go through mild depression over that sorry nigga K-Stone. Hopefully tonight would put her in a better mood. One of her friends told her about a bomb little restaurant in Torrance that she suggested to Uzi the other night. Kind of hesitant at first, Uzi agreed to let Ivie, come along this one time.

Uzi had never seen Ivie before. Nor did he ever really care to meet her. He preferred to stay away from friends and family. It wasn't because he didn't want to be around them. Just that past experiences had provided him with an accurate conclusion that bitches are scandalous and will try to snatch their sister or home girls man if given a chance, that was where the problem laid. If they threw the bait, he would definitely bite without hesitation. It was the conflict afterwards of doing so that irritated him. The, "Why did you do it?" and the classic "Why didn't you just tell me?" He didn't feel like hearing any of that shit. Besides, he had come to realize that bitches always want to show something off no matter what it is. When it came to a man, it was like expecting a kid to hold on to fifty-cents at a candy store. There was no holding back.

Surprising to Uzi, Ivie didn't act like her sister one bit. She sat in the back seat the whole ride, only speaking when asked an occasional question by Gina. From the looks of things she carried herself in a decent manner, Uzi thought to himself. But then again he also kept in mind that looks could be deceiving. One fact was definite; it wasn't just cars he was looking at when he peered into the rearview mirror that night.

"So Ivie why didn't you bring your boyfriend with you?" Uzi asked chewing on a bread stick.

"He's in prison right now."

"For what?"

"I think robbery, but I really don't know."

"Where is he from?"

"Does it really matter?"

"In a way it does."

"In what kind of way does it matter?"

"I have to make sure you are no proxy sent to get me," Uzi said in jocular voice, while holding a serious face. Gina looked at Uzi not knowing where the conversation was going.

"He's from your turf."

"What do they call him?"

"K-Stone."

When she mentioned his loks name Uzi's demeanor changed in a split second.

"I thought the name sounded familiar. K-Stone use to tell me about you all the time." Ivie's face lit up when she heard K-Stone use to talk about her.

Unfortunately the euphoria didn't pass on to Gina. Her face instantly started to frown as she saw Uzi light up in a way she had never seen before. As Uzi and Ivie chopped-it-up some more, Gina excused herself to the bathroom to go vent out her frustration and anger.

In the bathroom, Gina scrambled to gather her thoughts and her composure. The whole evening just blew up in her face. What made her the hottest was that she did it to herself. At least she found out that K-Stone and Uzi were tight, which meant all she had to do now was pry a little bit to get some information.

Looking up briefly to see Gina sitting back at the table, Uzi continued his conversation with Ivie as Gina ate the remaining portion of her mild meal.

Breaking from their conversation, Uzi asked Gina if she had ever met K-Stone. "A couple of times."

"Too bad you didn't get to hang with the homie too." On the way home, Uzi and Ivie continued talking about K-Stone as Gina laid her head up against the window rolling her eyes with every new story.

Fumbling in his pocket for a minute, Uzi pulled out a crumbled up ball of money and gave it to Ivie before she got out the car.

"Send the homie three-hundred and you keep a yard for yourself. I know how it can get when you are staying-down for your man. A lot of bitches leave a nigga leaking when he needs them the most."

"Thank you Uzi."

"Don't trip, if you need anything for my homie, let your sister know."

"Okay."

"Tell the homie I said what's happening when you write him."

Talking with Uzi brought numerous memories Ivie thought were too deep to retrieve. Tonight she would write her baby a long letter and get a money order in the morning before sending it off. That night Ivie held her pillow tighter than ever before, pretending K-Stone was in her arms. It had been too long.

* * * * * * * * * *

"Maximum security country club" was the first thought that popped into K-Stones head three weeks ago when he took in the full range of Delano. Manicured lawns with happy inmates mowing them didn't fit into the wicked image of what he thought a prison would look like. Between the birds chirping and the crisp fresh air, he could have sworn he was on the set of an up to date Andy Griffin Show. The scene he was absorbing definitely didn't fit the model of the prison stories and movies he had experienced growing up.

K-Stone stayed focused as they unloaded the bus into receive and release to get them processed before going to their assigned cells. Three hours passed by and he was still taking physical and mental tests on an empty stomach which was no longer responding to the constant drinks of stale water to substitute for food.

Another two hours passed before they brought in the lunches. The officers made sure to let them sit another hour before passing them out. At the sight of the lunch bags approaching the cell, K-Stone's mouth began to water. Being deprived of light, food, and women often reduced him to a primitive mental state. This he realized as he tore open the bag, then tore at the plastic surrounding the bread and meat. Sloppily spreading the mustard on the sandwich, he devoured it in two hungry bites. After satisfying his hunger he was mentally stuck for a couple of minutes. Pensive about what his next move would be, K-Stone came to the conclusion that all he desired was a hot meal and some sleep.

Four hours later his name was called to line-up to be escorted to his building. He was re-energized when his name was called because he was finally going to see what prison was all about. As he stepped out of receiving and release in a single file line he, couldn't help but notice how big the sky was compared to how it looked in the city. It had been ten months since he last saw the sky at this time of day.

From the way the sun was setting, he could tell that it was around six o'clock p.m. Just before they reached the final gate the officer ordered them to stop. Up until that point the officer had said a minimum, but now that they were under the gun tower he had plenty to say. From the way he gestured, it looked as if he had laid down the rules countless times before. He seemed to take pleasure in explaining prison etiquette in a lewd manner.

When K-Stone entered the building he was expecting bars with arms hanging out and mirrors attached to their palms. Instead, he found himself looking at something that resembled an apartment complex more than a prison environment.

As he settled down in the dayroom waiting to get a cell, a Black porter hit him up. He let him know immediately where he was from. He was told that a couple of his homies were on the top tier. Before he could ask which homies were there, the porter quickly made his way down the tier.

Sitting on the bench, he thought to himself. "So this is the pen?" Sighing, he thought, what a joke, and he was the punch line.

"Mr. Pink you are going to cell 107, top bunk," the Correctional Officer (C.O.) informed him breaking his train of thought.

"When are they going to serve dinner?"

"They didn't feed you?"

"No."

"Well, I'll call over to the kitchen to get you a lunch."

Entering the cell, he noticed it was well kept. Noticing a cane lying against the desk, he knew it must have been occupied by an older male. Seeing an older man come out from under the covers, his assumptions proved him right.

"Hello young brother, my name is Word," he said in a mild gentle voice.

"My name is K-Stone."

"Well it's nice to meet you," Word said extending his hand.

"I was almost asleep when they cracked the door. I can move out your way if you want to make your bed up."

"That'll be cool; I'll be out your way in a minute."

"No rush, young brother."

While he was making his bed, K-Stone and Word got better acquainted.

"If you don't mind me asking, how much time did you come with brother?"

"Five years with eighty-five percent."

"How much time they hit you with Word?"

With a slight hesitation Word answered, "Life."

After an awkward moment of silence, K-Stone asked how did he get a name like Word?

"Because I know this here Word real good," Word said picking up the Bible that was neatly placed at the foot of the bunk.

"Why do they call you K-Stone?"

"Because I'm a solid killa."

"A solid killa," Word whispered to himself. "Hopefully that will change one day young brother."

"I doubt it, it's who I am."

Before they went further into conversation the door popped open.

"Here you go," the Black porter from earlier said handing Word a lunch. "That's for your celly. There's a kite in there from M-Dogg and Bone-Tone."

Word noticed when he heard those names K-Stone's face lit up instantly giving him the impression that he had knew them well.

"Good friends of yours?"

"Yeah, some of my homies from the streets I was in the county with. After I eat this lunch, I will hit the light."

"No rush brother, I can sleep with the low beam on," Word said getting situated back into his bed.

Looking further through his bag, K-Stone could see two kites inside. He read M-Doggs first. It informed him that he would "shoot" him a couple of smokes in the morning and that there were no enemies on K-Stone's side of the building. Bone-Tones kite informed him he would "shoot" him some soups and a couple of bags of chips. After reading the kites, K-Stone flushed them down the toilet and hit the light switch off.

Waking up feeling fully refreshed, K-Stone handled all his morning activities with plenty of time to spare. Lying in bed fully clothed, he waited for the breakfast to come to the door.

"Well brother, they'll be popping the door in ten minutes to walk to breakfast."

"Where are we walking to?"

"To the tables in the dayroom."

The difference K-Stone noticed from prison life to county life was the food. Prison food was a hundred times better tasting and hotter compared to the county jail.

"K-Stone! Up here to the right." K-Stone looked up to see M-Dogg in the window throwing up the Ransom hand sign.

K-Stone returned the hand signals, and curiosities were answered.

"We'll holla at you during dayroom."

"That breakfast did the trick Word. All it's missing is one thing."

"What's that brother?"

"Some tobacco in my lungs."

"How long you been smoking?"

"Since the age of twelve."

"You youngsters start out early nowadays."

"Not really, I got homies who have been smoking and drinking since nine."

"Really! That's sad."

"No, it's reality where I come from." Staring out the door window, K-Stone could see the porter from last night approaching the cell.

"This is from M-Dogg" the porter said, sliding some cigarettes under the door.

"It's about time," K-Stone said while licking one of the cigarettes.

"You got a lighter in here Word?"

"No, I don't smoke."

"Well, do you have an old pencil?"

"That I do have."

Splitting the pencil in half, K-Stone removed the lead and broke it into three two-inch pieces. Walking over to the sink, he placed a piece of lead into the left and right holes of the socket. The third piece he twisted between pieces of rolled up tissue.

"And Stone created fire!" K-Stone said in a humorous voice, lightly touching the lead attached to the tissue against the other lead. "And he saw it was good!" he said lighting the cigarette with the lit tissue.

"You don't know what you're missing Word," K-Stone said as he inhaled the cigarette smoke, instantly giving him a head rush.

"Better make sure they don't smell that smoke on you when they pick you up for testing."

"What kind of testing?"

"They're going to test your health, knowledge, and mental state today or sometime this week."

"That's cool. At least I get to leave the cell. But until then I'll be taking a nap."

"Don't sleep too long today is our yard."

"How often do we go outside?"

"Every other day for two hours, except weekends."

"In that case, I might as well stay up." Looking out the window by the desk, K-Stone could see people walking around.

"Who are those people out there on the yard?"

"Those are inmates from the other building. We go out one building at a time." While looking out the window, K-Stone thought he saw a pack of females, until further focus showed that they were far from being females.

"What the hell!" From the sound in his voice, Word knew he had seen his first sagoony.

"Saw one of those abominations of nature?"

"Call it what you want, but that isn't cool. The last thing I'm trying to do is be on the yard with She-men."

"Don't worry, there's none on the yard with us. Speaking of yard, it's almost that time K-Stone."

Warm with a light breeze, the temperature was just right as K-Stone walked out onto the yard. To the right he observed a bar apparatus that inmates were working out on. A couple feet away from him, he saw Black inmates playing basketball on one side of the court while the Mexicans and Whites occupied the other half. The yard was small and resembled the USC track he use to visit as a youth. On the outer circle there was a gravel track surrounding lush green grass.

Once again, prison had failed to meet his expectations. There weren't as many swoll guys walking around fresh off the weight pile or set boundaries between races. Instead, everybody was walking around freely. As he became more pensive about the environment he felt someone reaching for his shoulder. Instantly he went into attack mode until realizing it was just M-Dogg as he turned around.

"My loks," K-Stone said embracing M-Dogg and Bone-Tone.

"How much time you come with?" M-Dogg asked.

"A half of what you got."

"That's straight. You ain't heard anything from the turf?"

"Nothing recent, I'm waiting on a letter from Uzi now."

"I heard Uzi was coming-up decent in the turf," Bone-Tone said chewing on an apple stem.

"I've heard the same thing."

"What pen did you get endorsed for?"

"High Desert level four."

"How about you M-Dogg?"

"Pelican Bay, I'll be bouncing in a couple of weeks. This will be the last time we'll kick it unless you catch some more points and come to the Bay."

"Who knows what will happen between now and then?"

"You'll be going to a level three, anyways Stone."

"When do you think I'll see a counselor to find out what pen I'll be going to?"

"It will be another three weeks before you see a counselor, so get comfortable cuzz. Bone-Tone got here two weeks ago before you pulled up. So you'll be the last homie up here, that's if anymore loks don't come through. Besides that, what's up on a game of basketball?"

"You know I don't do sports cuzz."

"What about you Bone?"

"I'm cool, me and Stone going to chill right here."

With that, M-Dogg went and shot some hoops while Bone-Tone and K-Stone reminisced about functions and hood-rats.

Chapter 6

Life Goes On

Later on that day, K-Stone was laying in the bed staring at the ceiling when his name was called for mail. Reading the envelopes, he saw that there were two letters, one from his mother and another one from Ivie. The fragrance of Ivie's letter engulfed the small cell, instantly stroking his nostrils with nostalgia of Ivie's delicate presence. Hypnotized by the aroma, he almost overlooked the three hundred dollar money order stamped on the front of the envelope.

Noticing what he almost overlooked, he snapped back to reality and began reading the letter. Nothing significant stood out about the letter he already didn't know until he came across the second page, third paragraph, about Gina being Uzi's girl and how they all went out to dinner. That's where she got the money. Being in a slight denial about what he just read, he reread to confirm the information. Realizing its truth he placed it to the side saying, "Damn!" to himself as he proceeded to open the other letter from his mother.

All was going well as could be, from what she wrote in the letter. But he knew she was just saying those things to comfort him. With the day coming to an end, K-Stone found his reception to prison not being that bad. Two weeks flew by quick with M-Dogg leaving. Before he left, they made some fire pruno with the apples they saved from their lunches. They also came up on a couple of sticks they got from the homies on the main line.

Compared to the county jail, prison was a resort. When certain C.O.s worked they would turn the T.V. in the dayroom on from two p.m. until nine o'clock p.m. Luckily K-Stone landed in A-section because C-section couldn't see anything and B- section was too far off to hear the volume. Little perks like that and playing games in the dayroom, made time fly.

Another week passed, Bone-Tone was transferred, and K-Stone finally saw his counselor. The counselor informed him that he would be going to Centinela on Monday morning. That night he wrote to his mother and Ivie to let them know he was leaving Monday and would be calling soon.

*   *   *   *   *   *   *   *   *   *

Rarely did the barber come on time, but when he did, he worked efficiently. The barber was able to cut three to four heads in less than forty five minutes and K-Stone had been waiting to get his "afro" trimmed up. He started growing his "afro," and after some time he liked keeping it neat as possible. While running a game of Pinochle, K-Stone didn't notice the barber come in until he noticed inmates getting up at the same time. Peeping what was going on, he called the game quits to go get his hair trimmed before leaving. At first sight, K-Stone thought he was seeing things, as he approached what seemed to be a new barber. He was in disbelief as he recognized the barber as Chicago.

"Chicago," K-Stone said in a skeptical voice not wanting it to be his old school county jail partner.

"K-Stone, what you doing here youngsta?"

"What am I doing here? I'm supposed to be here." Seeing the embarrassment in Chicago's face at his reaction, K-Stone laid off from getting a haircut. Afterwards he and Chicago sat down in the dayroom to chop-it-up.

"You supposed to be on an island with the broads. Not holding clippers in the pen asking whose next?"

"Don't you think I know that youngsta? I just got caught up in the wrong place at the wrong time."

"Caught doing what?"

"Remember the White girl I was telling you about?"

"Yeah."

"Well she had flipped the money I had told you about and bought a pound of heroin. So we were riding down the street when the police pull us over for no reason. When they searched the car they found the pound. Me being on parole, they put the blame on me, youngsta."

As Chicago continued with the story, it sounded more and more suspect to K-Stone. He still continued to listen without interruption, inquiring at the end of the story, about how much time they dealt him. Chicago was barely keeping eye contact with K-Stone since their tragic reunion. K-Stone was trying to gather a response but was cut off by Chicago's tears.

"I told the judge I couldn't do life. You know what he told me youngsta?"

"To appeal when I got to the pen."

"No. He told me to bring him what I could."

"Did they offer you a deal?"

"Thirty years. When you're my age that's life. I had no choice but to take it all the way. With no inconsistent evidence in my case, all I have to look forward to is that they take life sentences off of non-violent offenders."

For the remainder of the twenty minute conversation, K-Stone said nothing and felt no empathy for a man who sealed his own fate over some dope. When dayroom recall was called, Chicago continued to hold K-Stone at bay, unloading as much pain as possible upon him. It was a side of Chicago that he didn't believe existed. But here he was using time he didn't have available to him, to reach deep within himself to a place he rarely visited. A place in which he intended to take K-Stone on a full tour. For the first time since being down, K-Stone was looking forward to following an order from an officer. There was already too much turmoil inside his mind to be adding Chicago's dilemmas. He quickly obeyed the officer's third warning to lock-up, thus escaping from Chicago's desperate attempt at easing his embarrassment and his hurt. Reluctantly, Chicago left the building with a look of permanent failure on his face.

As K-Stone stood in the doorway, crunching a soup for lunch, he still tripped off his brief encounter with his old acquaintance from county.

"I see you know a lot of folks?"

"Not really. That's just a dude I did the beginning of my time with in the county."

"Were you guys close?"

"No, we were just cool. He went home a couple of months ago and ended up coming back with life, which is a trip. He always bragged about how much he had going on out there in the streets."

"Things of that nature happen to men who continue negative behavior. God eventually hardens their heart like he did pharaoh."

"Harden heart? What is that suppose to mean?"

"Brother if you or any person continues to mold their actions around killing, robbery, or any type of sin, it will overcome their lives. It is the reason many people get caught-up in the three strikes net. Eventually their heart hardens, allowing their negative behavior to control their lives. Eventually, this behavior destroys them."

"So what did God harden your heart to do?"

"Jealously, which lead to the murder of my wife. After years of cheating on my wife she found out and returned the favor. A favor I couldn't accept. It was my entire fault. My advice for you on that issue, brother, is when married never do unto your wife anything you can't accept her doing to you. My pa gave me that piece of advice when I was a young man like you. But I failed to heed his valuable advice. Don't end up like me, young brother, spending your last years behind bars. I see young brothers come through here and there simply living wanton. Not worrying about what's going to happen when they're too old to hustle and gang-bang. Selling dope and robbing people keeps their minds clouded. With the "get-it-right-now" mentality, seldom do they think about 401K plans for retirement. More so, the only CDs they know about are those that they buy at a music store."

K-Stone listened intently, not knowing what Word was referring to by CDs and 401K plans were. The only numbers he put a K after, was when he was crossing out someone on the wall or books in juvenile hall. Word feigned that he was a decrepit man who just studied the Bible, but K-Stone was soon to learn that Word was far from being a religious zealot.

Word's comments were exacerbating the feeling of annoyance he held earlier when confronted by Chicago, with his silly antidote about being caught with a key of brown. Many of the subliminal comments Word was shooting out were not being missed by K-Stone. In fact, they were cutting deep within his brain giving him a feeling that he was not taking a liking to. As the minutes passed to what seemed to become a paid for a lecture, people heard on college campuses and with nothing else to do, K-Stone listened reluctantly answering questions. Word asked questions, when he noticed K-Stone's attention was wavering. A benefit from the lecture was it knocked off hours from the day.

"Let me ask you a question I've been wondering since you began talking, Word?"

"Go ahead."

"If you have all this wisdom and knowledge, why are you in this cell with me? For real, though, I've been racking my brain trying to come up with a reason you're in this position besides jealousy."

"Brother everyone has weaknesses within their character no matter how prestigious or intelligent they are. Second you must have control of your mind, body, and emotions at all times. When you allow any portion of your thoughts, emotions, and instincts to run over your life you will be led to seek out pleasures instead of substance."

"So what should run your life?"

"Will power, you should have full control over everything you decide to do."

Noticing K-Stone in a confused daze by his statement, Word went into further detail.

"When you're born, you naturally know right from wrong. It's instilled in everyone before their taught actual laws. Now, when you go against what you know to be right, your mind, which is controlled by your will, will let you know immediately. All too often, I, as well as others, ignore the will. Instead, they choose to let their emotions, instincts, memory, and etc. take control of their lives. My malfunction was caused by letting my carnal take control of my life. Remember K-Stone, that when we don't pay attention to negative thoughts and actions that take place day to day in our lives, we inadvertently surrender our control over to other people, objects, and non-productive instincts.

"Do you have control now?"

"Yes and no. Yes, in that I can control every aspect of my inner self. No, in that I am given orders daily. I must obey against my will. As long as I remain in control of myself, I remain at peace. What controls you?"

"Besides these punk C.O.s, nothing."

"Nothing, you sure?"

"If I wasn't sure I would have not said it. Obviously you feel something is controlling me I can't see myself. So you let me know!"

"When I tell you this brother I'm not passing judgment on you. I'm just pointing out what I see. The first thing I noticed when you came in the cell is that you turned your self-control over to tobacco."

"Let me get this right. You're telling me a cigarette is controlling me?"

"Yes, in that you look to it to calm and relax you. Something you can do on your own."

Listening further to Word break down the ways in which K-Stone wasn't in control of his life made him feel a mixture of rancor and respect for what the man was saying. The heavy thinking, along with the denial, was beginning to make his head hurt. He had never thought of himself as being out of control. That was one of the main reasons he started gang-banging, for some type of control in his life. Especially in a world where he had known no control.

Ransom was his solace just as it was for the majority of his homies. To hear Word destroy his beliefs made him feel inadequate; forcing his mind to seek comfort in the idea that Word was just some old man who just had a lot to say because he had life. As much as he tried to convince himself of this, his mind was incessant to believe what he had heard.

Sunday night was moving along as if a parachute was attached to it, allowing plenty of time for him to reminisce about the comments Word made the previous day. The comments seemed to linger in his mind continually, as he lay in his bunk impatiently checking the clock every fifteen to thirty minutes. He finally gave into the sleep he had been fighting for the last five hours.

When his cell door popped open at 3:35 a.m., there was a command to bring his mattress and his belongings. Groggily walking down the stairs with mattress in tow, K-Stone could see two other inmates waiting down at the bottom. Throwing his mattress to the side, he fell into single file line with the other inmates. As they walked into the awaiting cold air clouds blanketed the full moons dull light.

It was the first time since arriving at Delano that he had seen R and R again. Now he was sitting in a holding cell with ten other inmates waiting to leave out the same way he came in. It felt like he was returning back in forth out the womb. Patience was an attribute K-Stone was not known for having a lot of. Going through the jail process was beginning to change that second by second, minute by minute, hour by hour, and day after long day. The half frozen mystery meat sandwich he had for breakfast was taking a toll on his stomach. When the bus finally arrived, it brought along with it a yellow paper suit, leg and arm shackles.

Walking with the leg shackles took K-Stone some getting use to. They would cut into his ankle every time he took a step. Walking up the bus steps he expected to find some cushioned seats for what would be over a five hour drive. He soon realized he would be sitting on cold hard plastic the whole ride. As he got on the bus, he noticed at the back there was a dark greasy skinned C.O., with a shot gun, who reminded him of a Black out-of-shape Terminator, glasses included. At least the driver was eye candy. A coke-bottled-shaped sister who's uniform fit just right. Once everyone got situated on the bus she drove slowly out of Delano onto the open road. Snoop Dogg's *Murder Was the Case,* ironically, played on the radio.

The beginning of the ride was cool despite the shackles, paper suit, and already numb cheeks. Everybody was talking to their passenger next to them when the mood instantly changed.

"What you muthafuckas think you doing?" The C.O. in the back of the bus yelled unlocking the cage which separated him from the inmates. "You muthafuckas just a-chit-chatting like some little school girls. Where the hell you think you're at, on a trip to Vegas? I'm going to give you one fucking warning! There's no talking on my bus! None, not even to your neighbor and if I hear you, we'll turn this muthafucka around and take that individual back! Take the time to sit and think why you're on this bus!" With that said, he returned back to his cage leaving a couple of grunts.

The rest of the ride, all that was heard was the radio and walkie-talkies. The sun was starting to come out twenty minutes into the ride. There was nothing to do but look out the window at gas stations, unknown markets, and farm land. An hour and a half passed when the bus pulled over to an Am/Pm somewhere in the boondocks. The bus parked along the curb while the driver and another C.O. ran off to get something to eat. This instantly sent a hunger pain to K-Stone's stomach and every other inmate. For some reason, a lady pumping gas was waving at the bus. This was something people seemed to enjoy doing whenever they saw a jail bus. It seemed like the C.O.s purposely made the stop just to annoy the inmates. The C.O.s came back on the bus telling jokes with bags full of goodies, making K-Stone realize why freedom was so valuable. The small things like pumping gas in his car, going to the liquor store when he pleased, and even talking when he pleased seemed like a distant luxury. To think he took those things for granted made him angry at himself.

Two more hours passed by, and the bus was so quiet you could hear an ant fart. The only thing plaguing K-Stone's mind was when he would eat. They had driven on five different freeways and K-Stone had already lost feeling in his cheeks which was adding to his hunger. He desperately needed something to ease his anxiety. Finally, as if they had read his mind, the bus pulled over into a gas station and the C.O.s passed out lunches. They had to be eaten slowly because the hand cuffs gave little room for motion. A sense of relief overcame him as he took the last bite of his peanut butter and jelly sandwich. With something in his stomach, he could bear the ride a little better, and from the looks of the other inmates they indeed felt the same way.

By this time they were in Palm Springs, almost to their destination. The first prison stop they made was at Calipatria. From there they headed towards Centinela. K-Stone was trying to figure out where they were taking him. All he saw was a couple of houses but mostly farmland and desert. It was hard to tell what the temperature was outside because the bus was air conditioned. But from how the sun was beaming, he could tell it was scorching.

After what seemed to be a labyrinth the bus pulled into Centinela's R and R, an unloaded all the remaining inmates to their custody. The inmates were then put into holding cells until they were called for their assigned yards. K-Stone breathed a sign of relief when his lower body began to regain normal movement and the cuffs were taken off, leaving his ankles swollen. While relieving himself, his name was called by a C.O. along with four other inmates, to go to A-yard. One last strip down and the five inmates were on their way out the door single file. Surprisingly, the weather wasn't as bad as the other inmates had led on to be. It felt like a typical day in South Central.

Since he was the only Black in line, he was placed by himself in the orientation building. It was just his luck that he had come on a lockdown that had just started the other day. Closing the cell door, K-Stone proceeded to making his bed and organizing his belongings on the locker. Once that was out of the way he took an exaggerated deep breath and laid out across his bunk preparing himself to adapt to prison life.

Chapter 7

Negative Influence

"Nothing stays good forever. Eventually shit changes, causing you to resort to drastic measures, be they negative or positive. Someone has to do the dirty work. Nothing in these streets comes without sacrifice. Feel me cuzz?"

"I can't help but feel you," Lil G-Liz responded unsurely to Uzi's comments, not really knowing where he was going with the conversation. It had been a week since the L.A.P.D ran in his spot getting him for two birds, three assault rifles, and five thousand dollars in cash. Fortunately, he was out of town when it happened.

"Sacrifice is the key to survival, being willing to do what others only talk about doing, you know?" Uzi said, putting emphasis on the "you know," pausing in mid sentence to take a pull on his blunt.

"This right here is the blue print to how we going to shine for along time. This plan right here is going to have us right. In two weeks we are going to hit this bank. I got an inside plug on the whole bank operation. They'll have at least four hundred thousand. It's going to be us four involved, that's all. So don't go telling anybody, especially your little bitches at night time when you're laid up. Like I mentioned earlier, sacrifice is the blood of balling. So if you're not willing to sacrifice your life for this grip, don't bother listening to the rest of the plan, because if the police get involved in any part, I'm busting. Whoever involved in any part is busting, and whoever else doesn't bust when it goes down, I'm busting on them too. You must understand. I'm willing to sacrifice your life as well as mine, to maintain my lavish lifestyle. One more thing; it doesn't matter how you spend your grip but if you get caught-up, ride your own beef. That should go without saying."

With that said Uzi's homies left his apartment and returned back to the turf. Since the incarceration of many of his homies, Uzi had become somewhat of a leader to the younger homies who inadvertently wanted to be controlled and told what to do. Annoyance was mainly what he felt when he arrived back in town to hear the news about his spot. He knew, eventually, it was going to happen based on the fact the spot was becoming too hot. The lost work hurt, but not that much. He had saved enough to get him by until the lick. Besides, he was getting tired of running a dope spot.

It was time to come anew. He was contemplating serving chronic and e-pills to attract a different type of clientele which would make it harder for the police to get up on him. Meticulously going over the plans one last time to see what roles everyone was going to play, he was finally comfortable with how it was laid out. Then Uzi decided to call Gina to come and kick it with it him.

It had been a couple of days since they talked and from the messages she left him on his phone, he knew she was eager to come kick it. She had only been to his apartment twice since he got it a month ago to save money on hotel bills.

"What's crackin' Ivie, your sister there?"

"Yeah, how you been doing Uzi?"

"Straight, just chilling. Everything straight with you?"

"I can't complain, just waiting to hear from K-Stone again. They sent him to Centinela last week."

"Tell him I said what's up next time you write him."

"Okay, here's my sister.

"What took you so long to call me?"

"Stop trippin, I was busy taking care of business, besides your phone was off."

"I had it charging."

"I'm about to come get you in an hour, so be ready."

"You just assume I don't have anything to do."

"If you had something or somebody to do, you would be doing it or them."

"I'm just playing Uzi, I'll be ready."

A smirk cracked across Uzi's face as he was vacuuming his apartment. The last time he had seen Gina she told him during sex that she loved him. His natural reaction was to just keep stroking pretending he didn't hear her. Ever since that incident he would spontaneously reflect on her voice that night giving him a personal laugh. It was comical in that she didn't even know his real name, nothing about his family, all she knew was he's Uzi from Ransom. He knew the only thing she loved was the image of Uzi. But if she thought she loved him, who was he to stop her, he would just have to see how far her love went.

Getting out of the shower, Gina slowly patted her new tattoo dry making sure the ink wasn't bleeding. It had come out just the way she expected. Tonight she would let Uzi really know how she felt about him. When he didn't respond last time, she thought he didn't hear her. Two weeks ago she found out that Uzi and K-Stone had matching tattoos of guns on their stomachs. It was good

information but nothing concrete enough to accomplish her goal.
It was becoming more difficult to obtain some dirt from Uzi
about K-Stone because he knew Ivie was her sister. This made him
watch what he said around her concerning K-Stone. Nevertheless,
she stayed tenacious and hoped something would eventually arise.
Until then, Gina would continue to indulge in Uzi's company,
canceling her previous male friends. Uzi was the only one who
would be sampling her goods. She realized it was stupid to continue
spreading herself when she already had the full package in her grasp.
Uzi didn't realize it but she was slowly getting deeper in his life.

As time passed, she noticed he was becoming more
comfortable around her. She noticed on the day they were chilling,
he asked her if she wanted something out of the kitchen. It seemed
small but it really wasn't when it came to Uzi, who always served
himself only. In her mind, dust would eventually become a hill she
would control.

Being maligned, Uzi started to feel a void emerging from not
putting in work. Since he started making money, days turned into
weeks with him not emptying a clip or two. On his turf, you were
only as good as your last kill. Yesterdays score didn't count for
todays. It was of great importance that his ruthless reputation
remained intact, at all cost. He rather enjoyed being lionized by his
homies and his rivals. Emptying clips was his solace. The thrill of
the hunt gave him an indescribable high which couldn't be
substituted by anything else. Gina would have to wait while he fixed
his jones.

*   *   *   *   *   *   *   *   *

Making a slow right when the light turned green, Uzi headed
in the direction of the K4's who frequented the gas station on
Figueroa. Pulling over to the side street he waited patiently while
blowing smoke out the slightly cracked window. Ten minutes
passed with no K4's or police in sight. This was expected, the
homies had been on them viciously, and lately it wasn't a hot spot
the police monitored. Sparking up his second Camel, Uzi decided to
wait another fifteen minutes before circling the block and hitting the
back streets. It was something he didn't want to do with just a 40
glock. He just wanted to get one or two stragglers. Just before he got
to the middle of his cigarette, he saw a white Regal pulling into the
gas station. Instantly his adrenaline started pumping as a grin spread
across his face seeing it was a K4. Leaving the keys in the ignition,
he stepped out the car and walked casually towards the gas station.

As he approached the side of the gas station he quickly made his way to a nearby pay phone. From the position he observed the full scene before moving into action. Noticing that there were five other cars at the gas pump with others still coming in, he knew it was time to play ball. The traffic distractions would make it easy for him to creep up on his victims. Easing closer to his victim he pulled his glock from his back waistband, placing it by his side. He was about eleven feet away when he quickly saw that the car closest to the K4 contained three females. The K4 noticed too.

Slowing down, Uzi let the K4 take the unintentional bait of the females. Throwing his guard down completely, gave Uzi the chance he was looking for. With his back to Uzi, Uzi knew this mission would end in death, in an unstoppable impetus. Uzi placed the glock to the exposed part of the K4's head squeezing the hair pen trigger tightly. Before the female in the back seat could warn the K4, five hollow points had already entered his braided scalp, instantly flopping his body forward inside the passenger side window.

The females screamed uncontrollably until he started firing inside the car. The back seat driver tried to crawl underneath the driver's seat when the first bullet shattered the window exposing her back to seven shots. The driver didn't see his face up close so he fired three shots into the front seat to keep her down. Every other individual inside the gas station was either lying on the ground or hiding behind their cars. Uzi shot four more times to keep the witnesses at bay while he made his way back around the corner.

Walking quickly to his car he heard sirens flaring up the street in his direction. He instantly dove down to the ground a couple inches away from his car. Uzi crawled to the side of his car and opened the passenger door. Sliding in and breathing with controlled breaths, he jumped into the driver seat and put the car in drive. The police passed him, and he busted a quick u-turn, heading in the other direction as he reached for a Camel. He took a couple of slow pulls while looking in his rearview mirror, as the helicopter hovering ahead was going to the scene.

Ten blocks away he pulled over to a quiet street where he put his gun in the stash spot then got out of the car to urinate on his hands. He spread the urine over his arms to get the gun powder off. Once he was finished, he headed back to his apartment to take another shower and redress. He then called Gina who was highly pissed, to let her know he was on his way.

Uzi let out a sigh of relief as he drove to pick up Gina. It had been a long day, but after getting his much needed fix, he was all right. One thing he could say about Hollywood movies is that they were on point with the feeling of shooting a gun at another person. It definitely felt like he was suspended in time moving in slow motion. Then bam he was back in real time. That's when he knew he got a potent dose. As he got closer to Gina's place he called to tell her to be outside. From the tone of her voice he knew she was madder than his first call. But he didn't give a fuck. He had to get his and she would never understand anyway. As usual, Gina was looking good, standing in front of the house with her lips poked out and hands on her hips.

"How much?" Uzi said, laughing to himself. Flipping Uzi off Gina walked to the car.

"Now that's unlady like."

"At least you could have called me, Uzi."

"I was, but something unexpected came up preventing me from getting to the phone."

"Something like what Uzi?"

"Something like… none of your business. So leave it alone. All that matters is I'm here now."

"Next time call to tell me you're going to be late. So I won't be sitting around dressed for nothing."

"That's all you had to say in the beginning."

One thing that pissed Gina off when it came to Uzi was his duplicity whenever she asked about his whereabouts or what he did with his time when he was not making money. She couldn't understand why he didn't trust her. They had been seeing each other about four months now, obviously he liked something. He kept coming around. It had to be more than just the sex because he could get that from anywhere. That's what made her know deep inside that he really did like her. He was just fronting like he didn't feel for her.

No this bitch didn't. Uzi thought to himself when he noticed Mrs. Uzi one-hundred and seventy-five percent tattooed on Gina's upper left arm in ten inch cursive writing. He grabbed her arm at the red light to make sure he wasn't hallucinating, and realized it was official. Gina wasn't going anywhere.

"Why you grab my arm like that? You like it? I got it when you went out of town."

"It's cool," Uzi said, as Gina stared at Uzi to see what she could get from his facial expression which was nearly impossible to do. His face was so dark and often had a blank expression, that is, unless he was getting his way with something.

"What made you do that?"

"I told you how I felt about you last time we had sex. You thought I was just talking?"

"To keep it real, I didn't even hear you when you said it with all the moaning you were doing."

"Well, since you didn't hear me then, you hear me now. Uzi, I want us to be together."

"We together now. What you talking about?"

"Together in a real official way, with no games or others involved in our relationship."

"So you telling me you want to be like Bonnie and Clyde."

"Stop patronizing me Uzi. I'm serious. I want to be your only girl and you my only man."

"You don't want that," Uzi said pulling underneath the parking garage.

"Wait before you open the door we need to finish talking about this."

"We can talk when we get inside."

Sitting on the couch, Uzi lit a cigarette while listening to Gina plead her case, which was amusing to him. Uzi was about to answer one of her questions when he noticed the breaking news from earlier that day come on the T.V. Uzi quickly changed directions away from Gina to the television and turned the volume up on the T.V. to hear clearer.

"No suspects have been found yet in a shooting that happened today at a south L.A. gas station, which left two dead and one critically injured. Witnesses reported seeing an African American male between the ages of twenty and twenty-five about five-foot five inches tall to five-foot six inches tall and about one hundred and fifty pounds flee the scene of the crime. At this time, this is all the information we have. If you have any information, please call the L.A.P.D. tip line. I'm Sid Garcia reporting with Channel 7 News."

Turning down the volume Uzi leaned back smiling and thinking to himself "mission accomplished." The description given was so vague, he was in the clear. Noticing Uzi's demeanor at hearing the report, Gina felt a cold chill run through her body.

"Why you smiling now?"

"What you talking about?"

"When you heard that news you started smiling."

"It's not that type of smile; I'm just tripping off all the violence that takes place now a day. It's a shame you know?"

"It's sad people still killing each other for nothing."

"Killing for nothing! How you know what they killing for?"

"I know it's over colors and streets they don't own, and that's stupid."

"There you go talking about something you don't even know about. It's deeper then colors and street signs. It's keeping it real for the homies that than died for this and behind bars for life for this. You never thought about that. We suppose to stop because outsiders don't understand this gangsta shit?"

"Make me understand why you gangbang besides that."

"Why? Why not? This is what I was raised to do. It was three categories when I was being brought up: athlete, gangsta, or entertainer. As you can see I'm not into entertaining. My love for drinking, smoking, and sex won't allow me to be Jerry Rice. So I fell into the category you see before you."

"But what do you get out of it?"

"I don't do this to get anything out of it. I just love being a Ransom and the respect that comes with it. It's not the money, bitches or anything superficial. I just like gang banging and I refuse to quit. You may see something wrong with it, but I don't. The people who got something to say about gang banging are just mad because they ain't got it in them."

"What about the innocent victims?"

"The majority of those victims ain't innocent. It trips me out when I see somebody's mom on T.V. crying about how good little Reggie was, showing an old picture from when he was in Jr. high school looking all sweet for the cameras. When his family knows little Reggie was squeezing triggers too. Niggas know in the ghetto where it ain't cool to hang at. They especially know what clothes not to wear but it's always some hard-head wannabe who steps out of character and gets his hat brought to him. On the female issue, bitches gang banging too. So I feel no remorse for them either. Take you, for instance. You know I gangbang. Say one day we driving and someone swiss cheeses my car. Who's to blame? The gangbangers or you, for knowingly being with a gang banger knowing the consequences involved?"

With that question posed, Gina was mad at herself for opening up the can of worms. But she quickly rebutting with, "What about the kids?"

"What about them? Casualties happen in war. Nothing is said about the kids killed in Iraq daily and in other third world countries. Me personally, I go to get my target. If there's a kid in the way I'll try my hardest to avoid shooting them. But if they're in the way I won't lose any sleep."

Uzi's apathy when discussing such delicate issues disturbed Gina. At times she thought he was putting extras, but now she was realizing, he was no feigning this was who Uzi was. This prompted her to; ask what if he had a kid?

"My kid wouldn't be around me in my turf or anywhere gang activity took place. If I was stupid enough to have my kid with me in my turf then I'm willing to accept the consequences for my actions. What? You thought there was a rule book to this shit. It ain't any more rules. The niggas who made the rules don't even follow them. It's to the point where there are generations of snitches running around on the streets. Homies killing homies, leaving solid homies with kick stands and a ton of time on their own, to rot in prison. That's why I make my own Ransom rules and stay solid in all I do. I knock anyone or anything down who goes against my rules, be that police, enemies, or homies. I'll continue doing what I want, when I want, to whom ever I want to answer all your questions. Knowing the consequences involved in being with me, you still want to make it official?"

"Like you said as long as I know what I'm getting involved in, it's on me. So that's a yes."

"All right then. That's enough of that type of talk, it's time to chill."

Chapter 8

Choices Made

"Blood, let me hit the smoke?"

"Like I told you before being they are a dollar for one you ain't hitting anything," Bazooka said taking his last pull.

Months had flown by and Bazooka still wasn't feeling the prison atmosphere. He preferred to have gotten life in Y.A., where it was active with gang banging activity. The majority of his homies had been down awhile and seemed not to have it in them anymore. When he first pulled up wanting to trip on the Crips, they looked at him strangely, telling him he wasn't in county or Y.A. anymore. In prison there's no fighting, especially on the four yards, just knife-play. Furthermore, they told him that boy's fight, and men kill. Hearing that, he asked for a knife, which was graciously provided. When they got wind that he was going to stab a Crip for no reason but gang banging, his homies had a meeting on him.

Reflecting on it made him angry. He could remember vividly them telling him who the real enemies were, and if they weren't trippin we weren't trippin. When Bazooka told them he didn't need their assistance they reminded him that they moved as a group and if one tripped they were all going to trip. His actions would jeopardize the car in which ten out of the twelve homies was hitting not to mention they all had kickstands. Seeing it was a no-win situation, he left it alone and kicked back waiting in the cut for the slightest opportunity to trip.

"Hayes last two?"

"Five, nine." Reading the outside of the envelope he noticed it was a letter from his mother who hardly wrote.

Hopping back on his bunk, he opened the envelope and proceeded to read the letter. After finishing the letter the opportunity he was looking for presented itself. Between the constant lock-downs, routine arguing amongst homies, Bazooka was already reaching his boiling point. The letter made it clear what had to be done, even if it went against the grain of his homies. He didn't come to jail to be on some peace treaty shit. He often wondered who made these soft rules. He was angrier that he was kept in the blind about these prison rules, which seemed more for the comfort of bustas that didn't want to get active. The more he thought about it the more he felt deceived and confused about why a prisoner would want to obey rules after they had a life sentence. Obviously going against the rules of society got them to this point. One thing he knew for sure, was that he wasn't about to fall victim to that mind frame.

Three options crossed his mind to where his life was going at this point. He would end up in the shu with an undetermined time, a C.O. would put a mini fourteen in his brain, or his homies would stab him. If he didn't die from his homies stabbing him, it would be war with them too. It disturbed him deeply that it could end with him warring with the same individuals that would die for what he believed in. But he refused to discuss or compromise about what he was about to do. He wasn't about to ask permission from anybody to take revenge for his brothers death.

The thought of his only brother being gunned down in a gas station caused him to inflame with anger. He refused to walk on the yard with the same individuals that represented a gang that had just killed his brother. Hopping down from his bunk, Bazooka stood at the cell door for hours looking at nothing in particular. He just stood there crumbling up the letter his mom sent. It was no reason to keep it. He wouldn't respond anyway, there was no reason. The emotional bond he shared with his mother as a child had been severed over the years with him constantly disappointing her. There was no point in pretending his brother's death would some how mend emendable wounds or bring them closer. It only made it clear that both her sons were dead. After finishing the letter he reached in his waistband to retrieve his knife. He began to sharpen it against a piece of wall that was suited for the purpose.

After much procrastination in Wayside with medical issues, M-Rat was finally about to start his life sentence in prison. No one was on the yard as he walked to his building escorted by a C.O. Looking at the C.O.s watch, he could see it was ten o'clock in the morning. The yard was on lockdown, which was basically the normal program for a level four, especially at High Desert. Walking through the dayroom M-Rat stared expressionless at the many hardened faces implanted in the cell windows staring out at him. None seemed familiar to him as he continued walking to his new cell. Approaching his cell he noticed a face he kept embedded deep his memory. The sight of the face caused his teeth to clinch together tightly, as he thought to himself it couldn't be. When the face gave him a head nod followed by a B-hand he knew it was no hallucination. The first thought that passed through his mind was to attack the door and diss his turf, but that would be a P.C. move, so instead, he just entered his cell with no response. Once inside the cell M-Rat introduced himself to his new celly who was a Crip from San Diego named W.S. After getting settled and putting his property in the lockers, M-Rat stood by the door as W.S. explained why they were on lockdown.

"Basically the Woods owed the Mexicans a dope debt and wouldn't pay, so the Mexicans took flight. We've been on lockdown about three weeks. They searched the last building yesterday. So we should be coming off in a couple of days. There are a couple of your homies in building one and three."

"What's up with the Crips and the Damus up here?"

"Nothing really, you have a fight here and there. But that's rare. Mostly it's someone getting stabbed."

"Who's all in this building?"

"As far as the Crips, they have fifteen cells and the Damus have ten."

"Where are our neighbors from?"

"One is from Skyline. His name is Bev. The other is from K4CB. His name is Bazooka. He hasn't been on this yard long. I talk to Bev, we know each other from San Diego, and he's cool. His celly be putting too much on it. We don't even talk. Besides that, the building is straight."

*   *   *   *   *   *   *   *   *   *

"That's on Bloods. Blood next door looks familiar." Bazooka kept repeating to his celly as he paced the floor.

"I know he's an enemy. I just can't place the face, but I know I know it."

"What happened when you hit him up?"

"Nothing, busta just looked and walked in his cell."

"Where you think you know him from?"

"That's what I'm trying to figure out, but it will come to me."

"You better get ready M-Rat there about to run showers for our section today. Walking out of his cell to the shower, M-Rat took off his shirt to reveal his remaining tattoos after the attack in the county.

"Blood, I knew it. I knew I recognized Blood. He's from Ransack. I had him tied up in the county last time I was there. He had long hair until I got a hold of him. This must be a sign to go ahead and finish him off."

Coming back from the shower, M-Rat could see Bazooka waiting in the window mad-dogging him with that same smirk he had in the county. As he got closer he could see Bazooka rubbing his index finger underneath his throat. Unable to control himself M-Rat threw up the middle finger with his left hand and the B-hand with his right, before going back in his cell.

Startled by the cell door slamming, W.S. jumped to his feet with a nine inch knife in his right hand he had stashed underneath his mattress. He was ready to attack M-Rat if he made any aggressive moves towards him. In his anger M-Rat had forgotten W.S. was in the cell. When he turned around to apologize, he noticed the thick long knife in his hand. Realizing that a violent altercation could happen, M-Rat quickly explained the situation. After hearing the story, W.S. slowly put his knife away as he forced himself to look at M-Rat's mutilated skin. He couldn't help but sympathize with the anger he felt. The only comforting thing he could tell M-Rat was that the knife was available to him if he wanted to handle his business. With no hesitation, M-Rat informed him it would be handled as soon as the door racked.

That night M-Rat felt a strange sense of comfort inside his mind as he lay on his bunk staring at the back of his eyelids. Bazooka's face had plagued his every thought since the incident in the county. Whatever he was doing, on any given day, Bazooka's face would appear on his mind causing him to look off in an angry daze. His mind constantly kept the memory button mashed down. When dazed, the thought of how the situation could have gone differently, also consumed him. But the most frequent thought that ran through his mind was the many ways he could inflict death upon the guy. Solace came with the fact that he finally knew how he was going to kill Bazooka.

* * * * * * * * * *

Hearing a knock at the door, K-Stone didn't have to walk far to answer because he was washing his hands at the sink.

"Pink last two," the C.O. said holding a white ducat in his hand.

"Eight, three."

Hearing his last two, the C.O. passed the ducat through the side of the door. At first glance he thought it was a ducat for the dentist. He had filled a slip out a week ago and was waiting for a response. Looking closer, he saw it was a job ducat for the p.m. kitchen shift. He would be starting tomorrow, that was cool for him. It usually took a year or longer for an inmate to get a job from what he had heard.

So far, everything was falling in place for him. He had moved into the cell with one of his homies last week who had a T.V. and two radios. His mail was finally running regularly and Ivie had just sent back the marriage package. She was coming to visit him in a couple of weeks which he was looking forward to. It had been far too long since he had squeezed those cheeks. Now all he had to do was get in contact with Uzi to see what was going on in the turf and to get some flicks of the homies.

"Well Ox, you don't have to worry about me cramping your style anymore, they gave me a job today."

"You're not cramping my style K-Stone. I've been down fifteen years. Shit, when Big Burt was in the cell with me in San Quentin he didn't work the whole five years he was down. I'll tell you what's cramping my style, these punkass niggas around here acting tuff. One of these days I'm going to kick one of their asses, K-Stone. You just watch."

K-Stone often tripped off of Ox. He had heard some stories of him from the older homies but nothing in detail. The homies who really put the name out there in the turf were Little and Baby Ox, who were highly active and didn't even know Big Ox. He assumed that his celly was with the business. From what he had seen so far, Ox was a cool older homie. He listened to rap and oldies and had a cool sense of humor for someone with life, even though he denied it. He would always say he had four more years left when the subject of paroling came up. One thing was for sure, Ox liked to drink coffee and pruno and talk bad about everybody. He always seemed to be irritated by what someone did in the building, on the yard, or on T.V. When he would come in the cell and tell K-Stone about how close he came to kicking someone's ass, K-Stone would just laugh and tell him he was crazy. A lot of inmates were scared of Ox because he was built like his namesake, but he always told K-Stone that the real reason they called him Ox was because when he hit someone they would fall out as if kicked by an ox. Hearing about this amazing fighting style, he couldn't wait to see him in action one day.

K-Stone's first day in the kitchen was interesting. He just kicked back and observed everybody working. There were six Mexicans, six Blacks, five Whites, and three Others that worked on the afternoon shift. The Blacks and Others kicked it on the B-side of the kitchen until they were needed to work. The Mexicans and Whites kicked it on the A-side of the kitchen until they were needed. Nobody started working until one o'clock p.m. Up until then they would play cards, dominos, or sleep until they were needed on the lunch line. His first experience on the lunch line was frustrating. They had him putting the bread in the brown bags at the end of the line. He busted a little sweat his first time on the line. It moved really fast and he had to catch on quickly to keep his position. After surviving the lunch serving line he walked around the main kitchen located in the back to get a real feel of his new work environment. The huge ovens made the kitchen extremely hot and it was very compacted, making it hard to maneuver around without bumping into somebody.

K-Stone was about to walk on the back dock outside, when a free staff called him and told him he had to leave the kitchen when he was through packing the lunches. The first week working in the kitchen went by quickly with K-Stone learning all there was to learn about the kitchen job. At first, it seemed strange to him, that certain inmates would throw tantrums to get on the lunch line. Why, he wondered, as it was one of the hardest jobs, excluding the scullery and pots and pans. Three days into his second week of working the line, he found out why. Almost every inmate who worked the line would pocket as many chips, mayo, peanut butter and jelly, or anything else that would sell on the yard. Some even had secret stashes set up for particular days they knew a certain item would be on the line. Watching the inmates put so much skill into stealing to sell, reinforced the reality that he was in a different world. It also explained why he would be missing cookies and other items in his lunch. K-Stone use to get mad when his lunch would come up short and he would have to eat a dry sandwich. After making it to the store he didn't even care anymore. All in all it wasn't that much of a surprise to him. He was in prison. Inmates were going to do what they do. Because K-Stone didn't have to hustle, the only thing he snatched off the line was an extra bag of chips. Overall the kitchen job was cool. It killed a gang of time in the day. When he got off work he would be beat. After taking a shower and chopping-it-up with Ox he would crash out. This process would continue on and on, nothing changing, but his boxers and the clouds in the sky.

"What took you so long to call?" Ivie said excitedly into the phone.

"I was A2B and could only use the phone once a month. So the first person I called was my moms. Now that I'm A1A, I can use the phone whenever I want from the hours of nine a.m. to nine p.m. if I'm not at work or have yard. Besides that, what have you been up to stranger?"

"I've been all right, but I'm much better now that I've heard your voice today. I hope nobody trying to mess with you in there."

"I see you have jokes; we'll see how funny you are when you come up here."

"I'm looking forward to it. I'll be taking the route the computer gave me. It should take about three hours to get there. I'll leave the house about five thirty am."

"That's cool. Did you send the marriage packet?"

"Yesterday, it should be getting to you next week."

"When it does, I'll call or write to let you know if it got approved and what date you need to come up to get the paper work done to make it official."

"You have one hundred and twenty seconds left on the phone." The prison recording informed them cutting into their conversation.

"Why does that voice keep doing that Kay?"

"To annoy me as much as possible. I don't need a recording telling me or you that you're talking to a California state prisoner."

"Calm down K-Stone, it's nothing. Just remember I love you and will be here until you come home to me, no matter what." Before K-Stone could respond the phone automatically hung up.

Walking back to his cell he looked back twice at the phone debating to himself whether to call her back or not. Once he reached his door he decided to wait until the visit to pick up where he left off. It felt good to hear Ivie's voice. There was no denying that it had him feeling good the remainder of the day. Yet, with all that, he was still reluctant to tell her he loved her without feeling strange. He was fully aware that he was stuck in his ways. He honestly didn't see a problem with that. In many ways he was content that the phone hung up prematurely. On Thursday he bought some visiting clothes from an older Black who worked in the laundry. The only thing he couldn't buy was some decent visiting boots because there were none in his size. Luckily, Ox had some that he never wore, wrapped up under the bunk. They were a half-inch too big, but fit fine when he put on an extra pair of socks. That night he took down his chain braids and put his hair in a tight fro after washing it. The following day, K-Stone ironed his shirt and pants in the dayroom. While doing so he couldn't help but to think that Saturday was coming around slower than usual, or maybe he was just a little anxious.

When Saturday morning came, he lay awake in his bed cracking his knuckles thinking to himself, today is the day he would be in a female's company. Hopping down from his bunk he walked to the door to see what time it was. After his vision cleared, he saw he had awakened an hour earlier than usual. Instead of trying to get another hour of sleep, he knew wouldn't happen anyway, he just lay in the bed until the sun slightly peeked through his window. Now it was the proper time to get ready for breakfast.

On his way to the chow-hall it seemed that every other Black in line asked him, if he was going on a visit. They must have assumed he was going on a visit because he always wore his hair in chain-braids. With a simple head nod he answered their questions. The only thing he ate off the breakfast tray was the oatmeal; he gave his coffee cake and peanut butter to Ox, who grabbed the tray with no hesitation. He didn't want to get too full on breakfast. He planned on tasting every food they had in the visiting vending machines that day.

"Why you not eating your coffee cake today?" Ox asked between bites.

"Have to keep room in the belly for later. I'm a little guy. Can't hold as much as you."

Instead of going to morning yard he stayed in and channel-surfed while waiting on his visit. Every time he heard the tower announce someone's name for a visit he bolted off the top bunk to the door to scan the dayroom. Maybe his name would be called next. Around eleven thirty he started to feel a knot twisting inside his stomach. It seemed to get worse when he saw inmates come back in from yard. Before Ox could make it up the stairs, K-Stone was back in his bed with his visiting pants and T-shirt on pretending to watch T.V., as if he didn't have a care in the world. When two thirty came without his name being called over the intercom, the knot had turned into concern, then to anger in a matter of minutes. His deodorant started to fail him as his body temperature rose more and more and the realization sunk in that he wasn't going to get a visit. All that kept running through his mind was that he had done all this preparation for nothing. Furthermore, he was going to be looked at as the guy whose bitch flossed him. At that point K-Stone realized he had discovered a new level of anger that he had never felt before. It felt strangely relaxing as he lay in his bed thinking that he had learned another valuable lesson in prison. Nothing is promised. Not his freedom, not to walk out fully intact, not to be sane, not to change, nothing. The list just kept increasing in his mind as he stood at the door swishing around sour spit in his mouth.

"Bet you wish you ate that coffee cake now."

"You damn right, that's another reason I'm hotter than lava."

The next morning K-Stone was up early waiting on the dayroom to open. He had signed up last night for a nine fifteen phone call and wanted to get all of his minutes in. When the dayroom opened K-Stone walked calmly down the stairs to the phone concealing his anxiousness as much as possible as he dialed Ivie's number. After six rings he hung up the phone and took a deep breath. He redialed the number again, telling himself that he must have dialed the wrong number. After eight rings on his second try and no answer he hung the phone up slowly. He held the phone down on the forks for five seconds before going back to his cell.

While in his cell, K-Stone paced the floor with his eyes closed. He was angrier then the day before, but this time the anger was directed at him self. The whole jail experience made him feel vulnerable and helpless. The thought that he put himself in an uncompromising situation made him sick. He was use to being in control of his life and not being in control always made him feel abnormal. In past situations he was able to use a plan to gain control over any obstacle. What frustrated him the most was that this new obstacle seemed inequitable. It restricted him to a particular area of thought, movement, and action. There was only so much he could make happen in a letter or a fifteen minute monitored phone call. Nevertheless, he had to work with what he had. That was his reality, no matter how he dissected it. He came to a final conclusion that there was no need to stress himself out. He could figure out a way to gain as much control over his life as possible, and that was a fact. He refused to sit around moping like a broad, feeling sorry for his self, any longer. He never did it before and he definitely wasn't going to start now. With that thought thoroughly ingrained in his mind he plugged in his hot pot to make a hot shot of coffee to go along with his cigarette. The rest of the day he just chilled and watched T.V.

* * * * * * * * * *

"I should've not let her use my car, I should've known better!" Ivie kept telling herself looking in the bathroom mirror. Wiping underneath her eyes, she flushed another tear soaked tissue down the toilet before going back in her room. She knew it was K-Stone that called this morning, but she was too scared to answer the phone. She knew he was highly upset and would have probably accused her of knowing better then to let Gina use her car. She was hurt because she did know better. She just didn't think Gina would do something purposely like this to prevent her from seeing her man.

"What's wrong with you?" Gina said smirking as she walked in the house throwing Ivie's car keys on the kitchen counter.

Without thinking, Ivie picked up the closest thing next to her which was a jar of pennies and threw them at Gina's head. The jar skinned Gina's head knocking her to the ground before it shattered against the wall.

"You crazy bitch! What's wrong with you?" Gina said holding the side of her head.

"You knew I was going to see K-Stone yesterday morning and needed the car!"

"If I would have known you needed the car I would have come back Friday night."

"Gina I specifically told you before I gave you the keys that I needed the car back Friday night!"

"Obviously I didn't hear you, because I would have come back."

"Why didn't you answer your phone when I called you?" Stuttering, Gina let out a quick, "My battery was low."

"So why didn't you charge it like you always do."

"Because I was with Uzi and you know how he gets about making unplanned stops."

"I still believe you did it on purpose and because of you K-Stone is mad at me." Hearing Ivie say that made getting skinned in the head worth it. She knew that by making Ivie stand K-Stone up, he would no longer trust her word, or her, which would eventually lead to them separating.

"Look, I'm sorry Ivie. I know how much it probably meant to you to go see K-Stone. It won't happen again."

"It won't happen again because you won't be using my car again!" Ivie said sternly walking to her room and shutting the door. Seeing that Ivie was really upset about what she did, Gina knocked on her door, pleading with her to come out and go to breakfast with her.

"Stop knocking on my door Gina!"

"Don't make me beg, Ivie."

Even though Gina held deep resentment for K-Stone, she loved her sister and was very protective of her. She was her best friend, which made it crucial that she knew they were square before she went through with her day. As much as she wanted to, Ivie couldn't stay mad at her sister even though she did something extremely irresponsible.

"Come in you scandalous female."

"Scandalous?" Gina repeated, relieved that Ivie let her in. "Let me take you out to eat or something to make up what I did unintentionally."

"The only way you can make it up is if you drive me to see K-Stone next week." Before Gina could respond, Ivie cut her off by saying, "I'm not asking I'm telling you."

Trying to get out of it, Gina reminded Ivie that she didn't have a visiting form to go inside.

"You don't need one. You can sit in the car and read a magazine or book until I'm finished inside. So where are you taking me for breakfast?" Ivie asked, grabbing some clothes off her bed.

"Where ever you decide," Gina said with a fake grin.

Dinner was running late which caused K-Stone to wonder what was going on. He thought he heard the alarm go off outside but wasn't sure. From his cell he could stand on the toilet and peek out the window and see the track leading to the chow-hall. When he looked he didn't see any movement. It was strange because it was six thirty p.m. Night yard started at seven o'clock. Returning to his bunk he heard keys jiggling in the distance. He headed back towards the door to see where the noise was coming from. He knew it was bad when he saw a C.O. opening up the food slots on the doors.

"Damn, I hope it's some bull shit," K-Stone said leaning against the wall by the door. Lying on his bed with his beanie covering the majority of his face, Ox asked what was going on.

"Their preparing to cell feed us. Nine times out ten if they're cell-feeding, something serious has happened."

"Well it looks like I won't be making any phone calls this week."

When he saw Blacks and Others pushing food carts in the morning he knew that something must have happened between the Mexicans and Whites inmates. That meant that the Blacks and Others wouldn't be on lockdown long. The institution didn't want to search every building anyway. That only happened when someone got stabbed or weapons were found on the yard. He would just have to play it by ear and see what was going on.

K-Stone was on his tenth domino game with Ox when the Black Mac-Rep came knocking at their door to tell them that the

Blacks would be coming off of lockdown Friday. Finally, some good news K-Stone thought, as he called domino.

Tired and hot, K-Stone worked the afternoon away in the back of the kitchen washing pots and giant sheet pans. It caught him off-guard when they called him into work the day after getting off lock-down. Thursday night, he had stayed up drinking coffee and chopping-it-up with Ox. Four hours passed and his fingers were pale white and wrinkled from the hot water constantly entering his gloves. He couldn't wait to end the day that seemed to be moving at a steady, slow pace. Heat from the ovens along with the steaming hot water had him exhausted by the time his shift was over. With the remaining energy he had left, he took a lukewarm shower then locked it up in the cell, calling it a night.

Sunlight lightly baked K-Stone's eye lids causing him to wake up seeing crimson Saturday morning. This sent him into a frenzy trying to get out of bed to go to breakfast. Whenever the sun raised before him, he knew he had over-slept. Grabbing his toothbrush off the locker he jumped down to the floor. The cold floor sent an instant surge through his body causing him to jump a couple of inches off the floor. Sitting down on the toilet he quickly reached for his socks and boots under the bottom locker and proceeded to brush his teeth. With water dripping down his face, K-Stone looked out the door window to see what time it was. Then he suddenly remembered that they were still being cell-fed. Hopping back on his bunk, he thought to himself. I must've been really tired yesterday because I'm tripping. From that little episode he could tell it was going to be one of those crazy days.

Picking out his hair he decided to get it braided when he went to afternoon yard and play a couple of games of chess with the older cats. More importantly, he would finally get a chance to call Ivie and see what had happened last week.

* * * * * * * * * *

"You got enough juice and water to keep you hydrated?" Ivie asked, taking off her coat to put in the back seat.

Looking through a stack of magazines Gina asked how long she was going to be. "We already discussed this the day before and on the way up here. When the visit is over, it's over. That's all you need to know."

"Know this, if you leave me in this car for too long, I'll leave you."

"Not without these," Ivie said grabbing the keys off the arm rest.

"It's too hot to be leaving me in this car for a long period of time!"

"You've been in hotter situations, you'll be all right."

"Hold up Ivie, I almost forgot I need a couple of visiting forms for my home girl."

"I'll bring you some on my way back.

One thing Gina was right about was it was hot and it was only nine in the morning." Ivie said to herself as she got closer to the visitors check point. She had gotten her hair done the other day in a wrap with waterfalls the way K-Stone liked it. She even went and bought a new outfit for the occasion that she knew he would like too. The only thing negative that occupied her mind was if the spark would still be present between them. It had been a long time since they actually touched each other or talked for over fifteen minutes.

When she got inside the visiting room, Ivie took a seat and waited for the C.O. at the podium to page K-Stone. While sitting on the hard plastic seat trying to get as comfortable as possible she observed her surroundings, taking notice of all the females inside the visiting room. They ranged from young to old and were of various races, most with small children or babies. For a brief moment her thoughts drifted away as she tried to imagine how difficult it must be for the mothers, grandmothers, girlfriends, and wives to take care of their children and grown men. She tried, but couldn't fathom the thought of being in a financial or emotional position like that. She commended them for their enormous inner strength.

"Pink, you have a visit. Flash your light when you're ready," the C.O. said over the microphone.

Lying in his bed, K-Stone thought he was tweaking when he heard his name called. Nevertheless, he was sure enough to flash his light. When the door popped open he knew it was official. Without further delay he pulled his visiting pants from underneath his mattress, grabbed his shirt off the wall hook, and pulled out Ox's boots from underneath the bunk. He spent five minutes in the mirror adjusting his afro, which he was glad he washed the day before. He stepped out of his cell to see who had come to visit him. He knew it could only be one of two people. Waiting at the gate for the C.O. to come get him, he could feel the nervous scoops in his stomach as he paced from the gate to the curb thinking to himself. Who could it be? At this point, it really didn't matter. He was just grateful to get a chance to escape from the prison atmosphere for a couple of hours.

Once the C.O. arrived, he patted him down and then walked him through the gate to the visiting room. Stepping into the visiting room for the first time, K-Stone felt like he discovered a secret paradise in the middle of the desert. The sight of normally dressed people amongst the blue shirts and jeans felt unreal. As he scanned the crowd for who came to see him he got nostalgic of how he felt as a child when he got lost in the grocery store. The feeling was a combination of nervousness and curiosity. Continuing further through the small visiting room he could feel eyes fixed upon him. When he looked to his left to meet the stare he was met by slender, out-stretched, dark-skinned arms coming his way at full-speed. Without much thought he recognized who it was and scooped Ivie up, hugging her tighter than ever before. He held her so tightly she had to signal for him to loosen up, which he did so slowly. They followed up with a long kiss in which he slid his tongue through every area of her warm, sweet-tasting mouth. All the while he was grabbing her cheeks firmly pressing her neatly against his ever-increasing bulge. As this warm embracement continued, K-Stone forgot he was in the visiting room. Though his eyes remained open during the whole encounter, he allowed himself to get caught in the moment as he caressed every curve of Ivie's shapely lower body moving to the upper region with his left hand. He was almost to her breast when his trance was temporarily broken by a microphone yelling his last name to report to the podium.

"Mr. Pink! The rules clearly explain that you are only allowed a brief kiss and hug. It's obvious you either don't know about these rules or simply don't care. Anyway you look at it, its grounds to terminate your visit. Mr. Pink, do you understand what I'm saying?"

Does it look like I understand or care, was the response he wanted to give. But he simply stated it was his first time in the visiting room and didn't know.

"Well, next time read the rules, Pink. This is your last warning." Walking back to his assigned table he was beyond pissed at being told how to greet his lady by another man. Nevertheless, K-Stone wasn't going to let that minor interruption ruin his day.

"What did they want Kay?"

"Nothing, they just swinging on the nuts of a Ransom nigga. It's nothing new that's what they do, swing. Besides, to what do I owe the surprise?"

"Don't play Kay, I know you're mad and want to know what happened last week."

"Go ahead state your case," K-Stone said pulling his chair closer to the table leaning his body forward.

"First off, there is no real excuse. I let Gina use my car the night before and she didn't come back until Sunday. I know how she is and I shouldn't have let her use the car, I'm sorry Kay."

"Don't say you're sorry because you're not. Sorry people are sorry and you're far from that. You made it a point to come up here this week, so that shows me way more than an apology could ever say. So don't even trip. We'll put that behind us and stay moving forward. Like I mentioned in the county, is that cool with you?"

"Of course it's cool with me. Stop playing."

Two hours went by in a matter of minutes with K-Stone and Ivie conversing like they had never been apart. This made Ivie feel totally at ease as she played with how Ivie Pink would sound, in her mind. The spark she was so worried about leaving, was not. For this was a new spark and was more intense. This brought a new surge that seemed to be missing before.

Standing in the microwave line waiting to warm up some buffalo wings, K-Stone couldn't help but notice how good Ivie was looking. She had filled into her body in the last year. She was wearing a pink, short-sleeve shirt that held her c-cup breast well with some white, khaki pants that were fitting every curve right. Sneaking in a grind, while she was bending over to put the chicken in the microwave, he let her know how good she was looking when she raised back up. To which she said thank you.

"You're not looking to bad either. It looks like you've been doing some working out."

"I do what I can, when I can," K-Stone said walking back to the table.

"Did the directions on the internet help you find the prison fast?"

"Yeah, they helped out a lot more than the directions the prison gave me."

"I'm surprised you're not tired from driving all the way up here."

"I would've been if I'd drove myself."

"Who would drive you all the way up here and sit in the car?"

"Who do you think?"

"If I knew I wouldn't have asked. For all I know it could be Kermit the Frog who drove you up here."

"Ha! Ha! My sister drove me, if you must know."

"Like I said Kermit the Frog."

Laughing to himself, K-Stone continued eating his chicken while taking glimpses of the other female visitors that were looking rather nice. However, there were others that looked like they could start for the Raiders defensive line.

"I'm surprised Kermit, I mean Gina would do something like that."

"She had no choice after the stunt she pulled."

"In a way it sounds like you Black mailed her into bringing you."

"A lady knows how to get things done."

"Like that, huh?" K-Stone said sipping on a Squirt. "You seem to have gotten a little cold since the last time we saw each other."

"There's nothing cold about me. I just decided to stop letting people run over me, Kay."

"There's nothing wrong with that just don't deviate from the real you."

"What do you mean by that?"

"In the process of you discovering more about yourself don't lose what really makes you, you."

"Give me an example of how you see me?"

"You're nice, caring, and understanding. Those traits and many more make up who you are, in my opinion. When we were on the streets together I noticed that you let your friend's, and your sister, take advantage of you with you saying nothing."

"Why didn't you say anything?"

"I just figured you didn't notice or just didn't care. Obviously you did notice it and got tired of it. There's nothing wrong with putting your foot down when people try to run over you. It's important to have strength of character. Just don't allow that strength to make you mean, which can easily happen. Before you know it, everybody will be calling you a bitch. And your only weak reply will be, 'I don't care what people say about me, which as we know is a lie. People thrive off opinions of who they are, to a certain extent. Besides, I deal with enough hardheads daily, for my lady to be acting like one." Bawling up his fist, K-Stone extended one of his knuckles and placed it against Ivie's forehead telling her, "Don't be a knucklehead."

Ivie responded, pointing at K-Stone's head with her small knuckles. "I've missed you a lot Kay, I can't wait till you come home."

"As long as I'm in the left side of your chest, I'm always at home."

"I know, but there are times when I need your physical touch and there is nothing but emptiness to grab a hold of."

"At those times what do you do?"

"Write you a letter letting you know you're on my mind or just allow my thoughts to drift."

"Well you won't have to worry about your thoughts drifting for too long. When the marriage package goes through you'll have that physical touch we both need, every sixty days."

Smiling, Ivie put her hand in the middle of the table, which K-Stone met quickly. In an ineffable moment they sat at the table across from each other imagining their future together. Time came to an end quickly on their first visit, with neither one wanting it to end. Plans for another visit had already been established. Watching Ivie leave without him felt unnatural. Something inside of him didn't want to go back without her. Ivie glanced back at him every few steps she took towards the exit.

Having to denude after the visit, stripped more then his clothes, but his sense of being normal as the reality of being in prison sank back into his mind instantly. Returning back to the yard, K-Stone caught a glimpse of Ivie getting into her car bringing back another type of feeling that was hidden deep within the catacomb of his mind; loneliness. At that moment he realized that the feelings he had for Ivie were genuine and there was no further reason to keep trying to convince himself that they were anything else. Heading back to his building, K-Stone felt ecstatic. He couldn't wait to get back to his cell, kick back, and enjoy the good feeling he was having with a cigarette. Day room was just being recalled when he stepped inside the building. Walking to his cell, he was asked by a couple of inmates how his visit went. He answered cool, thinking to himself how else would it be.

* * * * * * * * * *

A couple of days turned into three weeks with the whole prison still on lockdown as the institution continued its investigation regarding the riot. As the days continued to mount, M-Rat's mind slipped further into a primitive state of killing. It came to a point where he would sit in the middle of the cell, hunched over, sharpening his knife on the floor. The only reason he stopped this practice was because W.S. reminded him he could dull the knife if he continued trying to sharpen it. Revenge overwhelmed his mind day and night as rumors circulated that the prison would come off of lock-down soon.

"Look Blood, I'm going to stab Blood next door when we come off lockdown. So you don't gotta trip and jump in. I got this blood."

"You sure?"

"Blood, I don't need any help on any Ransack nigga. You just be sure not to interfere with me getting mines on, or you might get some too."

"What's that suppose to mean, Blood?"

"Whatever you want it to mean."

"You are standing up like you about to make it happen dog."

Before Bev could respond, Bazooka struck him in the mouth with a hard left, followed by a right upper cut that skinned Bev's forehead. Bev fell to the ground from the first blow. Moving in to stomp him out, he stopped when he saw Bev covering his head with his arms. But that's not what stopped him. He remembered he ran out of tobacco and Bev had a fresh pouch sitting on his pillow.

"Get up Blood, it ain't like that. Just watch your mouth when you're hollering at me." Crawling off of the floor, Bev sat on his bunk and reached for a towel hanging on his laundry line to wipe his bloody lip.

"Look Blood I've been really irritated lately since this Ransack moved next door. I ran out of smokes yesterday and I'm nicking bad."

Hearing this, Bev passed Bazooka a cigarette seeing where the conversation was going. Deep inside Bev hoped Bazooka would get caught so he could get a new celly that was cool. Since he moved into the cell he had been cramping his style with his constant flare ups when things weren't going his way. Going into his last pouch of tobacco, Bev gave Bazooka a nice size pinch with some papers, in hopes he would leave him alone for a few days.

Lying against his rolled up mattress, M-Rat was staring at his cell door thinking to himself, open. To his surprise the door suddenly popped open. Grabbing his knife from his waist-band, he ran out the door making a right into Bazooka's cell which was also open, along with every cell on the bottom tier. Nudging the door

open a little wider, M-Rat ran in with knife in hand catching
Bazooka in the rib with his nine inch bone crusher. While
hopping down off his bunk and giving a loud grunt, Bazooka fell off
the bed sideways, crashing against the top locker as M-Rat extended
his right hand further back to take another stab at his body. Barely
gaining his balance from the assault, Bazooka had no choice but to
embrace the unblockable knife, which was thrust into his forearm as
he rushed towards M-Rat. Ignoring the pain and the blood spitting
out of his side and forearm, Bazooka and M-Rat struggled by the
toilet area. With his hands tightly gripping M-Rat's wrist, Bazooka
tried to knock the knife out of his hand by banging it against the
wall. With blood slipping between Bazooka's finger tips, he lost his
grip on M-Rat's left hand and M-Rat punched him in the face.
Squinting from the blow, Bazooka released his other hand. Seeing
his opportunity open up, M-Rat rushed Bazooka with as much speed
as possible, tackling him to the floor. They landed between the
bottom locker and bunk. Managing to get on top during the struggle,
M-Rat sat erect on top of Bazooka preparing to run his knife through
his chest, when Bev kicked him in the side of the body knocking him
off Bazooka into the locker.

Up until that point, Bev didn't interfere due to Bazooka's
request, but he couldn't allow for a Crip to come in his cell and
murder another Blood in front of him. In his rage, M-Rat didn't pay
attention to Bazooka's celly during the confrontation. The kick
caught him by surprise and caused him to pull up on the locker and
step back giving Bazooka the opportunity to grab his knife off his
bed. For a brief moment Bazooka and M-Rat were at a stand off.
M-Rat calmly stepped out the cell with his right arm extended,
pointing his knife at Bazooka. Skimming against the door on his
way out, M-Rat reached around awkwardly with his left hand to
slide the door open. Inching closer the whole time, Bazooka saw a
chance and attempted to stab M-Rat in the neck. Instead of hitting
his neck the knife penetrated in M-Rat's left shoulder blade, causing
M-Rat to twist outside the cell. Feeling himself begin to tire from
the blood loss, Bazooka kept continuing his assault. Soaked in
blood, M-Rat stumbled out onto the tier. When he regained his
breath, he saw Bazooka wide eyed charging his way. Crouching
down, M-Rat pointed his knife down and went into a stabbing
motion as Bazooka ran at him with his knife straight out. Tightening
his stomach as the knife sunk deep within his belly button, M-Rat's
hand came crushing down, stabbing Bazooka in the head, neck, and

shoulders multiple times. Bazooka pulled away, falling to the ground, holding patches of his scalp together. No matter how hard he tried, he couldn't stop the blood from clouding his eyes, nor could he gather the strength to attack. Furthermore, Bazooka kept slipping on his own blood as he tried with no avail to get to his feet. M-Rat stood over him watching. The tower guard hit the alarm when he noticed the bloody inmates and grabbed the mini fourteen yelling for M-Rat to get down. Discombobulated by the whole event and clinching his stomach, M-Rat stood over Bazooka content that he had avenged himself and his turf. M-Rat kept kicking him in the head every time he tried to crawl helplessly towards him. Consumed by Bazooka dying, M-Rat failed to see the C.O.s running towards him yelling at him to get down. Approaching closer to M-Rat, they noticed the knife hanging by his side. The C.O.s came to a halt informing him to drop the knife. Looking at the C.O.s, thoughts of an undetermined shu program ran through his mind. He decided at that moment, that he was ready to chill with K-Slim. With the decision firmly planted, he charged the C.O.s. Taking two steps towards them, a bullet was fired ripping a chunk of his skull apart. Clump was the sound M-Rat made as he hit the floor besides Bazooka's dead body.

There was no need for the MTA to check their bodies, and it didn't take a medical expert to tell they were dead. Once the alarm was shut off, the C.O.s stood around looking at the bloody bodies. The bodies looked like they were torn apart by wild animals. The goon squad finally arrived and took pictures of the bodies, bagged the knives, and picked up any other evidence to log in. The investigation lasted a couple of hours with the conclusion in that they came as numbers, died as numbers, for representing a number.

"Remember that nigga K-Stone I went to go see that day on seventy-fifth?"

"Somewhat. You mean like a year ago?"

"Yeah, that nigga. I need you to do me a huge favor girl and there is some money in it for you."

"I'm listening."

"Look I got this prison visiting form I need you to fill out and mail to K-Stone under the name Kevin Pink. I'll give you the rest of the information when I get it later tonight. After the form gets approved, I need you to go up there on a particular day I tell you and pretend to be his baby momma while my sister is there with him. You down?"

"How much money you talking about?"

"One-hundred up front, and one-hundred plus, depending on how good a job you do convincing my sister."

"I'm in."

"Smart girl. I'll be over there tonight." Gina said, collecting the mail from her box.

Sorting the mail, she found K-Stone's address and copied it on a separate sheet of paper. She was overly tired of driving Ivie up to Centinela to see K-Stone while she sat in the car baking. Her mother always told her to look for the best in people and situations. She always took it as a bullshit cliché until it hit her while driving. She wanted to have one of her home girls come visit while Ivie was on a visit. After many years of hearing the platitude, she finally believed it. This plan was better then the one she thought of before because it was full proof. To put a cherry on top, Gina would be there to see it all unfold.

Chapter 9

Intro to Failure

"Ms. Hayes, if there is anything you need just call me at this number." One of Bazooka's homies said at the end of the funeral handing her a piece of paper.

"No baby, I won't be needing anything. You guys paying for both my son's funerals is enough." Walking to their cars, Bazooka's homies huddled in the parking lot. "Blood this not the business. We lost two of our soldiers to those Ransacks, we need to set an example ASAP. It's up to us to step to the plate and knock down some of their main heads. Word on the street, is that nigga Uzi killed the homie at the gas station. This bitch I be hitting told me she use to hang with Blood. He drive's a midnight blue Monte Carlo.

"It's a must that this Ransack gets properly touched. So they can feel what we feeling now." With that said they jumped into their cars and drove back to their turf. Some went back to the turf to get high and forget about what happened, while others went to load up heats getting ready for revenge. The rest went and chilled with their females and did nothing.

That following week, the K4CB's declared a full-scale war on the Ransoms by striking up in their turf daily and shooting anybody who looked like they were affiliated with the Ransom gang. After two weeks of shooting at one another, the K4's saw a pattern occurring causing them to have another meeting amongst themselves to re-group. "Look Blood, we've been serving the Ransacks for two weeks and all we've done is killed a non-affiliate, a smoker, and sent a couple of them to the hospital with minor wounds. Furthermore, they have put some of the homies in the hospital too. Shooting wannabes and non-affiliates is not cutting it. It's time we find Uzi or another main head and make them lean back permanently. All this irrelevant shooting is doing nothing but making the turf hot. I want these fools crying over their casket wearing t-shirts with R.I.P., feel me Blood?"

"On Bloods."

"Then let's make it happen."

Since hitting the bank lick, Uzi was relaxing in his town house he purchased two months after the robbery; enjoying the lifestyle he thought was only possible for athletes and entertainers. Playing with hundreds of thousands gave him a new feeling of power he never felt before and planned to keep permanently. He thought as he stood on his balcony looking over the quiet Inglewood neighborhood.

He knew he had to hit another lick soon to maintain his new lifestyle. Though his ecstasy and chronic spot was bringing in a nice chunk, it only covered the rent for the town house but not his daily expenses that were growing. Uzi realized that he needed to get a new ride to match his new lifestyle. The Monte Carlo was cool for a minute, but the days of riding in cars of the past were over. It was time to elevate his game to another level.

Word spread to him quickly that the K4CB's had a hit out on him, but he didn't give a fuck. This was the lifestyle he lived for, the five W's: weed, wine, women, wealth, and weapons. However the K4CB's wanted it, he would give it to them.

Hearing a knock at the door, Uzi walked to see who it was with his mack-11 in his hand. Looking through the peep hole, he saw that it was Gina. Before opening the door, he gazed at his Rolex and thought it was too early in the morning for her to be dropping by unannounced. For a brief minute, Uzi contemplated not opening the door for Gina. He didn't like being bothered early in the morning when he was chilling. Knocking at his door again, Gina was about to shout his name, when he opened the door.

"What took you so long to answer the door?"

"Does it matter, I answered it."

"When am I going to get a key, Uzi?"

"What do you need a key for? If I'm here you'll get in, and if I'm not, you'll just be sitting at the door."

"That's a cold thing to say to your lady."

"But it's a real thing said. If you give me a decent reason you need a key, I might give you one. Hold on before you start to explain, I need to get something." Going into his room, Uzi got a neatly rolled blunt off his night stand. He then returned back to the living room, sat down on the couch, lighting his blunt as Gina started to explain while standing in front of him with her hands on her hips.

"And thirdly, I think it's time we stayed together." Inhaling the smoke from the blunt, Uzi shook his head in disapproval to all the reasons she put out.

"You're going to have to come-up with something better than that for a key. By the way, what do you think you'll be doing all day in my tilt while I'm gone?"

"Doing female things, like rearranging furniture."

"You can do all that at your place. Why do you feel the need to come over here to do that?"

"Oh, I know why you don't want me to have a key," Gina said sitting beside him on the couch. "You don't want me to cramp your style with your other little hoes."

"Here you go with that non-sense. Have you ever seen me with another bitch?"

"No, but I'm not stupid, Uzi."

"You must be, bringing up a stupid conversation like this."

"Why do you talk to me like that?"

"Why do I talk to you like what? I've been talking to you this way since we met. Now all of a sudden it's a problem. If you don't knock it off with the theatricals Gina…"

"I'm just trying to express my feelings and you're taking it as a joke."

"Look when I feel you need a key, you'll get a key. Beyond that, I'm not holding you here with any restraints. If you're unhappy, bounce."

"Just like that, Uzi?"

"Just like what?"

"You'll get rid of me just that quickly?"

"I'm not getting rid of you, I like having your funny looking ass around. It's you with all this drama early in the morning messing with a young Ransom Crip, when he's trying to chill. What happened to the days when you use to come through and serve me then hook-up some breakfast or dinner and just relax? You want to barge in here harassing Uzi, not worried about how I'm doing. It's all about Gina, and you say I'm tripping. Get a life."

"You're right baby."

"I don't need to hear all that we better then cheap words. Just kick it and do you. I'm not even tripping you still cool with me," he said as he put his arms around her waist.

After the argument Uzi asked Gina why she came by so early. "Because you've been hard to catch lately. It seems like you're always busy and never have time for me anymore like you use to."

"Things have been hectic for me lately. That's why it seems like that. It's not that I'm trying to avoid you. If it was like that, it wouldn't be hard for you to tell."

"Is that right?"

"It's not wrong." With that said Uzi pulled another perfectly rolled blunt from his robe pocket and lit it.

After deeply inhaling the blunt, he passed it to Gina who also took in a large pull, then passed it back. In an implicit moment, Uzi looked at Gina with blood shot eyes and exhaled a cloud of smoke, as she slid her hand gently into his sweat-shorts to find his penis fully erect. Sliding his shorts all the way down to his thighs, Gina looked up at Uzi to make sure she had his full attention.

Gina wrapped her moist lips around his penis, moving up and down his shaft slowly while maintaining eye contact. Uzi fell into a trance as he eased back on the couch with each stroke of her tongue. He thought to himself before releasing his man juices that this bitch was not worth it.

"Damn! I hate going to Capone's cell, it smells like cowboys living in there," Ox said coming in from work. "What you been up to, K-Stone?"

"Nothing much, just writing my broad to tell her the marriage forms has been approved. All she has to do now is send the two-hundred dollars to make it official to walk down the aisle."

"So you think she's going to send the money?"

"She better, if she planning on getting married. Besides I don't see why she wouldn't."

"Sometimes they change up when it's time to take that final step."

"I'm confident she won't freeze up on your boy. We have a solid understanding."

"You sure?"

"Why would you ask me something like that? You think I'm in denial about something?"

"Not at all. It's just you have to be careful with the information females give you while your up in here."

"Up until now, the information has been on point. I'm going on visits, going to the store monthly, and I'll be on a fam bam in a couple of months. Ivie's made that happen. So her information and actions are all right with me."

"If you say so."

"Cuzz, what's that suppose to mean?"

"Nothing."

"You saying nothing, but it seems like your trying to get at something without actually saying it directly. To keep it real, sounds like your border line hating."

"Hating! Hating on what?"

"That's what I'm trying to figure out. It seems like every since I started getting visits you've been having a little attitude or something smart to say when I ask you a question."

"I don't got no attitude. You just trippin, K-Stone."

"Do you see me on the floor? I'm not tripping on shit, you know how you been acting lately, whether you admit it or not."

"Man, I don't know what you're talking about."

"I don't know why your sitting on the bunk looking confused for."

"Like I'm making all of this up, or maybe I'm just seeing and hearing things. Maybe I'm not even here. I'm probably off sherm in a prison version of Alice and Wonderland. Tell me then magic cat, when am I going to wake up back on the turf?"

With no response from Ox, K-Stone left the conversation alone and hopped on his bunk to re-read his letter before sending it off. All he could think about besides the weirdo on the bottom bunk was how close he was to a family visit. Having a little extra time on his hands, he decided to write Uzi a letter and mail it along with the letter to Ivie because he didn't have his new address.

Ox's constant complaining day after day was starting to irritate K-Stone. It seemed odd to hear a person complain so much about everything. Ox's complaints constantly consisted of the program being boring, the food not tasting good, and not having enough T.V. channels to zone out on. Ox had a complaint about almost everything he could think of. At first it was amusing to listen to Ox talk about everybody in the prison, until it became an everyday thing. Furthermore, he noticed that the majority of the people he referred to as bitches and bustas, he drank coffee, played cards, and talked about sports with. This made K-Stone wonder what he was saying about him behind his back. Annoyance reached to a new extreme when K-Stone realized that Ox was obsessed with the sink in the cell. He often bragged about how it shined like a chrome Daton, which it did. Then he would marvel at how he could see his reflection in it. The annoyance began to grow immensely when he could sense Ox's eyes on him whenever he cleaned the sink on his clean up- days. Knowing that he was constantly watching over him, K-Stone would quickly turn around to try and catch Ox staring, but Ox would be pretending to watch T.V. when he turned around. What would be the eventual breaking point was when Ox evaluated the cell after K-Stone would get through cleaning the cell. Ox would get up, and without saying a word, re-clean the whole cell. After a month of this behavior, K-Stone couldn't hold back any longer.

"What the hell is that about?" K-Stone said, gesturing to him on cleaning the sink.

"What you talking about?"

"Cuzz, you know what the hell I'm talking about. Why you always wait till I get finished cleaning, then hop up and re-clean?"

"Because there is always streaks in the sink when you get through."

"There shouldn't even be clean up days if you feel that your cleaning method is superior."

"If you felt like that, you should've said something instead of doing that bitch shit."

"Bitch shit?"

"Yeah bitch shit nigga! That's what it is. Instead of you hollering about the cleaning situation like a man. You just keep quiet and resort to weird shit.

"You not about to be talking to me like that K-Stone!"

"Cuzz, that's said."

Grabbing a sock from his bed that contained a can of chili at the end. K-Stone waited to hear Ox's next response. After the awkward silence which caused the tension to steadily climb, Ox took a seat on his bunk and began to speak to K-Stone.

"You're young and all you want to do is fight. That's the reason I never said anything. You need to take your time when cleaning the cell, that's all."

While listening, K-Stone couldn't help but think that Ox's excuses were complete nonsense. He knew all Ox had to do was bring it to his attention. As Ox continued talking, K-Stone realized that Ox's whole tough image was just a front. Realizing that Ox was going to keep rambling on, K-Stone cut him off.

"Next time, if there's an issue, just get at me. You're painting a picture like I'm incapable to talk too. I'm just not with the funnies. We from the same turf, you know the business."

With that, K-Stone laid back on his bunk, clinching his sock by his side, knowing things would never be the same between him and Ox.

The days began to feel the same again, and it was as if their titles didn't even matter anymore. Mondays felt like Fridays and Saturday felt like yesterdays. K-Stone's boxed-in life was slowly beginning to feel controlled with the every day schedule becoming monotonous. War stories were told everyday, drinking pruno on the weekends and at work had become common, and sex talk happened every thirty minutes. Stale thoughts, breath, and conversation had become his new life. Breakage of this cycle came in the form of a letter from Ivie informing him that all the necessary steps were completed, and that they could pursue with the marriage. That night K-Stone sipped on some white lighting and smoked a couple of sticks he had stashed away for later use. He even felt kind enough as to offer Ox a drink, though their communication between one another had came down to head nods and body language. This caused a cloud of tension to engulf the cell whenever both of them occupied it. Ox, of course held his cup up, making sure it was filled to the rim. Seagram's Gin, was the signal his tongue sent to his brain as he downed the remainder of the first cup of sour pruno sweat. It didn't take long for the effects of the alcohol to take hold, as a feeling of being caught in the grip of a giant over took his body. Zombied out, listening to CBO on his radio, and watching T.V, K-Stone's thoughts drifted from the intoxication.

Ivie's image ran through his mind, as it did often bringing him solace the alcohol only pretended to do. Waking up in the middle of the night, with his eyes hurting from the TV's blaring light in his face and a dry mouth from the alcohol, weed, and cigarettes. K-Stone rolled over facing the wall to regain his focus before getting up to get some water.

Turning back around, he untangled his head phone cord from around him and reached out to turn the T.V. off. While doing so, he caught a glimpse of Ox standing in the door way looking out the window butt-naked lathered up in baby oil. At first he thought he was hallucinating from the drugs. He looked again and saw that Ox was masturbating to a female C.O. in the tower. In a split second, the signal to attack reached his brain causing K-Stone to grab his can in a sock from underneath his pillow. Without Ox noticing, K-Stone silently came down from his bunk, stepped on the desk to the stool, and winded his sock up as he crept towards Ox. When K-Stone came in striking distance, he swung a maelstrom of

blows to the back of Ox's head. The blows were so sever the
corners of the chili can became disfigured as they cut deep into
Ox's skull giving off a squishy sound as blood spattered all over the
mirror, front window, and walls surrounding the bathroom.
Completely surprised from the assault, Ox could barely turn around
to defend the unexpected assault, losing consciousness with each
vicious blow delivered to his head and arms that he used to protect
himself. Seeing that Ox's was losing consciousness, K-Stone got
entrapped in the moment, as he worked the chili can in a sock like
nun-chucks coming down hard against the front of Ox's face leaving
lacerations with each blow.

     Naked on the floor, lying between the door and toilet, Ox
was completely unconscious while the blood continued to pour out
of his head into a pool of blood. K-Stone stood over Ox holding the
bloody sock breathing heavily like an insane tyrant. For a brief
moment K-Stone stood there staring at Ox's bloody clothes
contemplating how he was going clean up the mess he created.

     The first thought that came to his mind was to get rid of the
weapon. Without hesitation, K-Stone flushed the bloody sock down
the toilet along with his bloody muscle shirt. Then he washed and
cleaned the disfigured can, placing it in the paper bag they used as a
trash bag. Looking down at Ox one more time, he decided to cut
some strips of sheets so he could tie him up before Ox regained full
consciousness. Before doing so, K-Stone threw his pants that had
specks of blood on them under the bunk. Grabbing an extra pair of
pants from his laundry bag, K-Stone opened a razor and began
cutting the sheet.

     Then he heard some keys jiggling. Before the confrontation,
K-Stone didn't realize what time it was. He just knew it was late.
Hearing the keys, he realized that it was too late to clean up his
mess. The only way he was going to get a chance was if the C.O. in
charge of the count passed by the cell like they normally did. Taking
no chances he hopped in the bed turning off the T.V. and pretended
to be asleep. K-Stone lied on his back with his heart beating
furiously to the point of discomfort. Peeking through the small holes
he watched for the C.O. to flash his light in the cell as he heard the
keys approaching nearer. When the C.O. arrived to the door, he
flashed the light in the cell, and then walked off as usual.

     Exhaling a deep breath, K-Stone was about to hop down;
when the C.O. doubled back knocking on the window. At first, K-
Stone stood motionless as the C.O. knocked a little harder with each

non-response. Flashing the light again inside the cell, the C.O. noticed some blood at the bottom of the window and immediately hit the alarm button. Hearing the sirens go off, K-Stone knew he had to get up and meet his punishment. Before doing so, K-Stone put together a plan and pretended as if he didn't know what had happened. As long as Ox didn't snitch, he had nothing to worry about. Getting out of bed, K-Stone walked to the door and acted surprised at what was going on. Ten C.O.s trailed along with a medical cart and a few M.T.A.s rushed into the building while K-Stone stood staring out the window. When they made it up stairs to his door, they looked in and told him to turn the lights on. Then, they opened the tray slot ordering K-Stone to turn around and place his hands through the slot for hand-cuffing. Once the process took place, they popped the door open and escorted him down the tier to the dayroom.

"Oh my God!" Was the scream he heard coming from the top tier when a female M.T.A looked into the cell and found Ox. Another C.O. threw up on the tier from the bloody scene. From their reactions, K-Stone started to question himself if he had killed him.

"So what happened?" The sergeant asked sitting opposite him.

"That's the same question I'm asking myself."

"You mean you don't know what happened?"

"Your guess is as good as mines. When I woke up he was like that."

"Mr. Pink. You're telling me that you didn't notice anything strange going on while you were asleep?"

"No, how could I? I was asleep."

"And I guess you don't know how he got that way?"

"I have no idea. You should ask him."

"What bothers me Mr. Pink is you don't seem moved."

"It's kind of hard for me to take all this in at once. I'm a fragile dude." Tired of K-Stones sarcasm, the sergeant walked over to the medical cart where Ox's laid naked strapped to the bed.

"Are you all right?" Barely conscious, Ox could hardly utter a word to respond to the sergeant's question. "What happened?" When the sergeant saw that it was frivolous to continue questioning Ox in his current condition he gave the okay to take him to central health for medical attention.

Sitting at the table, K-Stone couldn't help but notice all the inmates in the building glued to their doors. Some where even standing on their toilet seats so they could look over their cellie head

staring with curiosity and admiration. For a moment, K-Stone
felt like the man, as he was silently lionized by other inmates and
C.O.s for his violent act.

But that changed in a matter of minutes when a member of
the goon squad came and read K-Stone his Miranda rights. He asked
him if he wanted to make a statement, which K-Stone replied with a
decisive no. The reality of him being charged with another case
didn't give him a feeling of being hard-core as they escorted him to
Ad-Seg, placing him in a cell by himself while pending an
investigation.

Chapter 10

Hole Time

Ad-Seg was like a prison within a prison. When he first got there they made him stand in a steel cage smaller than a portable bathroom. After a long hour, a C.O. came to the cage ordering him to take off his pants and shoes, and then pass it through a small slot. His second order was to squat and cough.

When the denuding process was over and the paper work was finished, they assigned K-Stone to a bottom tier cell with a bed-roll that consisted of: a blanket, one sheet, two pairs of socks, two t-shirts and two pairs of boxers. Closing the door behind him, the C.O. ordered K-Stone to back up and place his hands through the tray slot. With the cuffs back on his waist belt, the C.O. slammed the slot shut, locked the lock, and proceeded back to the podium.

Surveying his new cell, K-Stone noticed that some K4CBS occupied the cell before him because they left their graffiti all over the cell. There was also Ransom whacked out on the walls. With some pieces of lead he found in the lockers, K-Stone took to whacking out all the sets that beefed with Ransom. An hour later he managed to strike the whole cell up. Stepping back towards the door, he scanned the cell to make sure he marked every inch. Satisfied with his work, he began making his bed.

Lying on his bunk, he couldn't fight the sleepiness that was overtaking him, as his mind tried to figure out different scenarios he could use to outwit the investigators. Plenty had happened between the last two days, and it was putting a severe mental strain on him. Before K-Stone knew it, he was out cold only to be awakened for his dinner that was brought on a huge plastic tray. Stumbling to the door, K-Stone grabbed the tray and walked back to his bunk. Sitting the tray down on top of the locker, he began to wipe the crud from his eyes so he could see clearer. Looking out the window, K-Stone saw that it was dark out and thought to himself, "Damn, I slept too long." With his senses still dull, he picked through the beef stew and crumbled the stale cornbread on it before eating.

Morning came around fast, and K-Stone forgot he was still in Ad-Seg. Reaching for his toothbrush in his locker, he realized that his bed was on the top and not the bottom. It seemed unreal, and in a way he wanted it to be unreal with a baby toothbrush, karate shoes, and barley enough toilet paper to blow his nose let alone use the bathroom he knew things were going to be rough. After rinsing his mouth out repeatedly with warm water, K-Stone walked over to the door to view the food carts coming in for breakfast. Besides breakfast, K-Stone was more concerned about getting some toiletries and writing materials. Luckily he had put in a canteen ducat before he came to Ad-Seg.

"Are you taking a shower?" the C.O. asked while picking up his tray.

"Yeah, but I need some toiletries to wash up. I just came yesterday."

"I'll bring it to you when I get done collecting trays. Be ready in ten minutes." "Ten minutes?" K-Stone thought to himself.

His food had barely digested, when they started running the showers. When the C.O. came back for K-Stone, he thought he was going to be escorted straight to the shower. Instead, he learned quickly that all movement was under restraint, even in the showers.

"You get ten minutes," the C.O. said unlocking his handcuffs through the metal door.

For a few seconds, K-Stone contemplated leaving his Karate shoes on or entering the shower barefoot, risking the chance of acquiring a foot fungus. K-Stone went ahead and entered the shower stall with his only pair of shoes.

Once he got back inside his cell he asked the C.O. when they were going to pass out laundry and other materials. The C.O. informed him that laundry ran on Tuesdays only. Materials and library books were passed out every Fridays around 10:00 a.m. Being that it was barely Wednesday; K-Stone would have to rough it out for the time being.

Shivering from the cold air that came from the vent, K-Stone paced the floor in his socks while his karate shoes dried on the top bunk.

Supply day finally came and as the cart passed by his cell, K-Stone made sure he got some paper, pencils, forms, and a new toilet roll with soap inside. When all his necessities were acquired, he felt a brief moment of contentment. He was lost in his thoughts because he had nothing to look forward to, but mail that wasn't guaranteed to come.

With the hours passing like years, K-Stone sat on his desk looking out the narrow window gazing at the sparrows chasing each other on the desert sand. For the first time he felt inclined to take a pencil in his hand and write down his thoughts. His thoughts weren't about the sparrows, but about the correlation of them playing. At that moment he felt like he was playing also, but it wasn't in a good way nor was it friendly because he was playing with his life.

When that brief thought was jotted down, others thoughts started flowing in but were ineffable to write. For an hour, he stood motionless and went into a deep thought like never before about the direction his life was heading.

Gone were his thoughts of hanging in his turf, getting high, chilling with pound cakes, and busting on K4s. Gone were his beliefs he had from when he was a youth, to thinking that prison was down and fun. Those beliefs were fading on a daily basis as he was never told theses kinds of stories, real stories. Those thoughts had to go, for there was no more room left inside to think like that. Just the thought of his entire life fitting into a plastic bag made him realize that music videos, rappers, and entertainers didn't speak or show this part of the gangsta life. Glamorization of wet boxers hanging to dry from a pencil stuck in a vent was never mentioned, nor was being put in a cell with complete weirdoes.

Numb from thinking, K-Stone stepped away from the window to lie on his bed, waiting for the last meal of the day to arrive. When it finally came two hours later, he knew the day was over. His only accomplishment for that day was having a new level of thought. The night brought nothing but restlessness; no mail came for him again and he didn't get a chance to exercise because he had to take an early shower. So the only thing left to do was look out his door window at the empty dayroom.

After fifteen minutes of staring out the window, something caught his attention. At first he thought it was a mouse from the way it moved, but with further focus, K-Stone saw that it was a piece of soap, wrapped with a string, attached to some more string that made a line.

Catching his attention from his boredom, he watched as the soap slid from A-section all the way to the middle of C-section with ease.

Once there, a similar device flew out of another cell from C-section, wrapping around it pulling it into the cell.

A loud "Alright" came from C-section, signaling the inmate that shot the soap in A-section to pull. Not knowing what was going to happen next, K-Stone watched intently as several soups and magazines tied to the soap line moved across the dayroom floor like a midnight cargo train. The sight of the soups sent violent hunger

pains throughout K-Stones stomach as he scanned the cell for
something to soothe his appetite. After a short search he found
two pieces of bread he saved from his lunch.

Standing in the doorway chewing on the bread he thought to
himself, he needed to make a car to fish once he got some extra line.
As the night went on, K-Stone witnessed all the different ways
fishing could be used. There was no limit to where the fishing line
could go.

After taking a look at himself in the mirror for the hundredth
time, K-Stone knew the day wasn't going to be much different from
the other. Having nothing to do was the worse part of being in Ad-
Seg. If only he had a book or magazine to read he would be alright.
The library slip he filled out wouldn't be processed until next week,
so he was basically doomed to boredom.

At around two-thirty p.m., an inmate was rolling a cart in the
building with store bags. In an instant, K-Stone's whole drawn-out
bored day was filled with a little excitement.

Standing at the door, palms sweating by the minute, K-Stone
stared at the cart waiting for the C.O to pass the store bags out. He
had hoped that his ducat made it, even though he turned it in on
another yard. When the C.O dropped the bag in front of his door his
hopes turned into satisfaction. Finally a break, he thought to himself
as the C.O. opened his tray slot and began handing him items out of
his store bag.

K-Stone quickly noticed that the C.O. was placing all his
cosmetics to the side. Grabbing some zip-lock bags, the C.O. began
pouring his lotion in one bag then his toothpaste in another. He even
twisted the deodorant all the way down and placed it in a bag. Not
even the soap was spared. There was no point in getting upset, even
though he thought it was some bullshit putting his cosmetics in bags.

Overall, K-Stone was better off now then he was a couple of
days ago. Now that he had stamps and envelopes, K-Stone decided
he would write Ivie and his mother over the weekend, to let them
know where he was. Just when he was about to kick back and eat a
honey bun, K-Stone heard a knock at the door. Before he could
make it to the door he saw an arrangement of different color papers
come through the side of the door. Grabbing the papers, the C.O.
informed him that they were the first couple of his one-fifteens.

Sitting down at the desk K-Stone read over the one-fifteen
forms slowly, making sure not to miss anything. When he finished
reading he was aware that he was in Ad-Seg for an assault on an

inmate with serious injury. K-Stone started wondering if Ox was cooperating with C.D.C. As he sifted through the papers he came across a D.A. referral informing him that he could be tried for an assault in court, and if found guilty, it would be a felony.

Reality had its way of stinging deep into a person with no apathy or remorse. A barrage of court appearances started flooding K-Stones mind as he thought about how much time he could receive if charged. It would be a mandatory ten years. Taking a deep breath he grabbed his remaining honey bun from the bed and walked to the mirror. Staring at himself in the mirror, K-Stone began to look over every scar, bump, and freckle on his face. He told himself, "We've made it this far and through worse. We'll make it through this, between bites."

It was no point in stressing over the referral. He knew the job was dangerous when he took it; the life of a lok was never easy. Hard times weren't about to crack him now.

Sleep came easy that night despite the stress on the papers. Saturday morning came with the sun shining bright in his face. Today he felt decent, for he had something planned for the day that would occupy some hours.

Once breakfast and showers were taken, K-Stone sat at his desk and began to write his mother. Then he heard his name being called over the intercom for a visit. He didn't know he could get visits in Ad-Seg. The C.O. approached his cell with an orange jump suit, handcuffs, and chains. K-Stone figured that this would be his wardrobe he would wear on his visit.

Walking with leg shackles on again instantly brought back memories of when he first arrived at Centinela. When he entered the visiting building, the C.O. escorted him inside a small room similar to the ones at County and Wayside. Looking up from his stool he reluctantly locked eyes with a teary-eyed Ivie. Her face bared a look of confusion and hurt he didn't like seeing. For a moment they just stared at each other searching their minds for something to say.

"I would ask you how you were doing, but it's obvious that you're not doing well," Ivie said wiping her face with a tissue.

"Well you're right about that, but it's not as bad as it seems."

"What happened, Kay?" Ivie said shaking her head at K-Stone.

"You don't even want to know."

"Yes I do, if I didn't I wouldn't have asked you."

"If you must know here's the directors cut. I woke up to my celly pleasuring himself. So I put a proper beating to him that put him in the hospital."

"You couldn't just ignore it?"

"Ignore what? I know you're not talking about him beating off."

"Yes, if he didn't notice you, you could have done the same."

"Look Ivie, I'm not about to discuss this issue with you because obviously you don't understand and I'm not about to explain my actions."

"See Kay, you haven't changed. You still have that I'm right and that's it mentality."

"No I don't, I am right. Besides, I know you didn't come all the way up here to talk about this. I'll be out of here in a couple of weeks so don't trip."

"Don't tell me not to trip. It's like you're just thinking about yourself Kay. In county you told me things would get better, things would be different, remember? You told me we would be able to hold each other. I can't hold you through this," Ivie said thumping the glass. "I can't kiss you through this. The only difference is I have to drive three hours instead of twenty minutes to see you behind glass. Kay, this is what I look forward to. This is all I have, and you took it away form me."

Ivie's outburst didn't sit well with K-Stone. All that was running through his mind when she was talking was she done lost her damn mind getting at him like this. Sitting there listening to her rambling took a lot of self-control which he barely had.

"Alright, stop talking you're making no sense. You act as if I did it on purpose. Like I just decided last week that it would be fun to be shackled up, lose my visits, and go sit in the hole. Have you lost your mind?"

"No, but I will if you keep putting me through these changes."

"Ivie, I told you from the start that things are unpredictable in here and unavoidable at times. You can't tell me how to function in here day to day. Just like I cannot tell you how to function day to day on the streets. Reason being, you're going to do what's best for particular situations you encounter. There's nothing me or another can tell you to change. Do you feel what I'm saying?" As much as she hated to admit it, Ivie had to agree that K-Stone made a valid point.

"Five more minutes!" the C.O. said leaning into the booth.

"It's only been forty-five minutes. What is he talking about Kay?"

"Since I'm in Ad-Seg my visits have been cut down to an hour. Just wait until I'm out of Ad-Seg before you visit again."

"You don't want me to come see you anymore?"

"It's not like that; I just don't want you wasting your time and money coming up here for only an hour. I'll write you and tell you more in detail."

"Don't forget to write me."

"How could I do that when you're the only one who writes me besides my mother?"

"I love you Kay."

"I love you too," K-Stone said standing up.

Before hanging up the phone, he asked here to deliver the letter he wrote to Uzi.

When he got back to his cell he found his lunch sitting on his bunk. Placing it on his locker, K-Stone laid it out while thoughts of Ivie were still on his mind. A month passed by and the D.A. did not pick-up the case because Ox wouldn't cooperate.

This was a huge relief to K-Stone. Ox confessed that he had had a seizure and passed out, but the prison wasn't accepting Ox's excuse for his head injury. They found K-Stone guilty of assault on an inmate with serious injury when he went before the committee they gave him ten extra points and a suspended shu term of six months.

Chapter 11

Never Learn

After making K-Stone wait another month in Ad-Seg, they kicked him out due to overflow on C-yard. With no blues available, K-Stone hit the C-yard in an orange jumpsuit. Being out of the sun for two months made K-Stone a few shades lighter. While walking the track with an escort he tried to focus his eyes clearly, but was having difficulty because he was absent from the sun so long. K-Stone could barely make out who was on the yard.

Dayroom was in full swing when he entered his new building. Exaggerated loud idioms focused his attention to the left side of the dayroom where the Blacks resided as they slammed pinochle cards and dominoes on the table. A few looked up to see who came in, but no one introduced themselves or banged on him. Placing his property on a table in the dayroom, K-Stone stood with his arms crossed observing the building. He found it to be just like all the yards he had been on at Centinela. The Hispanics out numbered the Blacks seven to one and the C.O.s were so busy eyeing the Blacks' side that they missed half of the violations taking place on the Hispanic side.

"Pink you're going to cell two-o-five," the C.O. at the podium informed him. Walking into his new cell, K-Stone instantly noticed the extremely polished sink and immediately thought to himself, another lifer. For some strange reason, lifers took a special pride on having a shiny sink. Their sinks couldn't just be clean, they had to sparkle. The cell could be decaying, paint peeling off the wall, floor raggedy, light broken, but the sink would definitely be shining. With his attention caught by the sink's luster he didn't notice the pictures of Black figures posted on the wall until he closed the door. Surveying the new cell, K-Stone saw a couple of pictures he recognized like Malcolm X and Muhammad Ali. The others, he had never seen before. These pictures struck him as odd because most cells were decked out with half nude women and low riders.

His new cell had a certain energy in which he could do the remainder of his time. All he had to do now was meet his new celly and hope that they would be compatible. Sitting on top of his bunk, K-Stone noticed a mountain of books neatly stacked on the top locker. He assumed they were novels. If so, he would have to hit his new celly up to check some out. He had gotten hooked on westerns, urban books, and Jackie Collins while in Ad-Seg.

Looking out the door window, K-Stone saw that the yard was coming in. As he stood there he tried to guess which Black inmate would be his celly. K-Stone spotted a couple of gang members and quickly ruled them out as being his celly. When no one came to his door, he figured his new celly must have been at work.

Since K-Stone didn't have any blues on he wasn't allowed to go on the yard that afternoon. After sitting around for about an hour he decided to go ahead write his mother and Ivie to inform them that he was out of the hole.

By the time he finished, two hours had flown by, and when he stood up to stretch from the writing, the door popped open. K-Stone grabbed his lunch bag which was now trash and walked out of the cell to throw it away. On his way back to his new cell, he saw his new celly walking towards him. Giving him a head nod, they both acknowledged each other before walking into the cell.

Once inside, his new celly reached on top of his bunk, grabbed a towel, and placed it on the door for a shower. Closing the door behind him, he quickly turned around and extended his hand to K-Stone to introduce himself.

"My name is Askari," his voice sounding strong and deep.

"They call me K-Stone. How do you pronounce your name?"

"A-scar-ri."

"I'll have to say it a couple of times to get the pronunciation down."

"No rush, you'll get it brother K-Stone." When the door popped open, Askari grabbed his shower bag and walked out of the cell.

"We'll finish talking when I come back in."

When Askari left, the door stayed cracked, so K-Stone gathered his letters off the desk to place them in the mail. On his way down the stairs he had a refreshing feeling about his new celly. From his first impression, Askari seemed like an alright dude. But K-Stone was also aware that many cats played that cool role the first couple of weeks, then the real person would come out.

"So you just got out the hole?" Askari asked while reaching underneath the bottom bunk for a bag.

"Yeah, I was in there a few months for assault."

"Sometimes things must be done. A little violence often brings about a great deal of peace." Confused yet intrigued by the violence part, K-Stone inquired to what he actually meant by that comment.

"What you did is what you felt necessary to do. The word will spread quickly that you're prone to violent acts. That fact alone will give second thoughts to whoever thinks about trying you. In the process of them thinking of doing something to you, the majority of their thoughts will be geared to talking themselves out of actually doing something."

Seeing the nefarious smirk spread across K-Stone's lips, he quickly retorted.

"Now don't take it out of context K-Stone, and think violence is the only resort to solving problems, because it's not. All problems should be handled with decorum first. When that doesn't work, other techniques will have to suffice."

"I hear you, but I've learned that violence is the only language understood in prison. Everything else is foreign."

"To a certain degree that's true, but only because the average inmate doesn't know how to think outside of violence. Here you go." Askari said handing K-Stone some blue pants, a shirt, and boots. He figured it would fit him.

"I know you're getting tired of being in that pumpkin suit."

"Man you must've read my mind. Good looking out As-Ka-Ray."

"If you need anything else just let me know."

"I'm straight right now, but I do have a question. What does your name mean?"

"It's Swahili for warrior. By the way what does the K in your name mean?"

"Killa."

"How long have you been down?"

"About a year and some change, I got about four years left if I don't catch anymore time."

"A short-timer, that's good to hear."

"How long have you been down?"

"Seven years today."

"How much time you got left?"

"An eternity, the courts gave me thirty-four to life."

"How old are you?"

"Twenty-five, how old are you?"

"Twenty-two."

"A young brother."

"You're not that much older then me, I thought you were older."

"Why is that?"

"It's the way you carry yourself, it's like an older type of person."

"Funny you say that. How is a twenty-five year old supposed to act?"

"It's hard to say, most I know act like teenagers. Before we finish talking, I have to know why you don't have any hair on your face?"

The entire time they talked, K-Stone didn't notice that Askari didn't have any eyebrows until he really paid attention. He was use to looking at people without noticing small details in a person.

"I have a disease that prevents me from growing hair."

"At least you don't have to worry about haircuts."

"That's what my parents told me as a child."

With a further look, K-Stone also noticed that Askari had size as well. He was the size K-Stone was trying to get to before he paroled.

"Who are those two dudes by the mirror?"

"Nat Turner and Marcus Garvey."

"Who are they?"

"They are two Black African men who fought for our freedom in different ways. I consider them my yin and yang. Nat Turner leaned towards violence, while Marcus Garvey leaned towards decorum in liberating his people. If you want to learn more about them I have books."

"I can see; I'm more into novels right now. Do you have any?"

"No. I don't read novels, only literature."

"Why is that?"

"Because there is nothing tangible I can acquire by reading them."

"What do you mean?

"There can be something learned from everything."

"I agree, but you must read a whole novel in hopes that there is something valuable inside. With literature, you know with every page there will be something your mind can devour and grow from.

Most, but not all novels and magazines are the equivalent of feeding your body nothing but candy. While literature, is a healthy full course meal. Whenever you're ready to feed your brain something healthy that will strengthen it, feel free to grab a piece of fruit from my locker."

"I'll have to do that one day. Do you have any cell rules?"

"I have no rules brother, just conduct yourself as a man, and if you don't know something, ask. Basically just clean up after yourself and respect my space and I'll do like wise."

"I can feel that."

"Well K-Stone, I'm about to read a couple of chapters before chow. If you want I can put the TV down for you to watch."

"That'll be cool. You want me to put it back when I come back from chow?"

"Go ahead and keep it down there, just put it back on my locker whenever you go out to the yard."

"When do you watch it?"

"I don't."

"Wait. You mean to tell me you got a TV in here for nothing?"

"When I first came to prison it was my pacifier. But as I grew out of my baby stage of thinking, I put it on the locker. It no longer served a purpose brother. Hopefully you will no longer need it."

Adjusting back to the mainline made the time move quickly for K-Stone. He was due for a visit from Ivie this weekend and one from his mother the following week. The only thing he lacked was his property that was held up in the R and R. It would take another week before he got it back. K-Stone wasn't really concerned because he had enough soups to last him two months, plus every time Askari made a spread he shared it with him. K-Stone wasn't suffering for anything. He had access to the TV and radio whenever he wanted. The only problem was that he was use to having his own.

There were a couple of his homies on the yard. Most of them had been down awhile, but couldn't relate to the line he wanted to push on the enemies as well as how the homies were to conduct themselves. Though he was only on the yard a couple of weeks, he knew that changes had to be made with how the homies operated. They didn't have a care package made up for homies. They didn't greet each other when they first hit the yard, and none of them exercised on a consistent basis. Furthermore, half of them had some type of dealings with an enemy. This type of behavior couldn't be tolerated as long as he walked the line. K-Stone couldn't wait until one of his loks would hit the line who was on the same page as him, because the page the homies were on was definitely out of another book. No matter how hard they looked, their behavior was nowhere in his script of gang-banging. His mind was made up that after his visits, he would call a meeting amongst the homies to let them know that a change was mandatory. It wasn't hard to see that they knew something was in the mist by K-Stone's body language when he caught them doing something out of line, especially if it was borderline busta behavior. He didn't run a soft program on the streets, and he definitely wasn't going to start now.

"Hey killa, is it safe to enter the cell?" Askari asked as he entered the cell looking at the devious look on K-Stone's face.

"Its safe, I just was running some ideas through my mind."

"From the look on your face, they look like they were not positive."

"You're right about that, but when they're applied they will have positive results."

"Have you ever heard the saying, that if you make hard faces your face will get stuck like that?"

"When I was younger. Why did you ask me that?"

"Because seven days out the week you have a mean 'mug' on. I'm a good judge of character; I know you're no ersatz gangsta. I can tell you're with the business by how you carry yourself. You just need to relax, K-Stone. Besides, it's not wise to let your feelings be showing on your face. It is a great disadvantage when you put your enemies on alert of your intentions."

"How do I look now?" K-Stone asked relaxing his face.

"Like you always look."

"Because this is how I look whether I'm chilling' or angry."

"But you didn't let me finish. You looked the same but not as devious as you normally look. If you practice facial relaxation techniques in the mirror you can change your problems, which will benefit you in a wide range of areas outside of gang-banging."

"Such as?"

"Society, were no one cares about how many stripes you have. Those type of things only matter in the small world we create in our ghettos. Outside of that, in the bigger part of the world, presentation counts for a lot as well as tangible sources stating your skills. Once you learn discipline over one thing, you have the power to master another no matter how big it may be. Your initial discipline can be over the way you show your emotions by contorting your face up which is unnecessary. If you're going to strike, do it with a look incapable of discerning."

"Speaking of striking, I need you to show me how to make a heat."

"As soon as count clears I will teach you," Askari said looking out the door window.

"Before we start, do you know where to hide it on your person?'

"No, I was going to put it in my pocket where it's supposed to go."

"That's not the most logical spot. If the C.O.s should randomly search you, you'll be caught instantly."

"So where else am I going to hide it?"

"In between your gluteus, the C.O.s can't feel it unless they strip search you all the way down. As you know, that never happens unless something serious happens on the yard. Before they get to you in that situation, you'll have ample time to bury it."

"What about the residue left after using the bathroom?"

"That's an issue you've got to take up with yourself brother. Besides, that's not the only spot you can hide it. It can also be hidden in the seams of your shorts or boxers, whatever's convenient. Once on the yard, you can place it in your workout gloves while making sure it's always in grabbing distance. Once you start to carry it you'll become accustomed to it like a gun on the street. I'm sure you can relate to that." Shaking his head in agreement, K-Stone was ready to begin making heats.

"There are basically two common types of knives you will find in prison you can make right off your shelf. One is the flat you can make from tops of cans, soda cans, and any flat metal. The other is an ice pick that can be made by melting down a lotion bottle over a bong. Grab about five can tops out of the box of trash." Going over to the box, K-Stone came back with five roast beef can tops.

Sliding the curtain over as he sat down on the bunk, K-Stone placed the can tops on the bunk.

"You'll practice with one first so you can get the hang of it. Usually I use two tops to make one knife. But since you're practicing, you'll start at the basics. First you want to bend the can over in a mini pyramid shape; this will be your point and blade which is the most important part. Reason being, it will determine if it will enter your opponent's body or bend. That's something you don't want to happen, that is the main reason I reinforce them. Once the first bend is complete, you want to bend the other side over to match it. Yeah, just like that." Askari said hunched over watching.

"You sure you haven't done this before?"

"Naw, this is my first time, but I get the fundamentals."

"Alright let me check that point out." Handing the point to Askari to check out, K-Stone began stretching his fingers which were stiff after all the bending.

"That's a decent point." Askari said poking himself in the arm with the sharp end of the can. "Now you need to flatten it, then you can secure a handle. The best thing to use when flattening is the butt of a state boot. First thing you want to do is lay a book down on the floor then place the can on it. After that, you want to stomp on it with all your force until it flattens. Alright, that's flat enough. Now you need to bend the two end pieces inward for the handle. Take your time; this part is as equally important as the point. You always want a decent grip, without it, it would be like firing a gun without a butt. Now fold that flap over just a few inches. Okay, now flatten it before you start on the other. Just like that, now flatten it one more time. Now you need to sharpen it. There are numerous ways to sharpen knives. Inside the cell I use the back of the wall behind the bottom bunk, or a piece of hard sand paper which sharpens it quicker than the wall. Since it's your first time, I'll let you use the sand paper so you get a feel for it. Sit at the desk."

While K-Stone was sitting down, Askari searched through some legal work for a piece of sand paper. When he found it, he placed it on the desk. Before giving the green light to start, Askari glanced out the door window then gave K-Stone the go ahead. Holding the knife in his hand, Askari further instructed K-Stone on sharpening techniques. After practicing the sharpening technique Askari showed him, K-Stone started to feel excited as he started to see the simple can top turn into a real knife in a matter of minutes.

"Let me see your work," Askari said leaning over K-Stones shoulder. After examining the knife's two edges, Askari was impressed.

"Now you need to sharpen the top of the point on the flat side. But instead of going real fast, go at a moderate speed until it gets thin, but not too thin. Then flip it and hit the other side."

While K-Stone was putting the finishing touches on the knife, Askari took an open razor and cut a seven inch piece of strip from an old sheet.

"Let me see the knife. Yes this is sufficient, now I'm going to show you how to reinforce the handle. First, you wrap the sheet around the handle of the knife tightly in one complete wrap around fold. Once that is done you keep wrapping it tighter and tighter. When that part is done you wrap a rubber band around the sheet to keep it from unraveling and it will provide a better grip. There you go." Askari said throwing K-Stone the knife. "Poke yourself with it to see how sharp it is."

"Damn!" K-Stone shouted when he felt the point against his wrist.

"Sharp huh?"

"Hell yeah! I can just imagine how vicious it is going to be when it's reinforced with two cans.

As K-Stone marveled at the knife, he moved through the cell pretending he was stabbing someone. Askari started cleaning up the cell; during this time he took notice to how K-Stone grasped the knife and his stabbing technique that were both wrong.

"Calm down killa. Show me how you would stab at someone."

Without hesitation, K-Stone lunged at Askari who quickly grabbed his extended wrist, twisting it hard around to the opposite direction, causing K-Stone to drop it.

"The last thing you want to do is hold a knife with your whole hand around the handle. You are vulnerable to your wrist being broken or someone doing what I just did to you. The proper way to hold it is to grasp the handle placing your thumb on top of the handle; try it."

"Now I see the difference," K-Stone said, practicing the new technique.

"Holding it like that gives you more movement and stability."

"So where is the best place to stab someone?"

"There are a lot of places, but it all depends on what you're trying to accomplish. If you're trying to get someone off the yard, you could simply give them a good body shot to the middle of their back which will collapse their lung. A hit to their lower stomach will hit their intestine, or directly underneath their armpit which will also collapse their lung. If you're trying to make an example, you could stab them in the eye or any other part of their face. If you're going for the kill, the best place to stab is the jugular vein."

"Five minutes until chow!" The C.O. said over the intercom.

"We'll finish when we come back, K-Stone."

"Where do I put the heat?"

"Just give it to me I have a spot."

"If they find it, do we both ride the beef?"

"Don't trip, I got life. I'll take the rap. Besides, you don't even have to have those types of thoughts. I think way beyond these pigs." Wrapping the knife in a tissue, K-Stone placed it in between his cheeks as the door popped open.

To his surprise, the knife stayed in place, his cheeks held it in place firmly as he made his way down the stairs to the chow hall. With a couple more test trials he could see himself getting used to packing his heat daily. The platitude remained true, He thought to himself. The more things change the more they stayed the same; from packing heat on the streets to carrying one in between his cheeks in the penitentiary.

Before laying it out that night, K-Stone made three more knives with intentions to bury them on the yard.

"Good looking out on showing me the get down."

"Don't trip K-Stone, it's my duty to teach you all the knowledge that you seek. Each one is suppose to teach one. A lot of older brothers have forgotten that. It's the main reason so many young brothers come to the pen and end up returning. Walking around their entire sentence lost with no direction of where their life is headed. The only request I have for you is to lace the next brother's boots you encounter."

"You got that, in the morning."

"In the morning." With that they both laid it out to repeat it again tomorrow.

*　*　*　*　*　*　*　*　*　*

"Have a good one, K-Stone." Askari said stepping out of his way inside the cell.

"All the time. We'll holla when I get back."

Walking in the visiting room, K-Stone instantly saw Ivie and grabbed her tightly resuming a long needed ritual.

"You feel like you've lost weight, Kay."

"I lost a couple of pounds in the hole due to the forced diet."

"Besides that, you're looking good. I see your hair is ready for French braids."

"I'll give it another month before I get it French braided."

"So what you been up to since you got out of Ad-Seg?"

"Nothing really just waiting on my property to be given back to me, that's all." "They haven't given me a job yet so I just chill all day. How about you?"

"I got a new job driving buses for the MTA."

"Is that right, what made you fall into that?"

"I just got tired of my old job. I needed to do something that has me moving around staying busy."

"Nothing wrong with that. You better get some maze for all the stalkers you're going to encounter."

"There are already some of those. This one guy I pick up on my morning shift always gives me flowers."

"Looks like Stone has some competition. Did he propose to you?"

"No! He's an old man, Kay."

"It's your story tell it how you want to. Other than that, do you like the job?"

"Yes, it's alright, just a lot of other females who be hating all the time on who looks the best and other stupid talk. There's this one girl who's cool. Her boyfriend is on D-yard. She said we could come up together sometimes."

"That's cool; at least you got someone you can holla at."

"Is your new celly cool?"

"He's real cool. He's the complete opposite of me as far as gangbanging. I won't have to worry about any strange behavior late at night."

"Well that's good to hear, that way I don't have to worry about you in Ad-Seg again. I almost lost my mind when I was unable to see you those last two months. You can't send me through that again."

"Believe me, I'll try my best."

"Uzi came by the house the other day; I gave him the letter you sent me."

"Is that right! I hope you gave it to him personally and not to your punk-ass sister."

"Of course I gave it to him myself. He said he would write you soon."

"That'll work; I need to holla at him about some things."

"Like what?"

"Just homie talk, it's been awhile since I have got at one of my real loks."

"I guess."

"You guess you know how it gets when you haven't heard from a home girl in a while. Due to whatever circumstances, and you happen to run into each other."

"Yeah."

"Then stop acting like you don't know what I'm talking about twig."

"Twig! You looking like the twig since you got out of Ad-Seg."

"Don't trip, I'll get back what I lost, plus some. Are things still the same out there?"

"Pretty much, everybody riding on rims or trying to get some. All the niggas is thuggin' or gang-banging and still trying to use the same corny lines to get the panties. What's so funny?"

"I was just tripping off the face you made when you said that. What kind of lines do they use?"

"I was at the mall last week when this nigga approaches me asking me for my number. When I told him I had a man, he quickly responded I have a woman. What they don't know won't hurt. I just walked off. I hear so many stupid lines that I hardly pay attention."

"So if I said that to you when we first met, you would've walked away?"

"You wouldn't have said something corny like that anyway,"

"How you know?"

"Because you think you're too hard to even let something like that slip out your mouth."

"Think, I know and you especially know." K-Stone said leaning into squeeze Ivie's side causing her to bounce around in her seat. "You better stop before the C.O.s calls you up here again," Ivie said between laughs.

"Let's walk on the patio before the visit ends." K-Stone said standing up.

While walking in circles on the patio, K-Stone listened while Ivie talked about their future together and how she could never be with another but him. With the visit coming to an end, they embraced each other tightly like it would be their last time together. From previous experiences, they knew it could be possible.

"My mom's is coming up next week, so I'll see you the following weekend."

"Okay." "I'll call you tonight to see if you made it alright." With that said K-Stone walked back outside and waited for the C.O.s to call him to strip down.

Chapter 12

Family Pain

Sophia Pink had been putting a little money aside every month since Kevin left the county jail. It had been too long since she had seen her baby boy. She would have gone and seen him sooner but her car needed repairs and financial problems seemed to constantly mount up. Nevertheless, she made a way to make extra cash.

Struggling had become a normal problem for her throughout the years. She was brought up in a loving single-parent home, but all that changed when her mother died in a car accident coming home from work late night. At the age of eight, she couldn't fully grasp the loss of her mother. She always thought her mother would someday return and that everything would be all a misunderstanding. With her mothers passing, Sophia was taken in by her mother's sister who had three daughters of her own, all a year apart and the oldest being ten at the time.

Living with her aunt was alright, until she started noticing how she was made to do the hardest chores all the time. She even received the strictest punishments when she did anything wrong. This treatment continued on and off well into her teenage years. The only solace she had was her auntie's husband whenever he was home. He was a timid man who barely spoke, but he noticed the treatment Sophia received and tried to intervene whenever possible. Once her aunt noticed the treatment wasn't working the way she planned, she resorted to mentally abusing Sophia. The older Sophia got and filled out into a young lady, the worse the abuse increased. The effects of what her aunt was doing took a serious permanent affect on her self-esteem. She would often lay up all night crying warm tears of pain and confusion. It eluded her mind why her aunt despised her so much when she did nothing but try to make her proud. How could she treat her sister's only child the way she did?

With no one to turn to, she felt trapped and slowly became a recluse to everything. Her cousins who she viewed as her sister's weren't any better; they all seemed to hold something against her also. At seventeen, Sophia slowly began to put the pieces together to why they treated her the way they did. She was very fair skinned and all of them were dark. She first noticed the difference when they all attended the same high school on a transfer.

When they would walk through the halls during period change, the boys would refer to her as red bone and other fair skinned epithets. Sophia received the majority of the attention at school from all the males and it greatly agitated her cousins who viewed her more as a stranger then a relative.

Consequently, the mental abuse surpassed the physical abuse, and her aunt constantly made diminishing comments about her beauty whenever possible. After graduating from high school, she started working at the local bank. Sophia started to perceive her job as a way out from her abusive situation. One important thing she learned through her early struggles was responsibility. She knew it was more important to save her money then to spend it on clothes, make-up, and shoes. Besides, she couldn't if she wanted to; her aunt started charging her rent while her cousins lived rent free. At the age of twenty, Sophia had saved enough money to move out and found herself living in the middle of South Central.

Life was good living on her own. Gone, were the senseless arguments and abuse from her only family members. Oddly, her aunt stayed in contact with her after she moved. She would sporadically check-in on her by calling her throughout the months. It was funny to Sophia, that her aunt had suddenly taken an interest for her safety after she moved out. Deep inside Sophia knew it was all a façade because her aunt was only waiting for her downfall.

Though Sophia knew this, she couldn't bring herself to disown the only family she knew. Little to her knowledge, she had developed an unconscious dependence on her aunt's and cousin's approval. Because of her low self-esteem, she stayed away from men and female friends. This behavior was beneficial in that she was able to save money and avoid stressful situations, but there were some draw backs. She had pushed away a lot of good people because of her insecurities, and brought about a pessimistic attitude because she kept herself in solitude.

The few friends Sophia did have were older women. In many ways, she was still looking for that motherly love she was deprived of as a child. One particular night her friends took her out to a popular night club. That night, her life changed when she met Jamal. Jamal was a dark skinned average built man with an abnormal amount of confidence about himself. With his deep articulate voice, he caught Sophia's attention as she sat at her table. When the night ended, Sophia learned that Jamal came from a well off family and held a decent job working for the city.

For the first time Sophia was happy. Jamal showed her
ways of life she never knew about. He took her to the finest
restaurants and made sure she had nicest clothes. While all this was
taking place, her aunt and cousin's envied her to the point of
constant predictions of her down fall, which was taking too long for
their patience. Her aunt felt the pressure the most. With all the
abuse she put forth on Sophia, Sophia seemed to be making well for
herself in all areas of life, while her daughters still remained at
home, jobless, eating-up her food. She just couldn't understand why
her plan to destroy Sophia's life had backfired.

* * * * * * * * * *

Jamal was use to fast women and the fast life. Sophia was
the complete opposite of what he usually went for in woman. She
didn't wear tight fitting clothing, nor frequented the clubs, or hung
out with numerous men. In many ways, she brought calmness to his
hectic lifestyle that he was beginning to enjoy. She was a
respectable woman he planned on keeping in his life. After a year of
dating seriously, Jamal Jr. was born with Kevin arriving two years
later. Jamal Sr. took great pride in his son's referring to them as the
boys. He took them everywhere he went, and planned on marrying
Sophia the following year. Earlier in their relationship, Jamal had
noticed that Sophia had many insecurities, but he couldn't
understand why. He thought she was such a beautiful strong minded
woman. When he would inquire to why she felt the way she felt, she
would withdraw and push him away. Seeing that his concern pushed
her in a corner, he would back off and ignore the troubling behavior.

Sophia's behavior seemed to worsen after having Kevin,
adding more strain on their relationship. She had gained more
weight than expected during the pregnancy, which added to her
insecurities.

In Sophia's mind, Jamal Sr. no longer desired her, which
caused her feelings of abandonment to increase, making her fall
deeper into depression. She felt that everybody she loved had turned
their back on her or treated her cruelly.

For the boys' sake, Jamal Sr. tried to deal with the crumbling
relationship and a woman he didn't know anymore. As the months
passed, the relationship increasingly got worse, to the point where
she wouldn't let him touch her. Then, Sophia began assaulting him
verbally whenever he didn't respond quickly enough to her phone
calls or requests. The last straw came when she wouldn't allow him

to take the boys to one of his friend's party. This small event set off a chain of events that led to legal battles over custody that Sophia won.

As the years passed so did the love of the boys for their father. Everyday Sophia thought about how life had been cruel to her and it made her bitter. Her words became the bane for the boys' resentment towards their father. Whenever they were unable to get a toy, clothing, or a pair of shoes at a moments notice, Sophia would just tell them it was their father's fault money was tight. Being children they never looked at the whole picture. All they knew was their mother was their solace in their lives.

Sophia's only form of completeness and happiness was her sons. They were the center of her life now. All decisions were based around them. She finally had something she could pour all her love into that wouldn't betray or abandon her. With this mind frame firmly intact, Sophia was overly protective of her sons. They were never too far from her sight. Though she was getting child support from Jamal, Sophia had it rough raising her two boys in South Central because her sons were targets of potential recruiters of the ghetto armies. To prevent them from joining gangs, she turned to the only family she knew to take care of them while she worked.

Without hesitation her aunt took them in, never missing the chance to say I told you so. Jamal Jr. and Kevin received the same treatment as Sophia did as a child. When she would drop them off, their aunt would be happy to see them, but as soon as Sophia left, she would lock them outside all day. The only time she let them in was at noon to eat a hurried lunch, then she would send them right back outside.

It didn't take long for Jamal Jr. and Kevin to realize that their mother's side of the family wasn't looking out for their best interest. From adolescent to their teenage years, the boys heard countless times by their aunt that they would end up in jail. When Sophia caught wind of this she was furious at the comments made to her sons. As much as she wanted to keep her sons from that side of the family, she couldn't. She had no where else for them to go.

Instead, Sophia implemented the best idea that came to mind. She trained Jamal Jr. who was eight years old at the time to be a man on her off days. Within a couple of months, Jamal Jr. knew how to cook basic foods, wash clothes, and other basic household duties. On his tenth birthday, she decided it was time for him to stay at home by himself and take care of his brother while she was working. The first couple of times she left them alone she would call every hour checking in on them. After a couple of months, she got more comfortable with them staying at home by themselves and the phone calls became less frequent.

Often, Sophia would place too much responsibility on Jamal Jr. and Kevin forgetting that they were just children. In many ways, she treated them as if they were her husband instead of her sons. When they failed to complete or perform a task correctly, she would lose her temper and without warning, she would physically abuse them. As the stress of living in the ghetto mounted so did the physical and verbal abuse. It came to a point where it was a weekly ritual. The slightest incident would set her off turning her into a person she hated. Without realizing it, Sophia was reacting the way her aunt use to do to her as a child. Sophia was becoming what she despised the most.

The abuse became so bad that the boys told their father one weekend while they were at his house. When Jamal Sr. confronted Sophia, she cursed him out and beat the boys that night for telling her business.

Having to pay child support, Jamal Sr. was barely getting by. He wasn't in a position to take in two more mouths. Furthermore, he wasn't prepared to give up the lifestyle he had become accustomed to as a bachelor. Realizing this, the boys knew they were on their own.

*   *   *   *   *   *   *   *   *   *

By the time Jamal Jr. reached the age of thirteen and Kevin ten, they had gotten use to the abuse and the ignoring of the abuse by both sides of the family. Tears were becoming non-existent as the boys became more cold hearted. She had beaten friendly emotions out of them permanently. Violence became infused within them and was their outlet. They would often fight each other and others to get their point across. In many ways, they began to believe that this type of behavior was normal even though it didn't feel right within. Jamal Jr. and Kevin both learned to block those feelings out and sought a way to funnel their anger and pain that accumulated over the years.

The only time they felt a release was when they fought others at school and around their neighborhood. Sophia often wondered why her sons got suspended so much from school for fighting. Every time she was called in for a parent conference she would defend her boys by accusing the other kids of starting the fight. In her eyes her sons could do no wrong. She remained overly protective of them even as they got older not realizing that she was their biggest threat and not the community.

While unloading laundry baskets one weekend from the car to the house. Sophia noticed the boys had left one basket behind at the neighborhood Laundromat. As usual, she went into a rage yelling how stupid they were for leaving the clothes behind. Seeing her fist balled up Jamal Jr. knew she was about to strike one of them soon. Before her hand landed in Kevin's direction, Jamal Jr. caught her wrist. Realizing for the first time the strength of her son, Sophia ordered him to release her wrist or else. Jamal Jr. replied by saying no, and let her know that the beatings were going to stop. Releasing her hand, Jamal Jr. stepped in front of his brother staring his mother in the eyes like never before. Backing up, Sophia let loose a flurry of obscene epithets at them both before telling them to get the fuck out of her house!

With nowhere to go, Jamal Jr. and Kevin left with no particular destination. After walking through a couple of gates, Jamal Jr. and Kevin found themselves walking through an alley the Ransoms hung out in. A couple of Ransom gang members spotted Jamal Jr. and Kevin and approached them.

"What set ya'll from?" one of them asked, while the others stood around.

"Nowhere, we stay a couple of blocks up," Jamal Jr. said shielding his brother.

"You never thought about turning the turf?" another one asked.

"No." Jamal Jr. responded trying to figure out what to do next.

"You and your brother want to come kick it?" The first Ransom who saw them asked.

"And do what?" Jamal Jr. asked.

"Just chill." Looking at Kevin, then back up at the Ransoms, Jamal Jr. decided to go hang out.

After a couple of hours of drinking thunderbird and Kool-Aid the gang-bangers convinced Jamal Jr. to join the gang. Because there wasn't anybody Kevin's size, they didn't even bother putting him on the set. Watching his brother get jumped into a gang made Kevin angry and confused. He wanted to jump in and help his brother who was handling his own, but he knew this was the process. Instead, he nervously watched as his brother fought Ransom, after Ransom for an entire five minutes that felt like hours. With a busted lip, a couple of scrapes, and bruises, Jamal Jr. was now from

Ransom Gangsta Crip. In a blink of an eye, Jamal Jr. and Kevin's life changed.

Driving through the neighborhood frantically, Sophia looked for her sons everywhere through her tear soaked eyes. It finally dawned on her while sitting in an empty house that she was an abusive mother. No matter how much she tried to justify it to herself, she knew she regretted becoming what she had desperately tried to avoid. The way Jamal Jr. looked at her sent shivers down her spine. His eyes were voided of love and filled with hatred a son should never have for his mother, and it hurt her deeply because she knew it was her fault.

Sitting on a dirty couch in the alley, Jamal Jr. put together a plan on what to do. He would go back home to use the phone to call his father to come and pick them up. Crying uncontrollably, Sophia parked her car on a side street and tried to gather herself. While fumbling through her purse she didn't notice her sons walking past her car until she raised her head, barely catching a glimpse at them.

A rush of relief ran through her body, causing her to run towards them with open arms, which were met with the stiff response of two boys who had had enough. Sophia made promises to change, prompting the boys not to leave the home they knew. For the next few days, Sophia's behavior was awkwardly nice to the point of shamefulness. In many ways, the boys felt empathy towards her, and could see the obvious desperation of wanting them to love her despite her behavior. At night they would hear her crying when she thought they were asleep. One night they both entered her room unannounced to let her know that there was no love lost, even though there was. The only reason she stopped the physical abuse was because they were too big to hit, but mostly because they were not buying into it anymore. They had learned early in life that some times things had to be made right even though they weren't. Certain situations just had to be looked at in the best way as possible. Clearly their mother's conscience needed to be relieved because it was tearing her apart and if she fell apart they too would fall apart and that wasn't an option.

Though things changed for the better from the physical abuse, the verbal still was apparent, but not as frequent. Eventually Sophia's aunt's prediction became true when Jamal Jr. went to Y.A. for armed robbery. Following in his older brother's footsteps, Kevin broke into someone's home, rendering him probation for a year. With Jamal Jr. gone for a couple of years in Y.A., Sophia had more time to invest in how Kevin would turn out. As much as she tried, she couldn't get through to him. It often frustrated her because she honestly didn't know how to turn her sons into men.

What she knew she taught them, but it wasn't enough and didn't work as planned. When she found out she was having a boy she told herself that her sons wouldn't be gangbangers. Somewhere along the way she failed them and herself. Jamal Jr. was in a gang and so was Kevin, both stopped listening to their mother's advice and kept running the streets. Harboring the guilt from what she did to them as youths, she wouldn't push too hard because she felt it was her fault for the way they turned out. All she wanted was someone to love and be better than her.

As much as Kevin reassured Sophia that he and his brother made their own decisions in life, she still found herself at fault. One son dead and the other in prison, her only real accomplishments in life were her boys, but they too seemed to be failures. Sophia tried hard not to think those types of thoughts, but they plagued her periodically. She just hoped she could get her composure before she reached the prison.

* * * * * * * * *

"Going on another one K-Stone?" Askari asked.

"Yeah, my mom's is coming up."

"That's good to hear, mines passed a couple of year ago."

"Did they let you go to the funeral?"

"No, but my family sent me some pictures. I really didn't want to see her in a box anyway."

"How did it feel when you found out?"

"Honestly, I look at death as being natural. To live one must die. I've never looked at death in a negative way. In many ways, I embraced it."

"I see we share the same beliefs," K-Stone said sliding into his visiting pants. "It's hard not to, it's an experience you can only experience one way besides sleep. There is no comparison, but speculation from a man. We'll pick up later," K-Stone said giving Askari dap before walking out the door.

When K-Stone entered the visiting room, he noticed his mother immediately who was sitting down waiting to see him.

"Kevin! Come here boy," Sophia said as they embraced each other.

Stepping back, she admired how much her son had grown since the last time she saw him.

"Kevin you're looking good. Sorry for the long delay."

"Don't trip moms; I know how it can get out there. So what have you been doing since I've been away on vacation?"

"Nothing really. Just working and staying off those crazy streets when I'm not at church. How about you? What do you guys do in here all day?"

"Nothing really. I exercise, watch TV, and read magazines. I really don't observe other dudes in here."

"As long as you're staying busy, do they have any trades?"

"Yeah, but I'm not back there where they're at."

"How do you get back there?"

"I have to wait for inmate assignments to put me on the list. Until then I'll just be on the yard program."

"Oh, I almost forgot. I went to Lacey's birthday party a couple of weeks ago. It was really nice."

"Where was it at?"

"The Marriot Hotel by the airport. There was a DJ who played all types of music. A lot of people asked about you, especially Lacey's daughter. She's going to USC now and her brother Tony is playing for the football team. You remember Tony?"

"Yeah."

"What's wrong Kevin?"

"Nothing, I'm just listening to you tell me."

While Sophia continued talking to her son about the party, he couldn't help but feel embarrassed for his mother having to explain to her long time friend that her last living son was in prison. The hidden sadness in her voice was unmistakable. For the first time in his life, K-Stone wanted to give his mother something to be proud of. Something tangible she could tell her friends about when she talked on the phone or saw them out and about.

"When I get out I'll throw you a party."

"You're the one that's going to need a party, Kevin."

"I remember when I was in the county; this old man told me he never understood why people celebrated when they got out of jail. I asked him what he meant by that. He responded saying

Shit, nigga you got caught, what you celebrating for?"

Hearing the anecdote made Sophia laugh like she often did when Kevin would tell stories. Sophia thought the visit would fill the void she felt inside, but it only seemed to make it worse. It was going to take a lot of strength of which she barely had.

"Kevin, I'm going to have to leave early this time. I have to go see your brother before the cemetery closes. I'll have to work on his birthday, so I'm going to see him today."

"Alright, just make sure you drive safe."

When Kevin embraced his mother he felt her trembling body in his grasp trying to fight back the tears.

"Don't worry mother, I'll be out soon." Was all he could say to a woman who was barely holding on to what she loved the most?

Driving back to L.A., Sophia recalled back to the days of Jamal Jr. and Kevin's childhood which seemed like yesterday. Where did the times go? She thought, as she peered down at her protruding belly coming out through the seatbelt. So much time passed by without noticing. Looking at a picture hanging from her rearview mirror, she let out a desperate sigh as she pushed the cigarette lighter in.

Traffic was light that day and Sophia made it to the Inglewood Cemetery in less than four hours. Parking her car, she walked up the hill to see her son. Kneeling down on her knees, Sophia wiped away the old leaves, and dusted the flowers covering Jamal Jr's. Grave stone. She then replaced them with fresh flowers she purchased earlier at the flower store.

The monthly visits to see Jamal Jr. were routine for Sophia. She visited twice a month mandatory sometimes more. Outside of his homies she was his only visitor.

"Hey Jamal, it's your mother again I know you're probably tired of seeing me, but you know how I get. I got some good news for you today. I saw your brother today and he's getting big, bigger than you. I know that's not saying much, but he's growing into a man. I'll bring him to come see you when he gets out." With tears streaming down her face, Sophia got off her knees.

*   *   *   *   *   *   *   *   *   *

"I was beginning to worry when I didn't hear from you Monday."

"They had to do some night time cell moves so they didn't run night program; I couldn't get my night phone call."

"How did your visit with your mom go?"

"It was cool, she just had to leave earlier than expected to go visit my brother."

"That must be hard on her."

"This whole situation is hard on her, but she's gotten use to it over the years."

"Your mother is a tough woman, you better not put her or me through this again Kay."

"You don't have to worry about that. By the way I talked to the counselor this week, our date to get married falls on Saturday." From Ivie's excitement, K-Stone had to place the phone away from his ear as she let out a scream of joy.

"Calm down crazy woman, we only have a couple of minutes on the phone."

"You can't call me back Babe?"

"I'll try but someone else signed up after me. If I don't I'll call you before you come up to visit."

"I'm finally going to be Mrs. Pink. I'm going to love being your wife Kay."

"Why's that?"

"Because you're going to be all mines."

"I've been yours."

"But, now its official. Now I have to go find a dress and something special for our honeymoon."

"I can't wait to unwrap that."

"I can't wait for you to see what's under the wrapping."

"Is that right, you keep talking like that and it might get torn off instead of unwrapped."

"I thought that's the way you do it anyway."

* * * * * * * * *

"Well son, this cold air is picking up and you know your mother is not as young as she use to be the cold makes my bones ache." Babe, your brother and I love you and will never abandon you". Sophia said walking to her car.

* * * * * * * * *

"What's up Ivie, is your sister there?"

"Yeah, hold on Tatiana. Gina the phone is for you."

"Why didn't you bring me the phone?"

"Because you have two legs."

"Who's this?" Gina asked.

"It's Tatiana."

"What's up girl?"

"The visiting form came back to me today, I got approved."

"Wait stop talking, I had you on speaker phone. How long are you going to be at home?"

"Another hour or two. I was about to go to the mall."

"Well just wait, I'm about to come over there."

"Don't take all day Gina."

"Don't rush me, whoever's waiting can wait a little longer." An hour later Gina was at Tatiana's house.

"First off, here's your hundred dollars. I'm going to need you to visit K-Stone this weekend coming up."

"Which day?"

"Saturday morning. You'll have to leave here around five in the morning to make it up there by nine."

"Do you want me to call you before I go up there?"

"No, just go. We'll be there anyway and I don't want Ivie to become suspicious. You have anymore questions?"

"No, I've got everything else handled. You want to come to the mall with me?"

"Probably another time, I have to go see Uzi when I leave here."

* * * * * * * * * *

"Huh, it's been so long I almost forgot."

"We'll see how much you've forgotten on the honeymoon."

"Yeah, we will see indeed. Call Uzi for me on three way."

"Alright, let me click over."

"Uzi this is Ivie I'm going to click you over to talk to K-Stone."

"What it do?"

"Nothing much, just taking it as it comes."

"What's going on with you out there?"

"Same shit cuzz. Just stacking these Ransoms and trying to live as comfortable as possible."

"What's going on in the set?"

"Nothing really, Crash got the set hotter than lava and the war is still crackin' with the K-Forts. A lot of loks miss you out here K-Stone. When you touch down we're going to throw you a barbeque with a wide range of pound cakes."

"I don't know what for!" Ivie said cutting in on the conversation.

"Don't trip, I just was making sure you were still on the line. You know I have to keep it lively for my nigga."

"I see you still crazy Uzi."

"Ain't nothing changed but my zip code, feel me?"

"Yeah, did you get the block off your phone?"

"It's been off, it's just hard to catch me because I am in traffic most of the time. I'm going to get calls transferred to my cell phone tomorrow so you can reach me whenever."

"Aren't you going to tell Uzi the good news?"

"What kind of news your girl talking about?"

"We are getting married this weekend."

"My boy getting married! The Killa Stone is going to make it official!"

"Yeah, it's about time I settled down."

"At least you got a decent one. Is there anything ya'll need for the event?"

"Naw, everything is taken care of."

"Well, if you need it holla."

"That's good looking Uzi."

"Don't trip, you know how we do it. Hit me up tomorrow. I have to take care of someone you both know."

"Tell my sister to bring me something to eat when she leaves your house."

"Alright, I'll holla at ya'll later. Five minutes lok."

"Five minutes."

"Okay, I love you Kay."

"I love you to Mrs. Pink."

Hanging up the phone K-Stone made his way up the stairs to his cell. Lately things had been coming together for him. He had his marriage coming up, and contact with his set through Uzi. Now all he had to do was get his homies organized on the yard.

The next day he called a meeting on the yard by the bleachers. All together there were ten homies: six old heads, and four youngsters. When he first arrived on the yard he immediately noticed the lack of unity and structure amongst his homies. All day all they did was play cards, chess, and get intoxicated. None of them exercised or kept the other homies up on what was happening on the yard.

Their behavior was intolerable and the older homies knew it. They had become so relaxed through the years they stopped following basic rules of gang-banging. As K-Stone spoke he made sure to keep an eye on every homies' face to measure how they were taking what he was saying. Ten minutes into the meeting, everybody involved was looking around skeptical like he was just talking until he revealed knives inside of a white bandana. K-Stone explained to them that they would bury them on the yard at certain locations where the homies kicked it. After that was said, he informed them that there would be mandatory yard for the homies that missed yard a lot. There would be mandatory exercise no matter what it was, and mandatory checking in at the beginning and end of yard. One of K-Stone's homies asked what if he didn't want to workout. K-Stone replied by striking him in the mouth dropping him to the ground. Holding his bloody lip, he tried to get up but K-Stone punched him in the eye dropping him again. Standing over him, he told him that he was only able to get up when he was told. After the display, those that didn't agree with K-Stone remained quiet, while those that knew they needed structure showed compliance.

"We all come from the same turf and done walked through the same alleys and pissed on the same walls. Some of us have even fucked the same bitches. So we all know how the turf operates. I'm not trying to control or tell ya'll how to operate. We all have hair on our nuts and know how to think. I just want the homies right and we can't be right with no structure. I don't expect it to happen over night, but at least make it happen ASAP! As for cuzz," K-Stone said motioning to his homie on the ground. "I don't even know him. Furthermore, we don't need and want any weak links. So this is your only warning. You have to get off the yard."

With that, his former homie walked to the program office to roll it up.

"If anybody else got something they feel needs to be addressed, speak up!"

"You basically said what needed to be said to get things into motion," one of the older homies said.

"If that's all then, the meeting is over. I'm going to hit the bars."

Thursday came quickly, leaving one more day to knock down before the big day. That morning K-Stone hit the yard overly observant of his homies body language and how long it took them to meet up. He was content about the rules stipulated the other day were being followed. After greeting each other, they all headed towards the apparatus bars to workout. During his rest periods between sets, K-Stone would observe his homies and everyone else on the yard.

It was important to show strength in his homies by having unity. Though forced, it couldn't be seen, veneers were common in the prison environment. By the time voluntary inline came, all his homies were through working out. Gathering their belongings, they

all headed towards the water fountain to fill their jugs. When that
was done, they made their way to the bleachers to hang out.
While at the bleachers certain homies told jokes while others told
war stories and bragged about females they use to have. It seemed to
K-Stone that the program was the same no matter what yard or pen
he was placed. Everybody had the same anecdotes and the same
gripes. Nevertheless, it made the time go by and in most cases that
was all that mattered.

"I saw you out there getting your money."

"Somebody's got to do it, Askari."

"You right about that."

"Speaking of working out, why is it you do so many
calisthenics?"

"You mean berpes?"

"I'm talking about when you do the push up, and then jump
up, and raise each knee to your chest and continue the process
repeatedly."

"Those are called berpes. I learned about them from
watching other brothers who were in the hole with me."

"What does it work on?"

"Everything: your wind, shoulders, chest, legs, and mind."

"How does it work on your mind?"

"To do a myriad of berpes you must be more then physically
fit. Your mind must be extremely conditioned. Once you have
mastered the berpes you will have gained a form of discipline within
yourself, enabling you to have discipline in other areas."

"From the way you do them it looks like they're either too
easy or you are a genius."

"I'm not a genius K-Stone. What I know you can learn if
you apply yourself. Too many inmates are in overt and covert
competition with their own people and other races to be the biggest
and strongest. I see them everyday practicing improper technique
and wondering why they make little progress. The average inmate,
if you ask him why he does certain exercise, he won't be able to give
you an answer beyond something superficial."

"Why do you workout?"

"For my health first of all, second to keep my blood flowing
efficiently so my brain works at its best potential. One thing to keep
in mind too, is that it goes just beyond working out. You must have
a proper diet."

"That explains why you eat all that fish and chicken. What's wrong with beef, chips, and sweets?"

"A lot, beef stays in your body ninety hours before it fully digest. That's why you feel overly drowsy whenever you consume a meal consisting of beef, though beef has protein that you can't find in most foods. Over time, it wears your body down. Being that you're Black, you've already been subjected to bad eating habits. In the ghetto we all grew up having a local ice-cream truck hypnotizing us with its sweet rhythmic beats and even sweeter delicious candy inside those trucks. Furthermore, we're all familiar with the local liquor store, fast food spots, or candy houses surrounding our neighborhoods. These facts contribute to Blacks having shorter life spans than other races. There's nothing wrong with an occasional burger and fries or a sweet or two, but only in moderation. We as people must learn to eat to live and not live to eat. A person must be conscious of what's going in their bodies as well as the affects that cause it to be positive or negative."

"You know what Askari?"

"What's that?"

"You need to put out a workout video if they ever grant your appeal!"

"I'll put it into consideration."

"I don't see why you wouldn't. You remind me of those paid commercials that come on TV late night. I don't know if I could give up junk food."

"You can, you just have to discipline yourself in steps. Most people fall off because they set unrealistic goals. Just take one bad food out of your diet once a month and gradually your dependency on it will reside."

"Before you make something to eat, let me see you do fifty berpes."

"No problem, that's it?"

"For right now just remember that whenever you do berpes to raise your left leg to your chest then your right leg."

Twenty berpes into the routine, K-Stone was out of breath. He barely finished as he struggled through the last twenty-two. Panting and trying to catch his breath, K-Stone tried to force some words out but couldn't until he sat down on his bunk. Between breaths, K-Stone managed to get out a few words.

"I have to get the hang of those. Why do I have to start with the left knee?"

"Because the system isn't right".

* * * * * * * * * *

"Gina, don't forget to come back tonight, it's very important I see Kay tomorrow."

"The last thing you have to worry about is me being late. We already established this once. I'll be back around eleven thirty tonight, no later. If you feel I'm taking too long, just call me on my phone. It will be on."

* * * * * * * * * *

"What's wrong with you babe?"

"Nothing, why you ask me that?"

"Because you're acting different."

"There you go imagining again. I'm acting how I always act."

"If you say so Uzi." Sensing the unavoidable hostility, Gina got up from the couch and walked to the refrigerator for something to drink.

"Pour me something to drink while you're in there."

"What do you want?"

"Whatever. There was this question I wanted to ask you but it kept slipping my mind."

"What is it?"

"You said you never met my homie K-Stone."

"Like I told you, maybe once."

"You sure?"

"Maybe twice, but nothing worth remembering, here you go Uzi, I poured you some fruit punch."

"So which one is it, once or twice?"

"Yes, I've met him more than once."

"Where at?

"Why are you asking me about your homie?"

"Because I want to know. Why are you acting so evasive?"

"Look! A long time ago Ivie wanted me to test K-Stone to see if he was faithful to her. So I did and he passed. That was the only time I met him."

"Why didn't you just say that?"

"Because I know you wouldn't believe me."

"Is that right, you just assumed I wouldn't believe you because maybe you're lying."

"What do I need to lie for?"

"That's what I'm trying to figure out. So if I call your sister right now she'll tell me the same story?"

"Now you're acting stupid Uzi!"

"Oh, I'm stupid now because I want to confirm your story!"

"No, because you're playing games with me!"

"I'll do whatever I want with you, now what?"

"I was just playing with you, but you went and took it all serious, so it must be more to the story then what you're telling me. Something is up; I just can't put my finger on it."

Just when Gina was about to move to the couch to calm him down the only way she knew, his phone rang. After three rings broke the awkward silence, Uzi answered the phone.

"Yes I'll accept." When Gina heard those words her heart sank deep below her belly. For she knew it could only be one person.

"K-Stone, I was just talking about you."

"To who?"

"Gina."

"What that bitch got to say about me?"

"Such vulgar language for someone you don't know cuzz."

"Don't know!"

"Yeah, she said she don't know you cuzz."

"She knew me when she tried to dome me off. She would get her little revenge back whenever I would call from the county by hanging the phone up on me. I've wanted to tell you about that hood rat. I just never pushed the issue."

"Cuzz, I wish you would've put me up. I've been having this bitch all up on me."

"Well now you know do what's best for you."

"Besides that broad, what's crackin with it Killa Stone?"

As they chopped it up on the phone Gina tried to formulate a plan to explain herself. Every time she moved closer to Uzi he pushed her away with his free hand. With three failed attempts, she just sat there on the other side of the couch quietly fidgeting her fingers.

"Check it out married cuzz, I'm about to eighty-six your sister in law."

"Watch out with all that. Just get at me next week to let me know how it went."

"Five minutes lok."

"Five minutes."

As soon as Uzi hung up the phone one of his other females called.

"What it do?"

"Whatever you want it to do babe."

"How long is it going to take for you to be ready?"

"No time, come get me."

"I'll be over there in twenty minutes."

"You're just going to disrespect me like that?"

"Next time mind your own business."

"Can we just talk for a minute it doesn't have to be like this?"

"Yes it does, there's nothing to talk about. Anyways you disrespected my lok."

"Just like that Uzi?"

Without responding Uzi walked in the bathroom to turn on the shower. When he came back into the living room, Gina was gone. Good riddance, Uzi said to himself as he got in the shower. Dressed and ready to leave, Uzi reached in his key jar but found air instead of his car keys. For ten minutes he searched his neatly kept town house and couldn't find them anywhere. Sensing something was wrong, he walked to the underground parking garage to find his car gone. Instant fury filled his body as he jetted up the stairs grabbing his cell phone from the counter and hitting the speed dial button to Gina's cell phone.

"Gina, you stupid bitch you better bring my car back now!"

"Talking like that won't get you anywhere. You won't be picking up any other bitches on my shift," Gina said hanging up in Uzi's face.

Gina knew she was playing with her life by stealing Uzi's car. She had heard of his reputation but at this point she didn't care. She was tired of being disrespected and he needed to learn a lesson. On her way to South Central she decided to have fun while she had the car. Pulling over, she searched for a CD to play. When she found her favorite CD she threw it in and hit track number three as she gradually turned the music up till it was thundering. Not wanting to be alone on her endeavor, Gina picked up three of her home girls who were all amazed that her dude let her use his car. They all laughed and joked as Gina drove to the gas station on Figueroa and Century to get some gas before heading to the movies.

"Blood, you see that blue car?"

"Isn't that Blood from Ransack?" Another man in the back asked.

"Blood, get the AK, we about to make this nigga lean back."

As Gina pulled out the gas station a shiver went through her entire body. Shaking it off, she drove into traffic. Swooping up behind the Monte Carlo the K4s discussed their plan.

"Look Blood, I'm going to pull in front of Blood when the light turns red, hop out and make him feel it."

"Don't trip, we got this Blood," the two K4s in the back said simultaneously cocking their AK-47s back.

Traffic was light that night with this no police was insight, giving the K4's an added confidence. They knew they had to kill Uzi because he was one of the Ransoms main gunners. Furthermore, it would give them major stripes to be known on the turf as the ones that killed Uzi. When they came up on the third red light they knew it was time. Hopping out the back seat like the swat team, the two K4s rushed the blue Monte Carlo with rifles blazing. By the time Gina realized what was going on, she was getting hit in the face with broken glass followed by three bullets to her chest and one in her neck. All this before she could unsnap her seatbelt. Her home girls suffered similar fates as one of the K4s fired into the back side windows. In what seemed like minutes only took seconds as they left a lake full of glass and bullet shells along with four dead females in a bullet riddled car, still moving in neutral.

The K4s celebrated by reenacting gun sounds and their kill all the way back to their turf.

"Blood, my new name is Rambo B from now on!" one of the gunners insisted while laughing.

Word of the shooting spread like wild fire on dry brush through the streets of South Central. Without thought the Ransoms present in their turf, loaded up a myriad of guns and jumped in their cars. Some headed to K4s turf, while others went to the crime scene. When the Ransoms arrived at the scene it was surrounded by spectators trying to look over the yellow tape at who had been shot. All they could see was detectives taking pictures and collecting bullet shells. Seeing that the ambulance workers weren't treating anybody, the Ransoms assumed Uzi was D.O.A. and left the scene. They knew the K4s killed Uzi, but weren't for sure, so they decided to hit every turf nearest the crime scene to make everybody feel the pain.

His homies went on a murder spree through all of South Central while Uzi was pacing back and forth in his house frustrated that none of his homies were answering their chirps. Infuriated, he called up another female to use her car. As much as he hated people knowing where he lived, he was more irritated that he would have to leave this female alone in his home while he went searching for Gina. He had already promised himself that she would take a bullet for playing him. When his ride arrived he told her not to answer his phone while he was away. With that, he ran down to the car, jumped in, took out his forty glock from his waistband and placed it on his lap. He didn't have to worry about the police pulling him over in a beige Camry.

The first place he swooped by when he got to South Central was Gina's house, but his car was nowhere in sight. So he smashed to his turf to find it completely dry, which was very odd to him. Driving through the back streets of South Central he noticed an abnormal amount of police traffic. Usually Crash was in full force Friday nights, but they along with the regular one time, meant the streets were very hot. Looking up through his front window he could see the ghetto bird circling over K4s turf and other various enemies' sets in the area.

Something was going on in the streets and Uzi hated that he wasn't up on the get down. Wasting gas driving around looking for Gina was making his blood boil. So he parked the car on a back street in his turf waiting for one of his homies to come out. Three hours passed, leaving him to get a bottle of Hennessey and return to the car and chill. Alcohol flowed through his system as the time went by and the night became more still. The passed time fueled his evil thoughts as he caressed his gun like a small puppy just waiting to squeeze a bullet into Gina's brains.

*   *   *   *   *   *   *   *   *   *

After making some last minute modifications on her hair for tomorrow, Ivie laid across the couch by the window flicking the remote and peaking out the blinds every time she thought a car pulled up in front of the house. She had a weird feeling she never felt before dwelling within her. For a minute she thought it was pre-wedding jitters, but as it persisted she knew it wasn't nervousness, something was wrong.

Though Gina had a couple of hours left to make it home, Ivie decided to call her cell phone to make sure nothing unexpected came up, which was the norm for Gina. Four rings into her call, Ivie began to tell herself that she should have kept the car herself. On the fifth ring the phone was picked up by an unfamiliar voice. Ivie thought she had dialed the wrong number.

"Who is this?" Ivie said quickly.

"Detective Benson, from the 77th Homicide Division. Who am I speaking with?"

"Are you serious?"

"Yes ma'am, I am."

"This is Ivie Norms, what are you doing with my sister's phone?"

"Your sister has been involved in a murder."

"A murder, is she in jail?"

"You may want to contact your parents and let them know they need to come down to the department immediately!"

"Concerning what?"

"I can't discuss this any further with you over the phone ma'am."

Hoping it was all some sick joke, Ivie redialed her sister's cell phone number, but this time no one answered. Realizing its seriousness, she reluctantly called her mother but no one answered. So in a panic she called her auntie. After running down what happened, her auntie was on her way to pick her up. While waiting, Ivie wondered if her sister was the shooter, accomplice, or victim. She knew that if it wasn't a practical joke, then Uzi was a part of the crime in some way. In that moment it came to her to call his cell phone. Buzzing heavily, Uzi could barely hear his phone ringing. When he finally heard it he reached over to the passenger seat to answer the phone but it cut off. Checking the caller ID, he saw that it was Gina.

"Bitch, you better never come back to L.A. again!" Confused and shook up by Uzi's comment, Ivie quickly let him know it was her and not her sister.

"Ivie, what's up? Have you seen your bitch sister?" Hearing the intoxication through his voice, Ivie overlooked his derogatory comment about her sister.

"No I haven't, that's why I called you. I'm looking for her."

"Last time I saw your sister she stole my car. I've been looking for her ever since." As much as she tried to deny it to herself she knew her sister had been harmed.

"Have you tried to call her?"

"Yes and a detective answered the phone."

"What the hell a detective answering her phone for?"

"That's what I'm about to find out. He told me to meet him at the department."

"When you come back, call me."

"I will, but you have to promise not to harm my sister."

"As long as I get my car back and she stays out of my sight."

"Done, my ride is here, I'll call you when I get back."

The street seemed dark and lifeless adding to the worry Ivie and her aunt already felt. Walking up the huge cement stairs to the front door an eerie feeling overcame both of them simultaneously. Once inside, Ivie's auntie took a seat while Ivie approached the podium to request an interview with detective Benson. Twenty minutes passed slowly while Ivie and her aunt sat anxiously. Just when they were about to ask what was taking so long, a tall lean white man in his mid forties approached them introducing him self.

"I'm detective Benson, follow me into my office so we can further discuss what has taken place. Here have a seat," The detective said gesturing to the seats in front of his desk. Taking a seat himself, detective Benson let out a deep sigh before beginning.

"Are you Mrs. Norms?"

"No, I'm her sister and she is her auntie."

"I'll assume you're Ivie the one I talked to on the phone."

"Yes, is my sister alright?"

"Your sister was involved in a gang related quadruple murder this afternoon, in which she and three other females were the victims. At the moment it seems to be a cause of mistaken identity. They assumed your sister was a known gangbanger when they saw her driving the car."

"Are you sure?" Ivie shrieked out while tears streamed down her face. Seeing the distress, the detective gave them a brief moment of silence before sliding the picture of Gina's face taken at the scene of the crime. He needed to make sure they could give a positive ID.

"Is this Gina, Mrs. Leonard?"

"Oh my God, oh my God!" Ivies auntie said repeatedly while nodding her head up and down.

"Do you have the shooters in custody?"

"Not at the present time Mrs. Leonard, but we have some leads to who was involved. If we come across any new evidence or information, I will be sure to contact you immediately."

After wrapping up a few more questions, detective Benson escorted Ivie and her aunt to the front of the department.

"We will get whoever did this to your sister and her friends off the street."

Without a response, Ivie walked to the car as her aunt continued talking with the detective.

"Ivie, do you want to come home with me or go home?"

"Just take me home."

"Detective Benson says they got their best working the case."

"Does it really matter?"

"Why would you say a thing like that?"

"Because it won't bring my sister back, and the niggas that did it, are probably dead or will be before they catch them."

"I know you're hurt baby, but you must have faith that things will turn out alright."

"No disrespect auntie, but I don't have much faith or words left at the moment."

Seeing cars pull up, Uzi snapped out of his trance and got out the car to lean against the hood with his forty glock loosely hanging from his side. As his homies grouped up and started walking towards the spot, they quickly took notice of the stranger leaning up against a car they'd never seen before

"Cuzz, who is that?" One of the homies asked approaching him while pulling a three fifty-seven revolver from the back of his waistline.

"It's your big homie, cuzz."

Getting closer, the Ransom noticed that the stranger was Uzi but couldn't believe it. Stepping off his lean, Uzi met his homies half-way as they continued towards him.

"Where the hell have you'll been?"

"Out putting in work for you nigga!" Two of his homies said at once.

"For what? I can do that myself."

"We thought you had got swiss-cheesed when we saw your car slumped on Figueroa."

"Punk bitch got my car shot-up!"

"Rule number seventy-four, never let a bitch drive the main ride. From what we remember you made that rule up Uzi."

"You know me better than that cuzz. The bitch stole my car keys when I turned my back. Just take it as a lesson of what can happen when the Uzi is crossed."

*   *   *   *   *   *   *   *   *   *

"Today you will no longer be a bachelor like the rest of us looming about this decrepit forest of lost souls."

"Askari, you always got some type of parable or message, but they seem to always be on point."

"I'm elated for you K-Stone, I hope you treat the new Mrs. Pink like the African queen she is."

"No doubt, they should be calling me in another hour. She said she would be leaving extra early the last time I talked to her."

"So how do you feel?"

"Like I always feel."

"And how is that?"

"Prepared for whatever."

"You sound as if you're going into war against your rivals."

"Naw, it's not like that, I feel better then usual and a little nervous to keep it real. I'll no longer be responsible for just me anymore."

"You're right about that. Too many people fail to look at marriage like that. They see getting married in here as just a way to get pussy when it's much more than that. Life doesn't revolve around pussy. Many men and women these days feel it does. Sex should be looked at as a bonding experience between two people, as well as to conceive life. Not how many nuts a person can bust in the least amount of time. Today's society is obsessed with sex more and more and less concerned with morals. It's getting to the point where nothing is sacred anymore. Everything is exposed, exploited, and empty in so many areas. So you have to ask yourself K-Stone, will you continue to be a part of this virus that's spreading through our community?"

"I'm just trying to get married for right now, not make a political statement. My view on marriage is not to do anything that you can't handle your women doing to you."

"That's a decent piece of wisdom, Stone."

"Yes it is because it's real. I got it from an older cat in Delano."

"Marriage must have trust. If it doesn't at least have that element of foundation then there is no point in marrying a person under circumstances that can be avoided."

"I feel you, but what kind of circumstances can't be avoided?"

"The ones where your back is against the wall and you must marry some one out of necessity. Let's say you got a double digit sentence to do and a female comes along your way. You're going to try to marry her for the benefits. If you know yourself well you know you're not going to be faithful, but you marry her anyway because you have to. In a situation like that you don't care whether she's faithful or not as long as she's sending packages every quarter, keeping your books fat, and doesn't give you a disease on the conjugal visit. So the trust issues are not really relevant in the marriage, when you're trying to survive you'll do about anything. In correlation to that, when you're short timing like me, there's no need to go through the motions unless you know you're going to be faithful when you touch."

"So you feel you have that type of discipline?"

"If I didn't, I wouldn't be going out to the visit today. Females come and go, but a loyal female is near impossible to find. It's easy to be with someone when things are easy. One sees who really cares for them when there is nothing to be gained at the moment. I wouldn't sacrifice what we have for a piece of pussy."

With that being his last comment, K-Stone made his way out the door to the visiting room. Dressed in some fresh creased- up prison blues, K-Stone was feeling immaculate as he strutted across the yard with his chest poked out and chin held high. When he stepped into the visiting room he looked around like he always did, knowing he would make eye contact with Ivie, but there was no trace of Ivie in the visiting room.

After scanning the visiting room one more time, he walked to the podium to find out where his visitor was seated. Pointing to the table on the far left the C.O. told him table fifteen. Sitting at table fifteen was someone K-Stone had never seen before. Taking a seat he instantly asked who she was. She told him her name was Tatiana and she was there to see him.

"Where do you know me from?"

"We met at a party a long time ago, we just never hooked up."

"How did you know I was locked up?"

"First I went to where you hang at, but your homies told me you were locked up. So I asked for your hook- up and one of them gave it to me."

"This doesn't make sense. You telling me we never hooked up, but you went out your way to come see me in prison. More so you're a piece, which really makes you being here suspect. So why are you really here?"

"I don't know what you mean."

"What party did we meet at?"

"This party in Compton, I forgot who threw it, but you were there with some of your homies."

"Is that right?"

"Yes."

"Okay, you're here. What do you want?"

"You baby!" Tatiana said reaching her hand out to K-Stone who quickly jerked it away.

"Well, you're too late, I'm getting married today."

"So what, I gets what I want!"

"All that's cool, but you're cramping my get down right now. If I wasn't getting married, we could've probably done something, but my future wife is going to be here any minute now."

"Well, can I keep you company until she comes?"

"Now you sound stupid. If you have any type of respect for me you'll just leave."

"I respect you, but I didn't come all the way up here for nothing."

"If you want to wait, wait, it's on you if you want to make a fool out yourself."

"The last thing I'll be is a fool."

"What's that shit suppose to mean?"

"Nothing."

After an hour of going back and forth, Ivie had yet to come. They both sat at the table wondering where she was and what was taking so long. They were both ignorant to Gina's death the day before. Tatiana knew if she left she wouldn't get the rest of her money, but the more she went back and fourth with K-Stone, the more she found herself liking him. Even though he talked little, he wasn't buying anything she was saying. Two hours passed and K-Stone didn't know what to think, the preacher approached him and Tatiana inquiring if they were ready. When he said no, the preacher gave him a weird look of uncertainty. He wanted to leave by that point, but had nowhere to go. He preferred to be out with a strange female then cooped up in a cement box with another inmate. He still had time left on his visit so he decided to wait it out.

By the time it turned 1 o'clock, the preacher left, which meant he would have to reschedule the wedding, which meant he had to wait another three months to get married. A feeling of anger and concern filled his mind as he tried to out think his clouded mind to what had just happened, but he had no answers, but death that could have caused her not to show up on such an important day.

Tatiana was upset she had ruined her whole day for nothing. It was clear to her that Ivie wasn't showing either. The more the visit played out, she couldn't believe she even agreed to do such a trifling thing. She had made up her mind that Gina was going to have to pay her all her money. It wasn't her fault Ivie didn't show up. She came close three times to telling K-Stone why she really came, but decided to keep to the script for Gina's sake no matter how foolish it sounded and made her look.

K-Stone had enough waiting, and without mentioning anything to Tatiana, he walked to the podium and got her drivers license. Standing over her he tossed her license on the table and walked to the exit door which led back to the human zoo.

* * * * * * * * * *

Reading his dictionary in the dayroom to pass time, Askari was surprised to see K-Stone back so early. His demeanor spoke volumes that his visit didn't go well. Or so it seemed. It was hard to tell what kind of mood K-Stone was in at times. Most of the time he was stolid about everything, but this time it was different. Askari saw it in his nefarious gait walking up the stairs. When dayroom ended, Askari knew he was about to walk into a fog of negativity once he entered the cell. Although it was nothing new to him, he hated being around those type of vibes. Being in a cell caused the negativity to affect both occupants. Over the years he had realized that having a celly was like being in a forced relationship. With some being short and most long, it was important he played close attention to any changes in his celly's mood or behavior. It was crucial to avoid a hostile environment within the cell.

Askari knew that if he was ever paroled he would make a solid partner in a relationship. Years in prison had taught him much understanding, patience, and control over his anger when dealing with others and their myriad of problems. His first couple of years were hectic with weirdo cellys. It took a long time to comprehend that no one was perfect not even himself. It was all a matter of could he deal with the other person's flaws who was living with him and vice versa. Knowing the difference between flaws and disrespect was also a key element in managing a healthy cell relationship. One of the qualities he admired in K-Stone was his willingness to listen as well as soak up what he was being told and apply it in his own way. He knew deep inside that if K-Stone would calm down on his gang loyalties and certain ideologies, he would be a strong leader for the people. Time had taught him many things and he also knew that to fully change K-Stone must first have the desire to change. With all the knowledge he possessed within himself and throughout the cell, it meant nothing if K-Stone didn't realize for himself that he needed a new path.

Books and intellectual conversations only provided insight to those who may share similar plights to ones own. More so, providing the seeker with a sense that they can prevail no matter what dilemmas they find themselves in. Askari knew reading and discussions helped exercise the mind giving it new ideas to play with and mold it to be analytical when faced with future problems. In the end all this meant nothing if one truly didn't feel the need whole-heartedly to make improvements in their thinking and behavior. He knew plenty of individuals that read great works of literature just for the sake of saying so. They rarely applied what they had read to the improvement of themselves. More so, he knew plenty who had the gift of gab but when it boiled down to it, they talked all day but said nothing of importance that could truly help themselves or the listener.

So much cupidity, duplicity, and stupidity is worshipped in prison that Askari often felt rancor for the older prisoners, that most called O.G.s who weren't properly playing their part in the lacing of the youngstas that came through the system with something tangible they could use to survive in society. For this reason, Askari had made a pact to himself that he would reach out to all brothers no matter their status in the prison community to teach them about their history. He felt that an average Black man only knowing about M.L.K. and Malcolm X, needed seeds to be planted drastically.

For those that didn't want to learn he wouldn't shun them nor try to force anything upon them. He would simply set an example of how they should try to carry themselves one day when they were ready.

As he expected, the cell was dark as well as the mood when he stepped in. The back window was covered with a towel keeping the last remaining rays of sun out. K-Stone laid on his back, fully clothed, boots and all with a blanket doubled folded covering his head all the way to his waist. Cutting on the low beam, Askari jumped on the top bunk and continued reading a book he had picked out earlier.   The cell kept a stale silence for the rest of the day, which was broken by an occasional piss by one of them.

Sleep was unavailable to K-Stone that night. His eye lids were sore the next morning from forcing them shut the whole day before giving himself an intoxicated look as he stared in the mirror and splashed water on his face. Looking up to his left, he could see Askari was up early, as usual. They made eye contact for a minute and gave each other a head nod simultaneously. The implicitly of the moment said a lot. K-Stone knew Askari understood it was nothing against him the day before.

K-Stone had never been so anxious for dayroom to open that morning. When the door popped open he didn't waist anytime getting to the phone. His first call to Ivie didn't get a response. Holding his composure as much as possible he called three more times before dayroom ended. He became so desperate that he resorted to calling his mother to ask her to call for him and let him know what was going on with Ivie.

The day seemed to be going by slow for K-Stone as he waited on a letter to arrive from Ivie to explain what happened. The next day proved even slower because he had to wait until he got off from work before using the phone or checking his mail. When he spoke with his mother, she had told him she was unable to get in contact with Ivie. Then she went on to inquire if everything was alright with them, to which she already knew the answer. Being that he never asked her to do such favors it was only obvious she always told him Ivie was no good, in fact she told him every female he was ever with was no good. So to hear her ramble in his disappointment irritated him greatly, especially when she kept asking him if everything was okay.

Gina's funeral was Friday and Ivie was still having a hard time dealing with the loss of her only sister in such a violent way. She knew K-Stone was disappointed and angry about her not showing up. She just didn't have it in her to go up to the prison and get married after such a tragedy. Every time the phone rang at certain hours she knew it was him calling, but she fought back her feeling for wanting to be comforted by him. She had a lot of rancor in her for gang-bangers at the present and it didn't exclude him.

Instead of the typical relief Fridays normally brought, this one brought with it a plethora of pictures ranging from the past to present mixed with flowers, and decorations surrounding her sister's closed casket. Pathos were felt every time a family member took the microphone to say a few words about her sister. Ivie was too choked up to say anything. Besides, she had more than just a few words to say, and to prevent from causing anymore pain to her family, she kept her mouth shut. Instead, she scanned the whole church looking for Uzi. At the end of the day Uzi was nowhere insight to pay his last respects, which hurt Ivie even more. She knew how her sister felt about Uzi and she knew Uzi had feelings for her also.

For Uzi not to come at all was total disrespect. At that moment, she decided that K-Stone would no longer be a part of her life. He would have to suffer the permanent loneliness she was going to feel even if it was only for awhile. Uzi hurt her, so she would hurt his comrade. This would be her gift to her sister, something Gina was craving. She found solace in the thought that maybe her sister was right the whole time.

Letters and phone calls stopped arriving after three weeks. Ivie assumed K-Stone had gotten the point. She didn't even bother reading the letters he sent to her, instead, she let them pile up until they stopped coming. Then she put them all in the trash, including the ones prior to her sister's death. The only thing she kept that was reminiscent of him was pictures that she could not bring herself to throw away.

Ivie's sudden absence hurt K-Stone more then he wanted to admit. Every time he sent off a letter, he shuddered at what a fool he was making of himself. There were only so many excuses he could make for sending letter after letter even though he received no response. It took some strong self checking for reality to settle in that it was over. Without any explanations, excuses, or reasons, he was aware that she was out of his life. His last letter ranged from anger to the basic concern of why?

Though he had put it behind him, he still thought of her and wondered why she just left him. Visits came to an end once Ivie fell off, leaving K-Stone with even more time on his hands for prison gang life.

Other gangs took notice of the impact K-Stone had on his homies. They were now organized like a small army just the way he planned. After each third draw, they would have a big spread for all the homies to reinforce the unity. There would also be at least a gallon of white lightening and weed after to consummate the moment.

The months came and went with K-Stone submerged into the illusion of prison life. All his conversations, actions, and thoughts evolved around negativity. Like so many others, nothing beneficial was coming from his time. He had subconsciously become comfortable with mediocrity, resorting to imitating his behavior from the streets in prison. Instead of a gun he carried a knife. Instead of hanging on the corner with his homies he hung out against a handball wall or the bleachers with his homies. Pruno, weed, and cigarettes stayed at his lips more then ever. He was allowing the time to exacerbate his already nefarious ways. K-Stone's plummet into further destruction affected Askari. He hated seeing young Blacks continue to let their brains decay with false ideologies of what an individual should aspire to be in life. He knew that prisons and institutions like prisons reinforced mental shackles already present; such as, the lack of responsibility for ones self and their actions. There was no responsibility in prison, no bills, no real jobs, and no expectations to be better than what one had learned in their previous environment. This was just the tip of the iceberg as to why parolees came back to prison. Few ever stopped to think why whenever the prison went on lockdowns the only privileges they took were yard, phones, visits, store, and packages. They never took away the TV or radios which were also privileges. Reason being is that they don't want inmates to pick up books and learn material. The prison officials will take away religious services before the TV and radio, this is how important it is for them to keep the ignorance bliss with a grown males' pacifier. Knowing the formula to stagnate inmates' minds, Askari knew K-Stone was very close to ending his mental development. Since the wedding dilemma and getting his property back, he noticed K-Stone's behavior taking a turn for the worse. All that plagued Askari's mind was to get to K-Stone before too much damage was done.

It was a known fact to him that people rarely realize the influence they have had on others until it's too late. Be it positive or negative, everybody's actions eventually influence those of others. After picking his mind and going within his cipher he came to the conclusion to continue setting the proper example for him and be there when he eventually woke up to his self destruction.

* * * * * * * * * *

Rubbing a small rock in the hard dirt to a make a hole while sitting on the curb, K-Stone looked around cautiously to see who was watching before taking his knife out to bury it. Seeing the C.O.s getting closer he smoothed out the remaining dirt over the knife as they approached him and three other Blacks to be stripped out for weapons search. It was in connection with the stabbing of a skinhead earlier that morning by his own people.

"Damn, we just came off the lockdown yesterday!" An inmate said gathering their clothes as they walked to their housing units. It was nothing to K-Stone. He had become used to the constant lockdowns that happened every month.

Chapter 13

Calendars

Two years and some change into his sentence had made him comfortable in his new environment. Prison had become his home now. With each passing month he felt more estranged from society. One day he noticed the awkwardness he felt when he first came was out of his system. Nothing in his new society raised an eyebrow anymore. Every act of violence was familiar, just with different races. In fact, if it didn't draw blood or the stretcher didn't come, he didn't even get excited.

That night he lay against his rolled up mattress while flipping the channels as usual with his head phones on while Askari read a book. Word had already spread that they would be on lockdown at least three weeks while the C.O.s conducted a search of the facility. TV watching was never an activity K-Stone did when he was on the streets. With the lame programs that came on the eight channels the prison provided he was constantly reminded why.

Being that he had read all the good novels available and had no one to write to besides his mother; he searched his brain for something to do to pass the next three weeks. Looking around the cell he kept catching the stack of books sitting on Askari's locker. Realizing that a book would be his only escape from boredom he asked Askari to shoot him something cool to read from his collection. Placing a book mark in between the book he was reading, Askari reached in his locker instead of the stacks on top that he had reserved for K-Stone. He was fully aware that it wasn't constructive to just hand a fresh brain anything to devour. The mind needed something it could form a foundation on, and then move to adding more complex knowledge to that foundation.

Without words, he handed K-Stone the book in hopes that he would grasp its powerful message and slowly begin to put fourth a stronger, healthier direction for his life. Asking for the book told Askari two things: K-Stone could be ready to change or just be bored, but either one was a step into the right direction. Boredom could mean he was ready to take the TV and radio pacifier away from his mind. Everyone had a pacifier in prison that they turned to for some type of solace during their time. It could be drugs, alcohol, tobacco, sex books, coffee, sugar, food, or actions like telling jokes, talking on the phone, gang-banging, and sleeping. Being that everyone had some form of pacifier they used, Askari had decided that his would be books, studying, and learning new things along with pacification; Askari also knew the adoption of a character was necessary in prison. When he first arrived, his character had already been carved on the streets. So all he had to do was adopt a little more toughness. It was easy for him to fall into the gangsta group when he entered prison. Fortunately, he was put under the wing of some solid brothers who opened his eyes to a more suitable character. Since being down he had seen people adopt many characters to present themselves as. Most adopted a spiritual character of a Christian or Muslim and there were many reasons why inmates chose to adopt the spiritual character. The main reason was safety, because they figured this type of character sent the message that they were neutral in the prison society. After a couple of months in prison they soon realized that no one was neutral to violent acts in prison, especially when it was racial. The religious character held many forms of pacifications that inmates used to find themselves. Most inmates that were spiritual eventually ended up functioning like gang members. That is they would only socialize with their members while condemning other groups. They would get tattoos of crosses, prayer hands, and half moon with a star in the middle. These common tattoos normally were accompanied with scripture from the Koran or Bible inked across their chest or forearm. This was contradictory to Askari because he felt both holy books condemned desecrating the bodily temple with marks and symbols.

Others adopted characters that they had seen a lot of non-affiliates adopt were the thug character. A non-affiliate would come in the system under his real name, two months later he would have a nickname hanging out with a particular gang. This adopted character was the most dangerous one to adopt in a place where one was guilty by association. Gang members came and left daily, taking with them a photo memory of all their enemies. The category of adoptable characters in prison was universal. All of the prisons he had done time with always had a hustler, pimp, baller, athlete, legal eagle, and intellectuals were the rarest adopted character that he would come into contact with. It had long become clear to him through the interactions with these adopted characters that if one should adopt, let him adopt a character that was positive and wouldn't place them in a position where they would fall under greater peer pressure to be something they were not, and to please abnormal individuals in an abnormal environment.

With so many adoptions taking place within the prison society along with no responsibilities, inmates were more like babies than men. They were like men inside a huge incubator that kept their minds suspended in a frame of thought. Askari was aware that the prison promoted this behavior and it was a constant struggle to keep himself in check. He could understand how difficult it must be for someone that has no sense of mental discipline. Helping a few graduate from the baby mind state to the man mind state, they in turn could help others break away and start the positive impetus. He was also fully aware of the road blocks most inmates faced when trying to educate themselves. With so much working against, one had to be strong in all areas of importance. Especially being they had their own working against them. Black movies often depicted Black men fresh out of prison that has some knowledge as a joke. So when he reenters society trying to share his knowledge, self love, and strength among his people he is met with jokes about himself as well as ridiculed for living in the past.

Being that the majority of individuals' minds have been unconsciously molded through the years to reject any figure with a positive message who isn't an entertainer, athlete, or slick talking politician, they're content with having no control of anything in their daily lives. They're content being governed by another. Unconsciously they reject anyone that looks like them and who speaks of being independent and unified. When these thoughts passed through Askari's mind it made him angry and sad. To see his people achieve so much made him proud, but to see them controlled by another culture with no place to call their own sickened him. He had to constantly remind himself that he could still make a difference regardless of his life sentence.

Early the next morning K-Stone was awakened by the tray slot being opened. Sticking out his hand he took the paper tray Askari passed to him. K-Stone placed it on the desk while still gaining control of his bodily functions from waking up. Picking through the runny oatmeal, he decided to just eat the half done pancakes and go back to sleep. About ten a.m., he was reawakened by Askari who was working-out by the door. Getting out of the bed, K-Stone removed the towel covering the back window to let the light in making his eyes squirm. Folding his covers, he sat back down on his bunk and reached underneath to get his laundry bag to put his shirt on. With Askari finishing up, he reached for his toothbrush, toothpaste, and face towel inside a huge locker. Brushing his teeth at the sink he decided that he would knock out a couple of chapters in the book Askari gave to him. He looked forward to seeing what kind of literature he was reading that caused him to be so militant. Flicking the channels he saw that the prison hadn't changed the movies yet. Then he remembered that it was a holiday which meant that there would be no mail, not that he received any mail anyway, but he was expecting a magazine. After reading two chapters, K-Stone placed the book by his side on the bed. Getting out of his relaxed position he stood up to stretch then made his way to the door to look out the window. From the two chapters he read, a nerve was struck. A few times the truth that he read made him upset at himself. Taking a deep breath he returned back to where he left off. Sometimes he would have to look in the dictionary for the meaning of words. Then it made him realize that for a person in his early twenties he was lacking mentally in his comprehension. This simple fact combined with what the book was saying put some heavy thoughts in his mind as to what he was doing with his life. He hated not knowing. It seemed like every other page he was writing words down he didn't understand. Hearing his stomach growl he realized he had forgotten to eat. He had lost complete track of time. When he looked at his watch it was three thirty and he was half way through the book. All the reading he did earlier made him sleepy. Unrolling his mat, he laid down to take a short nap.

Waking up re-energized, he picked the book back up and continued to read. With three more chapters to read he decided to finish the book the next day. Placing it on the shelf he plugged his earphones into the TV to see what was on. After ten minutes of pushing buttons, he took his headphones off and placed them on the TV. Noticing that K-Stone had read a decent portion of the book, Askari asked him how the book was coming along.

"The book is on point. My only hang-up is all the words I have to keep looking up."

"Don't let it bother you. I had to do the same thing when I started reading literature. The more you read the better you'll get. It's good you're writing the words down to review later. I did the same thing when I first started."

"So you taught yourself while in here?"

"Basically, I learned most of what I know behind these walls. With no distractions and the right guidance I set fourth on my journey."

"Yeah, I feel you on that. The book made me realize in a lot of ways that I need to do some self checking."

"As long as you continue being honest with yourself, you're headed in the right direction."

That night, K-Stone kept thinking about what he had read earlier that day. He had never viewed himself as a Black man before. He saw himself as just a Crip who was a man. Never before had he felt any remorse or second guessed his past or actions. It seemed that the book had opened up a new area in his mind that had been vacant and lost his whole life. For the first time in his life he saw and identified himself as Black, which made him admit to himself that the people he used to shoot and victimize were Black too.

Wrestling with his thoughts made sleep hard to find once again, causing him to wake up the next morning feeling extra tired. In a way he regretted reading the book, because it made him question all his beliefs and values. What bothered him the most was the book described him with complete accuracy.

Finishing the last remaining chapters he closed the book and starred at the cover with a scrutinizing look on his face.

"Are all your books like this one?"

"What do you mean?"

"I mean about Blackness and self improvement?"

"Mostly, I also have some autobiographies on a range of great thinkers. Although the majority of my literature is Black oriented, I don't limit myself to just that. Knowledge can be found in a range of works. You just have to be cautious of what you feed your brain, that's all. All literature is not good just like how all foods are not good for you. What you allow in your mind will eventually dictate your actions."

"So you're telling me that if I continue reading books like the one you gave me, I will change?"

"It depends on if you want to change. The books only lay out the blueprints to what can be accomplished if you apply yourself. Furthermore, the books enlighten you to what's going on, why it's going on and most important how you can stop yourself from being a part of the problem. More so, they will inform you of what our ancestors endured which should give you some respect for our women and brothers. If you look at our communities, as well as Blacks living in conditions around the world, it's easy to see that the majority lack roots of our culture. K-Stone it doesn't matter if you read a thousand books if you're not willing to set in motion the actions that need to be made for positive adjustments in your lifestyle. My main advice to you is don't wait till you're doing life in prison like me to want to change. Do you want to change?"

K-Stone hesitated for a minute before answering. He knew a yes would be a defining moment in his life, but he wasn't sure whether he was ready to make that change now. He still had loyalty to his gang and his many beliefs. Straddling the fence could be dangerous in the prison environment. Never one to see things as a coincidence or luck, he knew he had met men like Askari as well as other individuals who tried to point him in the right direction for a reason. Even he was aware it wasn't wise to keep ignoring what was obviously a sign that he needed to put forth and make a serious change.

"Askari, man, I want to change. It's just I don't know what I will be or do if I do change my life."

"Everyone goes through that stage, it's basically a fear of leaving your comfort zone, which is a normal reaction. No one wants to leave from were they've been established all their lives to walk on unfamiliar territory. It takes strength and courage to change K-Stone. To walk a known path is much easier especially if you've been conditioned to it your whole life. At this point in your life there's nothing you can do to gain anymore stripes or recognition in your set, unless you're still trying to prove yourself to others. Your homies know you're with the business concerning all areas of your gangsta life. So my question to you is, what else is there left for you to accomplish in gang-banging?"

"Nothing, I've done it all."

"That's where you're wrong. You have two things left to accomplish: life and death. You've done it all, now it's time to elevate your game to another level. You're no longer blinded by what you've been taught by others who didn't really know what life was about themselves. It's time to start living and stop existing."

K-Stone listened to Askari's words carefully. His words penetrated deep within his mind and soul. He was correct about what he was saying. Now that he was aware that his past actions were wrong; his pride in taking lives, destroying his community and corrupting others started to fade out. At this point he knew he needed to grow up. For the first time in is life he gave thought to what he was going to do outside of hustling and gangbanging. Not much came to his mind, but the fact that he was thinking about it made him know that change was inevitable.

* * * * * * * * * *

"Let me get a double chili cheeseburger with bacon and some large fries and a strawberry shake."

"Is that all?"

"Unless you're going to put your number on the receipt then that's it."

"Drive to the window please."

Looking at the receipt, he saw the number which looked like it was written in a hurry.

"I'll holla at you tonight so we can hook something up."

Pulling out the Quick and Split in his charcoal grey Mercedes sedan, Uzi's next destination was his turf to check on one of his spots.

"Open up the door I'll be there in three minutes." Hanging up his cell phone, Uzi pulled into a nearby parking garage. Reaching over to his passenger seat he grabbed his food bag and put his forty glock in his waist-band.

"You didn't bring me anything to eat?" His homie asked with his nostrils flaring from the aroma coming from the food.

"Do I look like your bitch? Send one of the customers to get you something to eat cuzz."

"You a cold dude."

"You just now figuring that one out. Mistakes like that get people killed."

Uzi's younger homie just looked at him as he proceeded to eat his greasy meal.

He knew what Uzi was capable of, especially since the mysterious death of Lil G-Liz a few weeks ago. Rumors were floating around that Uzi killed him because he thought the F.B.I. was watching and wanted to quiet Lil G-Liz before they got to him. Six months had passed since Gina's death and he had forgotten about her. With two new spots popping and thousands at his disposal, he didn't have time to dwell on anything nonproductive. The only thing eating at his mind was that he hadn't written to K-Stone in awhile. All the changes in his life kept him too busy to even stop and write a few lines. Well, that's what he told himself to rationalize his excuse for not writing. After a while, he just admitted to himself that he was bullshitting. Just before he went to the Quick and Split he stopped by One Hour Photo to pick up some flicks he had turned in a couple of weeks ago of his homies on July fifth. That was his turf day they celebrated every year. Drying his hands off he sat down on the coffee table in the living room and looked through the pictures,

placing the ones he was going to send to K-Stone in an envelope.
Along with the pictures he enclosed a short letter giving K-Stone
the new numbers to contact him.

"You still hungry?"

"Hell yeah, cuzz!"

"We'll get something to eat and mail this letter too."

During the two weeks of lockdown K-Stone had read two
books and was working on the third just before they came off. Since
coming off lockdown he saw everything in his environment
differently. He was no longer intrigued by the war stories he heard
or the sexual conquest that were spewed out the mouths of his
associates. He could recognize the fakeness in everyone he
encountered, young and old, who tried to conceal their true selves. It
was as if this new knowledge gave him x-ray vision letting him peer
into the souls of everyone that surrounded him.

Certain behaviors that he found enjoyment in, and thought
were cool now irritated him immensely. Seeing grown men talk and
conduct themselves in lewd, childish behaviors day after day
suddenly disturbed him. As his mind drifted back to what he had
read during the lockdown, he would place a face with each thought.
He identified his new thoughts and feelings as in comparison to
being born again. He thought of it as a refreshing mental bath that
would forever change his outlook on the world.

Later on that day he received a letter with a return address.
From the weight of the envelope, he knew pictures were inside.
Opening the envelope he noticed the pictures were of his homies.
Going through the pictures slowly, he came across the letter along
with the pictures. Reading it quickly, he noticed Uzi had placed
some new numbers for him to call. Wasting no time he placed the
new numbers in his phonebook. The rest of the afternoon he
rearranged his photo album placing the new photos with the old
ones. When he finished he kicked back on his bunk and stared at
each page as the sinking sun rays bounced off the plastic, holding the
pictures down. A myriad of memories hit him at once, and for a
brief moment he was back in his turf hanging out and carefree with
all his loks. K-Stone missed his turf in many ways, especially his
homies. He knew the love would never leave, and was also aware
that he no longer desired to live that way. Stacking his photo albums
neatly on top of each other, he placed them back in his locker.

Walking to the door he couldn't help but think about Ivie. His chance to finally get to see what happened was hours away.

Though it had been months since he had written or spoken to her since the day she stood him up, he couldn't help but think about her daily. Those late nights when he couldn't find sleep, stressing over her, had resided after a couple of weeks. All that remained were unanswered questions of why. The anticipation was gnawing at him so much that before dialing the new numbers Uzi sent, he had to smoke a cigarette, a habit he was trying to stop.

"Who is this?"

"K-Stone, who is this?"

"T.N."

"T.N, who is you?"

"I got put on the turf since you've been locked up."

"Put Uzi on the phone."

"He at the other spot, you got the number?"

"Yeah, good looking."

"Killa Stone what it do?"

"Not much since we last hollered. I see from the flicks you sent that the same can't be said about you."

"What can I say; your lok is touching more bread than butter and rubbing more cheeks than a tongue."

"Is that right?"

"No doubt, any homies in there with you?"

"A few, but none of the loks."

"You cool up in there?"

"Cuzz, I'm in prison, it can never be all that cool."

"Don't trip; I'll shoot you some cheese tomorrow."

"What's going on the turf?"

"Same shit, just new niggas with money. Nothing really changed since you left."

"You still are messing with Gina?"

"Gina! Cuzz, that bitch got killed some months ago. You not up?"

"Naw! Real talk, by whom?"

"The K-Forts shot my car up thinking it was me driving, but it was her instead. Silly bitch stole my car keys and got murked. Her sister didn't tell you?"

"She stopped hollering at me around that same time. That must be the reason why?"

"Probably so, I thought she would stay down like a ton. It's not your fault that silly bitch got murked."

"Did you go to the funeral?"

"Hell no, I probably would have kicked the casket over.
That silly bitch got my car, CDs, and one of my heats confiscated. I
had anything but respect to pay that bitch. On another note, the
homies that knew you miss you cuzz and the ones that don't, can't
wait to get to know you. It ain't the same without you cuzz."

"Don't trip, they ain't got me forever."

"Right, right! Like I told you before it's going to be all good
when you touch Killa Stone. How much time you have left
anyways?"

"Three years on the nose!"

"Cuzz, I almost forgot to tell you, guess who's been on the
nuts since I bust with the Benz?"

"Jackie?"

"Naw, I been hit that!"

"That's the only female I knew you was trying to hit before I
came to prison."

"Tanisha."

"Tanisha, I know you ain't talking about Bone-Tone's
wife?"

"Cuzz, whatever, she's been borderline stalking your boy!"

"You gonna take it down?"

"Soon, real soon. I've just been shaking her to see how
desperate she is. Ever since Bone caught that kick stand, she's been
in search of the next baller to pamper her needs."

"Sounds like you going to be doing some pampering."

"Pampering them cheeks that's all!"

"I ain't with the tricks; I keep it one-hundred and seventy-
five percent Ransom!"

"Right, right! I thought you were going Hollywood for a
minute."

"Never! This money doesn't make me cuzz."

"It's going to be dayroom recall soon, so I'll hit you when
that cheese arrives."

"Then that'll be next week some time. Till then keep your
chin held high and your chest poked out lok."

"All the time, five minutes lok."

"Five minutes."

It felt good to holla at Uzi and find out what was going on in
the streets, K-Stone thought to himself. But the news about Gina's
death weighed on his mind the most. Sitting at the desk in his cell

K-Stone stared out the window piecing together how Gina's death played a part in Ivie's falling off. Since Gina had been killed the day before Ivie was supposed to come up, it explained why she didn't show up. He just couldn't figure out why she left him over her sister's death, when he wasn't involved. After rolling the thought through his head, it finally hit him. She blamed him because of Uzi's involvement with her sister. This could be the only reason. Now that he knew the reason, he just shook his head in disbelief. All that kept replaying in his mind were all the promises she had made about never leaving him. It further embedded the fact that nothing was certain in prison. More so, it confirmed that he would definitely have to severe all ties with his former life if he were to survive in society. Even the caliber of females he associated with seemed to play a part in his development.

At twenty-two, individuals his age were in college or starting a career. Academically, he knew he was rusty in a couple of areas that needed serious improvement before he paroled. All the reading he did in the hole and in between his jail experience had made him a fast reader. Reading Askari's books made him start working on his vocabulary for the first time. Hearing and seeing Uzi have it his way also plagued his mind with temptation. Lately, he found himself drifting into fantasies of the baller lifestyle, but then the reality would settle in about the negative side. At this point in his life he knew whatever path he took he would have to go at it full throttle without turning back.

Being twenty-five, and fresh out of prison wouldn't allow him any room for uncertainties or mistakes, especially with one strike hovering over his head. Any miscalculations he made would send him back to prison with double the time or a string of violations, which would be a detrimental set back for a male in his mid twenties trying to get reestablished in society. Life had become so clear to him the past few weeks. For the first time he felt like he had the knowledge on how to operate normally in the outside world.

With a myriad of new thoughts going through his mind daily it often made him disgusted at himself that all this time he had been living below his potential, unknowingly. When his thoughts would focus on self attacks he reminded himself that he only portrayed the actions he assumed to be appropriate. Hearing the food carts roll in the building he grabbed his spoon and a piece of tissue to get ready to eat.

"Finally left out of the zone?"

"Yeah, I just had some things I had to put together."

"Nothing wrong with that, it's a practice that needs to be promoted."

"Why you say that?"

"Because so many people operate throughout the day with unclear thoughts going through their heads. It causes a lot of stress on individuals, as well as society; when the majority of people are unclear in their thinking."

"Have you ever traveled outside of the country before?"

"Once when I was a teenager my uncle took me to Egypt."

"What did he take you there for?"

"At the time, he was in college studying to be an archeologist. We went to Egypt for class research. He saw that I was headed in a completely different direction so he took me along hoping I would get some type of understanding that the world went beyond my neighborhood."

"Tell me what it was like out there?"

"When we get through eating I'll finish telling you."

"What does it look like we're having?"

"Baked chicken."

After eating the chicken and sides, Askari finished telling K-Stone about his trip.

"The weather was basically the same temperature as here, just a little hotter, but nothing unbearable. The women are beautiful, and they cover up more then the females here. I almost didn't come back. There were a few buildings that I saw, but mostly tents and clay huts in the area. The children ran around barefoot throughout the area playing like children should; unlike here, where sometimes our children have to stay in the house or yard for fear of being shot or recruited. They were amazed by my CD player, because they had never seen one up close before. It was as if I had stepped back in time. Their lack of technology made me appreciate what I had back in the states. The most significant thing that stood out, and remains with me still today, was that they used Benzes and other luxury vehicles that were associated with wealth and prestige, as taxis and moving vehicles. Once I started studying in prison, I noticed that this was the case in most foreign countries."

"That's crazy! I never paid attention to that. Why do you think that is?"

"Basically it's symbolism, we worship symbols over here in the U.S.A. It's easy for the average citizen to be led to believe whatever by the media, look at the war. Whatever is shown to be popular or a new fad people will automatically latch on to it without thinking. Like we talked about earlier, it's important that a person keep a clear head about things so they don't fall victim to the nonsense of things they don't need and more importantly don't fit who they are as a person. This is a mistake Black people make daily, year after year around the world. Blacks constantly play follow the leader in nearly all things they do, not realizing the power they have to create trends, movements, and business opportunities. Blacks or a Black individual can start out with something unique, and a couple of years later it has grown to something that the dominant culture imitates. One small example of this is when Blacks get tattoos of Chinese characters on their bodies. We as a people are too quick to embrace other cultures but neglect our own strong, beautiful culture. Symbolism has taught Blacks that they need expensive clothes, cars, jewelry, and certain status to be somebody. So when a Black does make it, they quickly adopt the "I made it philosophy" and they also adopt a "you can make it without my help" mind frame, rather than teaching each other. I admire Oprah as a strong Black woman who provides for Blacks and embraces her Blackness. But I can't help but notice the separation she places between middle class Blacks and inner city Blacks. One particular show I watched last week disturbed me. I forgot what the actual subject was about, but I recall her saying that Blacks don't refer to each other as nigga when she was greeted by some Black Africans in Africa. Though I don't use the word anymore, the thought entered my mind that she was referring to middle class Blacks. Where I was raised it was a common word that everybody used in the community. The problem I found with the comment was she was and had to be speaking of Blacks she surrounded herself with. She automatically separated herself and Blacks from the inner city. Subconsciously, she is telling her devoted viewers that there are differences between Black people. Furthermore, the middle class and upper class Blacks don't associate themselves with the lower Blacks that use such language and exhibit other unpopular behaviors. So if this Black icon and symbol doesn't respect them and doesn't relate to them, why should any other race or class?"

Listening to Askari was always enlightening for K-Stone, but it also made him question why he didn't see the subliminal messages that Askari saw so easily. Whenever Askari watched TV, which was rare, it would make him upset. When K-Stone would ask him why it got to him, he would simply state, "the lies."

"In your opinion, what do you feel could be done to solve these problems?"

"First off K-Stone, there in no panacea for the problems that plagues Black people today. But there are some paths that I feel need to be explored that could make a definite change in how we as people treat each other, conduct ourselves, and manage our finances. When I make references to how we treat each other, I'm referring to the lack of cultural pride. Too many Blacks don't possess the natural love they should for Black faces around the globe. Though I know this natural love is within us all, somewhere along the line of constant distractions the love was severed from the Blacks mind. I'm often apprehensive about what happened to the love I know still exists and read about in books regarding our history that transcends all other worldly things. The change begins in each individual. Each person has to play their part no matter how small it is, and as long as it is for the benefit of the cause. Rosa Parks is the epitome of that benefit. It's the mundane that will start to make a difference. Just imagine if Blacks didn't imitate the negative behaviors from other cultures, and started to adopt the positive ones like universal family ties similar to the Jews and Hispanics. Secondly, we need to work on our image as a whole. It is making us appear to the world as just people who entertain with a few exceptions who take other routes.

The reason I stopped listening to the radio is because it seemed like every song that came on was about partying, sex, and extreme wealth. This is not a reflection of what's going on in the world today or in the average Black person's life. With a faulty pyrrhic war going on, increasing gas prices, and unemployment, I want to hear something real that I can vibe to or make me aware to something I'm ignorant of. I've seen a myriad of brothers come through this system since my incarceration along with all the trends they identified with. Just a few years ago they wanted to be thugs like 2Pac, ballers like Cash Money, and gangstas like B.I.G. Now they want to be rappers, instead of striving to be something tangible and of service to the community.

The main reason our women are confused and exhibit the behavior they do is because every few months the Black man's image is going through some type of metamorphous, in which he tries to define himself. Yet, I hear songs and brothers in here say that our women aren't shit. My question to them is how do you expect them to be much different than what they are exposed to?

We're the only race that exploits our women to the fullest with no sense of shame.

Thirdly, Blacks are earning more money now then ever before. Yet, as a people we still control nothing or handle any political or global power. Many poverty issues in the Black community come from a lack of financial knowledge. The average Black doesn't know how to budget, save, or use their money as a tool to create business or financial independence. Further, I find it disturbing that with all the money our entertainers, musicians, and athletes earn, why are there so many poverty stricken Black communities when they have the resources to pool their money together to help rebuild one community at a time with Black owned businesses and schools. We don't need anymore faulty charities that only help the conscience of the donator and their taxes. At times it seems as if we do more when we have less. How do you see Black people's plight?"

"Until a couple of weeks ago, I never gave it much thought or cared. From what I paid attention to, there just seems to be a lot of ignorance and confusion on many levels. Now I see children with struggling parents, trying to keep food on the table and pay the bills. Everyone, like you said, is searching for some type of identity to cling to in an ever confusing, decaying environment. When I look at it now, I realize it has become a pattern. Dudes come to jail and the females have bastards. It's as if everybody involved in the ghetto life is doing some type of time. The babies do nine months confined to a belly, while females do eighteen years or longer raising a child by themselves, while the daddy sits in here doing a Buck Rogers date or an eternity in the cemetery. Either way you look at it, time seems to play a part in the ghetto. Some have too much on their hands and some not enough, while some wait for one time to come and rescue them and others avoid them at all costs. Knowing to get caught for any offense would send them before the Black robe that always has an unlimited amount of time to dish out. From the books you have given me, I see that Black churches played a big part in daily lives and served as more then just a house of worshipping. This made me think when you were talking about solutions. There are many churches spread throughout the ghettos and they don't do anything to stop the growing gang problems, deaths, pregnancies, or any other dilemmas that affect the Black communities. I feel they should be held accountable to some extent for the direction the communities have gone. The majority of my homies respect the people who attend the churches in the turf. To keep it real, I don't know too many homies that would go shooting up someone else's turf if church people were present. Church members, especially the elders, always get that automatic respect. That's one lesson nearly every youngsta learns as a child. Now that I'm sitting back tripping, I realize that the church members wield a lot of power, that for some reason they refuse to use. Instead, they prefer to hide in the comforts of the church behind stained glass windows for hours while ignoring the trifle going on right outside. I've never been an avid Bible reader, but I know that church goers are supposed to teach the Word to the lost. The people in my community qualify for that title."

"You have a valid point K-Stone. Once you're released and have your thoughts where you want them, you can address that and many other issues."

Askari and K-Stone continued their conversation for the rest of the night. Waking up two hours before breakfast, K-Stone had the conversation from the other day freshly on his mind. It felt good to talk about something positive that he could focus his mind on and create something powerful from.

Being that it was the last day of lockdown, they would be walking to breakfast that morning. Mondays were always slow motion, not because it was the beginning of the week but because the C.O's would be tired from their weekends and would delay the program as much as possible to appease their needs. This was something K-Stone had come to expect, as he constantly observed this through all programs. The day was going slowly as he expected. Getting tired of hearing exaggerated war stories, he went in early, on the first line. Standing in silence by his door, he observed the other inmates moving around the building delaying lockup. Once lower level dayroom began, his observance became more concentrated as he watched patterns of all the inmates rushing to take showers. The reason he did this was to see who had the dominance of each racial group. While doing so, he also caught an earful of his next door neighbor, a Southsider named Boxer, talking to one of his homies on the other side of the door who was holding a large brown folder which he assumed was legal work. Listening more, he found out he was wrong, it was college work. This took him by surprise, because he was unaware that an inmate could take college courses at the prison. Hearing so made him feel ignorant.

The other Southsider Boxer was talking to someone who lived down stairs; he would have to catch him later that week for the information to enroll.

"So I tell the nigga K-Stone, I'll slap him once to make him question his sexuality and slap him again to confirm it."

"Is that right?"

"Damn right, next time you run into your homie G-Liz ask him, he was on the yard when I put my check down. I know a gang of your homies K-Stone. Been doing time with them for years."

As the stranger rambled on about knowing all his homies and how much time he had done in different penitentiaries, K-Stone was stuck yet again, listening to complete nonsense he assumed the stranger thought he wanted to hear. All he was trying to figure out was how he allowed himself to be caught up in this conversation trap when he had seen it coming. Standing on the curb by his building waiting on the three thirty inline to take a shower, K-Stone was exhausted from being behind the wall all day in plumbing class and the hundred plus dry heat didn't add any breaks. All he was trying to do at this point of his day was chill and get his thoughts together. Then he was bombarded with conversation by a stranger who had seen his tattoos and thought because he had a relationship with another one of his homies at another pen it was cool with him too. It wasn't the first time it happened since he had been down.

There was always an, "I know your homie" character that would come out of nowhere with a string of stories. He had learned to just listen and say as little as possible hoping they would get the point that he wasn't the friendly "get to know a person" type.

Prison is the wrong place to try and accumulate friendships. Furthermore, the whole friendship thing was something he wasn't into. If he didn't grow up with the person he was skeptical of their intentions on getting to know him. Not all, but the majority of individuals he ran into inside prison were vultures or had ulterior motives for their dealings with another inmate. Since being down he had come to accept that relationships in prison between inmates no matter the race or gang affiliation were just that way. He didn't have thoughts of liking individuals in prison or seeing them as friends. It wasn't like they were in elementary; they were behind barbed wire fences, iron, and cement all day, year after year. The last thing the environment did was promote or establish relationships and people skills. In fact, he found it to do the opposite which was reflected in the lifelessness of the iron and cement. There were those who got respect and those who didn't. Under those categories, there were two kinds of individuals. There were the real individuals that carried themselves in an all around solid demeanor and knew how to do their time without affecting the next man. Then there was the busta who hides behind his gang, race, or C.O.s for protection. These individuals usually are the brunt of the problems in prison chaos because they're constantly trying to prove themselves trying to be something that they'll never be. A cold fact about a busta was it never registered to him that if he didn't have stripes or respect before he reached prison then it was too late.

Since he started gangbanging he had seen many bustas come and go. Some got their issues and others didn't. As long as they stayed out his way with their fronting he didn't care what they pretended to be. He had read a platitude awhile ago when he first started his time that stated, "It takes a life time to build a reputation but only a second to ruin it." That simple platitude explained the structure of prison life in its simplest form. One had to pick their persona for the rest of their term and stick with it and pick his battles wisely. When it came down to it, everybody's chin was the same size.

Hearing the call for voluntary inline, K-Stone quickly ceased his escape gathering his material from off the curb beside him, leaving the stranger still babbling as he made his way into his building. Once inside, he put his towel on his door so he could get popped out for a worker shower after lower tier locked it up. It had been nine months into the New Year and he found himself in the third semester of his college courses. He had enough time from what his instructor informed him to get his A.A. degree before paroling. Visualizing the college courses as a challenge, he made a pact with himself to get the degree before paroling. All the studying took up the majority of his time with barely enough to do anything else. But it was worth it to him in many ways. It made his time go by quickly with all the deadlines to meet, his mind barely stayed focus on anything else. He hadn't told his mom that he was taking the courses, but instead wanted to surprise her once he received the degree. She had been sick lately and he knew the news would make her feel better. To know he didn't waste his time away doing nothing would make her proud. His whole life he thought that the old cliché of whatever he put his mind to could happen was a bunch of lies. Whenever he read about progress in the books taken from Askari, he wouldn't really accept it. K-Stone realized he had to acknowledge the difference in the course he started out on and where he was now. Now that his eyes were open, he saw how just a little application of positive ness was yielding results. As soon as he started the college courses, a month later he had a ducat placing him behind the wall to learn a trade. Learning something daily made him realize how important knowledge was because it was all connected in some type of way. At times he couldn't believe he was taking the initiative to learn. When on the streets he would ditch, drink, smoke, and have sex rather than go to class. He hated school as a youth and didn't see how education would play any factor in his life.

While chilling one day, he thought back to when he first started gangbanging and how he put his all into it. The same rules applied then as they did now, but in a constructive way.

The bond between Askari and K-Stone was still the same if not better. They both would have their days when they didn't want to be bothered but that behavior didn't last long and neither took it personal because they knew it was just human nature. Askari made it his duty to help mold K-Stone's education as much as possible without taking away from his own creativity. He was proud of the strides K-Stone was making. From his time being in the cell he had seen him quit smoking and drinking. He also changed his diet from beef to just fish. More so, he had seen a decrease in his gang idiom, and their conversations had increased in complexity and were less one-sided. Askari was watching a strong Black man emerge and loved it.

Waiting on the single man shower to open up, K-Stone thought back to how he had to check himself earlier that year for becoming too comfortable in prison; something he noticed happening with each passing year. When he realized one day he was regularly taking showers in the two man shower, he put a stop to it. He tried to remain as normal as possible within prison by not straying from simple behaviors he did on the streets. This was something he kept intact daily, because it was so easy to become institutionalized and not notice. He and Askari talked about it all the time. His solution to this problem was to keep his mind sharp by reading, studying, and self-improving. Most importantly, he kept in mind that this wasn't his home, no matter the life sentence. He refused to call prison his home like so many others did.

Chapter 14

No Longer Blind

K-Stone also realized that every decision he made came with some type of drawback. His decision to advance his knowledge alienated him from his homies. He found it harder each day to relate to their way of thinking on how life should operate. The conversations were starting to irritate him and sicken him to the point of wanting to attack and beat some sense into them. It got to the point where he just nodded and smirked when they talked as he thought to himself, if they only knew what was going through his mind.

"What it do Killa Stone?"

"Not much, just preparing for these last two years."

"The time you been away so far seems like a minute."

"It has, but it's hard to tell from in here when you're doing it."

"So what you been up to since the last time we hollered?'

"Just getting my mind right."

"I know you didn't turn Muslim on your boy."

"Naw, I'm just sharpening my mentality so I can have more options to lean towards when I touch."

"If you say so gangsta nerd!"

"I see you stay with the funnies."

"If that's what you feel you need to do cuzz do you. The only thing I'm sharpening my mind on is how to get this money out here the quickest way without working."

"Okay Jessie James, from what I hear everybody's coming to jail."

"That's putting it lightly, since the police put out these gang injunctions, the turf then got dry and it ain't just our turf. Everybody's feeling it. With all the arrest going on, it's been a rapid increase of niggas selling out instead of bailing out. Snitching has become an epidemic out here."

"A couple of the homies that just came, been telling me how it has been out there. I thought they were putting extras on it."

"It's bad lok, that's why Uzi does his with the real loks and by my lonesome. That's why it's been hard to catch me lately. I've been laying low in the cut. The feds even been coming through snapping flicks of the homies."

"Like that huh?"

"Cuzz, like that. On another note, I was in traffic a couple of day ago, when I spotted your old broad round in the middle walking to the store."

"Which old broad is that?"

"Ivie, who else! She's been messing with some nigga from Hoover since last year. You know I keep my ear to the streets, I hear she's having a little girl."

"You are killing me with that one."

"Cuzz, it killed me, and you know I don't be shocked at what bitches will do. I thought she was going to make something out of herself before going the baby route."

"Well it happens to the best of them."

"Yeah, I guess. It seems like a bitch is always looking for something outside themselves to love. I see from your flicks you then got kind of chunky up in there Killa Stone."

"I try to get what I can when I can."

"Your boy is still silky slim out here. Bitches don't care about muscles when your paper is long."

"I don't exercise for females; I do it to stay healthy."

"Healthy! Who are you Richard Simmons? You're going to get out on some Tae-bo shit?"

"You just don't stop, what's wrong with wanting to stay in shape?"

"Nothing if that's what you want to do, but you know you not about to be busting down on the streets."

"Why you say that Uzi?"

"Because, you going to be tossing sluts, getting faded, and gang-banging when you touch down."

"No matter what you say or think, I'm sticking to my new program on the streets. It's not like I'm waiting until I'm a couple of months to the house to start changing. I'm putting forth the effort daily. I'm cool on getting high, tossing broads daily, and getting snitched on for shooting at other gang members who may possibly snitch if they live through the attacks."

"If that's how you feel, I can't do nothing but respect it cuzz. But I'm telling you K-Stone, that's just the time talking. It's in you to do this gangsta shit!"

"I'm not saying it will ever leave me, but it comes a time when a person just has to grow up and stop running into brick walls."

"Cuzz, I've been out here going on four years and I'm having it my way. I haven't come across a permanent brick wall and if I do come across one, I'll hop over it."

"All that sounds good but we both know that if you continue, you'll eventually get robbed, killed, or snitched on. Once those boys come get you they'll take everything, which means you'll have to start from scratch. The lifestyle you're living keeps you looking over your shoulder constantly wondering if an enemy is out to get you or if a female or homie is out to set you up. Furthermore, it keeps you alienated from other parts of society, limiting you to one particular area. As long as you continue you're going to be forced to lie about where you get your money as well as socialize with individuals you know you can't trust, all to maintain the baller status. I'm not trying to live like that if I don't have to. I'm aware it has its benefits, and I think about them often. But I also know it doesn't last forever, especially if you're not putting your money to work in a positive way. Eventually, it will come to an end. We both know that no one is beyond being duct taped in their living room."

"All I can say to that Killa is I hear you, but I've made my bed and I'm prepared to sleep in it, fuck in it, and whatever else I feel the need to do in it. When it comes, if it comes, I will be here waiting for it. In the end you have to do what works for you."

"This phone is about to hang up so I'll get at you later. Five minutes lok."

"Five minutes lok."

Hanging up the phone, K-Stone walked over to the benches in front of the TV area and stood on the corner of the last bench before squatting down. Thinking of the conversation he just had with Uzi, it didn't surprise him that they would eventually bump heads. He realized that the bond they shared growing up would no longer be that tight ever again. They were moving in two different directions. His was to carve a new life for himself, while Uzi's was to become the first drug dealer, robber, and gang-banger to make a living off of pure negativity without consequences. When he mentioned Ivie being pregnant, it only confirmed the pattern he already knew was taking place in the ghetto. All the news really did was let him know whole heartedly that she had moved on. Before the news, he occasionally thought about reconnecting with her once he paroled, but that was no longer an option.

      It didn't take long for the news to spread to K-Stone that a new K4 had hit the yard who was active. He had seen him on the yard a couple of times when he came from working during bottom tier yard. He would just laugh to himself when he would see him walking the track with the other K4s with the extra idioms and choreographed gait. There were other K4's on the yard, but they were older and kept to their side of the yard. He still held rancor for K4's, but he had been disciplining himself to stop hating other Blacks that didn't do anything to him. It was the hardest personal battle to overcome. Seeing the new K4 with the extras, ignited the gang-banging fuel within him, but he managed to control it.

      Being that he was released early from work he found himself on the bottom tier morning yard. Walking the track with one of his homies that just arrived, he quickly noticed the new K4 with his shirt off working out by the bleachers. As he got closer he noticed a big RGC187um written across his chest in block letters. The sight of the tattoo instantly sent a rage through his body that he knew the K4 felt as he continued to walk by. Coming toward the water fountain, K-Stone asked his homie if he had seen what he saw as they waited in line. When he replied yeah, with no sign of anger or surprise, K-Stone quickly informed him that he couldn't let it pass. Before they made it back around the track, K-Stone had let his homie know that he was about to smash the K4 by himself. Without much of a response to what he heard, K-Stone's homie pulled over to a nearby curve while K-Stone made his way towards the K4. Noticing that K-Stone was by himself, the K4 stopped his exercise sensing something was about to go down. He had heard about K-Stone before through his career of gang-banging. He knew they would eventually bump heads. Approaching calmly without a mean mug or exaggerated body language, K-Stone asked the K4 if he was with the business. Without a doubt the K4 responded back. It didn't take long after for them to square off and start fighting. Once they locked up it sounded like two rams were bashing heads. Each blow thrown by the two was a solid hit. Twenty seconds into the scuffle, the K4 took a hard right to the chin dropping him. Without hesitation, K-Stone jumped on top of him pounding him with rapid combinations to his face. Crawling and kicking, the K4 managed to escape from underneath K-Stones assault. Jumping to his feet, he attempted to square off again but K-Stone rushed him with a flurry of punches that caused the K4 to start swimming. By the time the C.O.s on the tower took notice of the stillness on the yard, the two had been fighting for some time under prison standards. Grabbing his binoculars, the C.O. scanned the yard to see why the movement paused. It didn't take long for him to spot the cloud of dust causing him to hit the alarm.

Seeing that the K4 was stunned, K-Stone decided to go for the knockout punch. Realizing he was losing, the K4 grabbed K-Stone and began to wrestle, but by that time the C.O.s made it to the fight with their batons and pepper spray. Listening to the orders, K-Stone and the K4 both laid down on the ground to be handcuffed. Back in the cell sitting on his desk, K-Stone found himself not feeling the way he usually felt when he smashed on an enemy. This time he felt shameful about allowing himself to become entrapped in something he knew had no end.

The knowledge he possessed within himself wouldn't allow him to enjoy it. In the prison community his changes meant nothing, because all his fellow prisoners would view him as K-Stone from Ransom. If he let that disrespect slide, it would have tarnished his reputation and that would have brought far more problems.

Coming from work, Askari quickly heard about the fight K-Stone had earlier that morning. It didn't take much to get the yard talking. When he entered the cell he found K-Stone reading a new book he had gotten from him the other day.

"What's going on Jack Johnson?"

K-Stone just smirked and placed the book he was reading to the side, knowing he was about to hear it from Askari.

"You know what George Jackson would say?"

"Yeah, it's funny how we tend to regress instead of progress."

"You got to give me the benefit of the doubt."

"What benefit is there in doubt?"

Sighing, K-Stone paused for a minute to think about what Askari said.

"None, it's hard to explain."

"Not if you take your time. I'm not here to judge, just to make sure you're aware of all the actions you are taking before paroling."

"I'm aware, I'm also aware I have two more years left in prison to do before I walk out those gates. If I had seen dude on the streets, I would not have tripped. When I first saw my turf disrespected on his chest, it got me hot. As I walked off before going back the anger resided, but I knew I had to do it regardless. I have to stay true to my turf up to a certain degree. In a fantasy world I could just hang up the rag and walk away, but the reality is that I still have strong ties that don't easily break. When I make my final departure from the gang, I want my file to be clear with no discrepancies. Stopping while in prison is a major offense where I'm from. At the same time I want to be able to serve as a role model to other gang-bangers that they can put forth the effort to change. Ridas are only going to listen to Ridas. In many ways I'm in a catch twenty-two, and I hate that it's like that but that side of my bed is already creased and folded."

"K-Stone, I hear you and I'm proud of the strides you have made so far. Yet, I still see that 'Crippin' in you ready to come out at anytime. My only advice is do not let it ruin all you have accomplished so far. You're needed out there on the streets more than you realize at this moment. Anybody can resort to violence to get their way, but only the strong can make a point without using primitive behavior. Continuing to use violence without righteousness only causes weakness."

"Sometimes Askari too much patience and talking builds cowardice. At times violence is the only solution no matter how you view a problem, especially in here."

"Righteousness, just remember there is a thin line between necessary and just conforming to what's easy. Most importantly, a lot of young brothers look up to you K-Stone."

"I'm aware of that, and I'm also aware that they respect my gangsta and not my journey to change. When I succeed in my new life, then they will respect that side of me too. You just don't know how much I wanted to avoid what happened today, but it was unavoidable."

"The fact that you wanted to avoid it shows a lot of growth within yourself. The hardest battles we face are within ourselves."

"Who are you telling. Up until this situation I felt in total control of myself. In that small moment I knew I had forfeited that control over and reverted to the wrong behavior I was trained in as a boy."

"What's done is done, no sense in dwelling on it any longer, just capitalize on your mistakes."

"All the time."

Constant hospital bills had put a strain on Sophia over the last few years. It had been over a year since the last time she saw Kevin. She was looking forward to the visit they were going to have the following week. She could hardly believe she let such a huge gap of time fall between them. She wrote him letters and talked to him once a month when he wasn't on lockdown, but it was nothing compared to embracing her son.

From Kevin's letters over the last year, Sophia could tell he was educating himself. It didn't surprise her because she always knew he was a smart boy. He just chose to use his talents in a destructive way. She didn't approve of that but couldn't neglect him because that was her son. He never brought any problems to her home or disrespected her with the behavior he exhibited on the streets. In his letters he wrote about changing his life, something that he had never mentioned before. She prayed that he was sincere and not just talking prison talk like she heard so many did. In her heart she wanted it to be true but she also knew Kevin was loyal to Ransom and enjoyed having an unlimited supply of money.

She knew her son well enough to know once he put his mind to something he would stick to it. This gave her faith in what he was saying. She also kept in mind that change could occur once out in about in the work field. Kevin had a temper that could erupt if someone gave him an order in a tone he didn't take a liking to. The last thing she wanted was Kevin hanging with the Ransoms and end up like Jamal Jr. The thought of failure often engulfed her mind daily. Sophia felt she had failed as a parent, especially after Jamal Jr. was killed and Kevin was sent to prison. It often seemed to her as if failure had taken possession of her life. With so many failures, disappointments, and let downs; it seemed like she and her son's were destined to fail. As much as she tried to bury her thoughts it was impossible. Smoking cigarettes had become her solace, offering her, a temporary numbness to her painful thoughts.

A hug from Kevin was long over due and she could easily feel the strength in his hug when he lifted her from the ground. She couldn't help but be stunned at how much he had changed since their last visit. His baby face was gone and was replaced by sharp features of a young handsome man with a full goatee.

"As always it's good to be in your presence mother."

"Really?"

"Yes, even when you're getting on my nerves."

"Real funny Kevin."

"Naw, for real it is finally good to see you after so long. Everybody in here probably thinks you're my girlfriend."

"That's why these girls keep looking at me all funny."

"You're a beautiful woman, can you blame them?"

"Okay Mr. Smooth, what exactly have you been learning?"

"A range of things, but nothing that would interest you at the moment. I'd rather hear about what's been going on with you?"

"Nothing much, just trying to stay afloat out here. Your father stopped by a couple of days ago. He said to tell you that when you're ready you can send a package form."

"Is that right?"

"Yes it is Kevin, I hate when you say that, it sounds so arrogant."

"Is that right?"

"I'm not messing with you. He also asked why you haven't written him?"

"That's an easy answer. The same reason he doesn't write me."

"And what reason is that?"

"There's really not a reason, there's just nothing really to discuss with him, that's all. If a person doesn't engage me with a decent conversation in a letter, it's hard for me to just come up with something and begin to write. But, I'll write him a letter this weekend."

"Oh, everybody at church told me to tell you hi."

"Tell them I send mines."

"I've been hearing about that boy you use to hang out with named Uzi."

"What have you heard?"

"That he is terrorizing the streets and making a lot of money."

"Where did you hear that from?"

"People at church."

"I thought people were supposed to go to church to worship not gossip."

"They're not gossiping they're sharing information."

"If they're not gossiping about him, then why don't they lend a helping hand to stop him from the direction he's going in?"

"I don't know maybe you can ask them when you get out."

"That's a good idea."

"You're not going to do that Kevin."

"Why not?"

"Because I said so."

"Why do you take everything I say in the wrong way?"

"I don't, I just know what you're capable of doing when a thought enters your head."

"Well, you put it there."

"I'm through with that part of the conversation Kevin. What do you plan on doing when you come home?"

"I've been taking plumbing as my trade. From what I've read, it's a decent profession to fall into when I get out. It's just one of my options, but I'm working more on an idea to start my own business so I can create my own wealth."

"That sounds good. At least you're trying to accomplish something while you're in here."

"I've wasted enough time running around confused, why add more years of confusion when I have a chance to remold my behavior. By the time I parole I will have a solid plan put together."

"Sometimes I feel it's my fault about what happened to Jamul Jr. and what's going on with you."

"I don't see why, we both knew what we were getting in to; it was our own decision not yours."

"I often think I was too hard on both of you when you were growing up and maybe that's why you guys rebelled."

"Honestly, it played a part, but so did a lot of other things. You had no control over our decaying community. I realize now that you had issues way before you had us and I strongly take that into consideration when I look back at my childhood. It's not an excuse, but I understand that sometimes you just didn't know any other way to express your own hurt without it affecting us."

"So you think I'm a bad mother Kevin?"

"No, you did the best with what you had and understood to be right. You never abandoned us or let us go. For that I commend you, and harbor no blame for you or for my present situation. That would be pointless dwelling on the past. Here we are, sitting now in the present mother, and we are all we got. I love you and I know you love me. That's what matters the most. You're always there when I need you the most, like a mother should. That's all your thoughts should consist of when you reflect on our relationship. Feel me?"

Sophia just shook her head in approval, and couldn't believe that Kevin was talking to her like that. It was as if she was the child. It finally dawned on her that he was no longer a baby, but a man, and she would forever view him as such.

"Kevin, it's about time for me to leave. I'll come back as soon as I can, once my money gets right."

"Don't trip, this visit will last me awhile. I'll call you tomorrow to see if you made it home alright."

After embracing each other for the last time, Sophia walked out the exit leaving her son staring. Before exiting the final door, Sophia waved goodbye trying to hold in the tears until she made it to her vehicle. It was always hard to leave her son behind even though it had been over three years. The pain still felt fresh.

Walking the track after the visit with his mom, K-Stone was relieved he had repaired their bond. Many years prior to him being incarcerated he held a slight resentment towards her for what she had done to him and his brother. His studying brought him more than knowledge, it also gave him great understanding. This made him view his situation with his mother differently. He knew for him to truly grow he would have to understand and forgive her past behavior. It felt good to remove the wedge that had always been present in their relationship. It took a lot of discipline for him not to tell his mother about his college courses. He had only twenty more credits to earn before he would receive his A.A. degree, which he would obtain before the end of the year.

Chapter 15

Timing

"All right cuzz, tell the homies on the lower level I send mines."

"You gots that, being you'll never see one having l.w.o.p."

"It is what it is, the tough guy sentence."

"Sit wherever you please Mr. Tapps, it's only a couple of you guys going to a level three. Without a response to the C.O., Bone-Tone made his way to the back of the bus. The only thing on his mind was if his legal work was going to make it safely to Centinela. He was making a critical issue on his appeal that was basically his last chance. He had sold most of his possessions during the past four years he had been at High Desert fighting his case. His freedom seemed to be slipping from his finger tips with each failed attempt. Just a year ago he came so close, and then the court shot him down for an incomplete habeas corpus. That mistake forced him to fire his first attorney and hire two more. One attorney was to sue his first, and other to reduce his appeal. It had been a hectic four years that seemed to be going nowhere. As long as he had a kick-stand attached to his sentence, everyday he woke up felt pointless, as if he was living for nothing. The only time he felt alive is when he saw his children which was becoming less frequent as the years passed by. His wife was just sticking around out of pity and because he still had money. At the moment Bone-Tone was content to be leaving High Desert where it was impossible for him to get to the law library because of the constant lockdowns. He assumed the level three would give him more access to it. While sitting in R and R. waiting to be assigned to a different yard, Bone-Tone couldn't help but notice a difference in demeanor the C.O.s had as to the ones at High Desert. They seemed more relaxed and quick to disrespect an inmate. Being on the four yard had made him demand respect instead of expecting it. It wouldn't be long before he would have to check one of the C.O.s, he just knew it.

There were three types of lifers Bone-Tone encountered since doing time: the ones that didn't give a fuck because they knew they were never going to see the streets except on TV and magazines, and the other type were the ones hoping the board would give them a date or that the three strike law would change. These inmates avoided any and all conflicts twenty-four-seven in hopes that they would be paroled by the board, or considered non-violent to slide out on the three strikes law if ever changed. Lifers were often permissive or deeply religious. Most knew they would never see the streets again so they would sabotage their chances before going to the board. It would give them a false sense that if they didn't get the infraction they would have otherwise gotten a date, and it was better then accepting an unquestionable no. Bone-Tone felt he didn't fit into either category because he still had action on his appeal and he didn't do anything to jeopardize his freedom. Dependence on his appeal took away his dependence on the board so he didn't walk around like he had been neutered either. Depending on how things went he knew he would fall into a category eventually, but didn't know which one it would be.

When he stepped onto the new yard, he could instantly tell the difference of his new environment. Inmates were laughing, smiling, and seemed to be enjoying themselves. This was something he had rarely seen where he had come from. When he made it inside the orientation building he didn't see anybody in the dayroom on either side. So he proceeded to go to his assigned cell until he was classified to go to the yard. After putting his property in the lockers, Bone-Tone cleaned up the most he could and posted-up on the door looking out the door window. He already had a kite ready to shoot out to whatever homies were on the yard. Seeing a Black porter emerge from A-Section pushing a push-broom in his direction, he grabbed his kite in hopes that the porter would pass it through the yard.

"A Black, check it out." Stopping at Bone-Tone's door, the porter listened to what he had to say by the side of the door.

"Are there any Ransoms on the yard?" Without hesitation the porter quickly told him that his homie K-Stone was on the yard.

"I need you to slide him this kite for me."

"That's all?"

"Yeah, for right now. Nice looking."

Hearing the porter respond to K-Stone's name let Bone-Tone know that K-Stone was still the same and had respect on the yard. It made him feel good to be on the yard with a lok he knew from the streets. The thought of if K-Stone knew Uzi was sexing his wife crossed his mind shortly after. He figured because they were tight, he probably did know about the situation and thought it was comedy. When he first heard the news he couldn't believe Uzi would disrespect him like that. With all the bitches out there he had to sex his wife. That was something Bone-Tone couldn't accept. He had made a pact with himself that he would kill Uzi if he ever got released, and if K-Stone got in the way he would murk him too. The helplessness along with the ass-kissing he had endured since being locked down made the thoughts flow through his mind occasionally especially moments like these when he was standing around trying to get the thoughts out of his mind that had been suppressed until a couple of minutes ago. He decided that he wasn't going to let what Uzi did cloud his judgment with how he greeted and dealt with K-Stone. If K-Stone was the same way he would try to go to war with him inside the prison, and most likely win. Besides, he always knew K-Stone to be a rational man, though he hung with that asshole Uzi.

"What's crackin KP?"

"Nothing much, I got a kite from one your homie's that came in yesterday."

"Good looking out KP."

"Don't trip you know how we do."

"All the time."

Standing by the basketball court, K-Stone read the kite KP handed to him. A smirk spread across his face before he tore it up and let the torn pieces scatter to the ground. "Bone-Tone," he repeated to himself, he thought he would never see him again. The thought of if he knew Uzi was sexing Tanisha crossed his mind also. Knowing Bone-Tone he knew, but wasn't tripping, because he had her on the team running for him. Doing his last remaining time with Bone-Tone would be decent depending on if his life sentence hadn't kicked in on him yet. If he was on a weird page, K-Stone had his mind made that he would just avoid him and continue on with his program alone.

A week had gone by and Bone-Tone was on the mainline. The only problem was that he was on the bottom tier and all the Ransoms were on the top. Instead of waiting months or longer for a cell to come available, Bone-Tone took the initiative and paid a non-affiliate to trade cells with him.

"Damn K-Stone, it has been a minute since I've seen you cuzz. You than got big!" Bone-Tone said while embracing K-Stone.

"When I first read the kite, I couldn't believe it was you. I thought it was baby Bone-Tone."

"That's the same thought I had when KP told me you were here. I thought you were on a foe yard somewhere."

"Almost was, I just lucked-out and got away with a few fights that would have given me level foe points. I see you looking around amazed at the yard. What you tripping off?

"Just being outside at night. It has been almost five years counting my county jail time since I've been outside at night. The foe program ends at four-thirty p.m."

"Yeah, I heard."

"I'm just tripping off the whole environment, period. So what's the program like up here?"

"Basically it stays on lockdown for every little incident. The majority of your time will be in the cells so it's wise to keep at least a hundred soups on standby because trays become real skimpy when we get cell fed. Besides that, the Blacks are disorganized. There's no real unity amongst us as a whole. You have a handful of solid cats from different turfs that I function with. The Damus hang out by the table in front of building foe. They run a tight script all the way around. The Compton and Watts Car hang out by the bleachers by the basketball court the Mexicans use. The Neighborhood Car is on the bottom tier and they hang out at the bleacher too. The I.E. Car hangs by the handball wall and the Hoovers hangout against the curb in front of the whole basketball court with the Long Beach Car. As you can see the Blacks all have their own little spots. The homies kick it along the curb by the Hoovers or behind the bleachers. The other sets get in where they fit in. The L.A. Southsiders usually hang to the left towards the baseball field and the San Diego Car hangs by the kitchen and water fountain. The Woods have one part and that's the bleachers by the baseball field."

"There don't be any bumping heads?"

"Here and there, but nothing major since I've been on the yard. We've had a few riots, but you know how that goes. The last one we had was over some coward who wanted to do something tough before he went home. He took off on a Southside in front of the canteen over something petty. The trip was that the coward went home a couple days later leaving us on a five month lock-down. Even though they out number us five to one, the respect is there on both sides. Overall, it's a cool atmosphere where you can do your time, but I still stay on point regardless."

"All the time, you seemed to have the yard mapped out."

"Somebody has to do it. It just irritates me that the Blacks won't come together like all the other races, and build some bonds that can be carried to the streets. We can start to fight the real enemy and stop mistaking him for the one wearing a different colored rag.

He could easily be a homie if they grew up just a few blocks closer. These judges, prosecutors, and crooked police that got us walking in circles mad at the world are the real threat to our existence. This shit is crazy BT, you haven't ever tripped that a gang-banger will shoot one of his own without a thought, but will drop his gun and surrender when a police pulls him over or approaches him on the streets. It just doesn't make sense. We've been trained and tricked to attack the weak instead of the system that has oppressed us and our ancestors."

"I feel you K-Stone, I'm just surprised to be hearing this come out the mouth of Killa Stone."

"I've been mentally sleeping a long time. Somebody decided to wake me up. So at times I'm a bit cranky."

"Alright little Malcolm."

"Little Malcolm, I see you got jokes."

"Naw, that's cool your starting to see life as it is instead of what it's painted to be. Speaking of painting, the sky out here seems like it was painted. It seems real wide."

"We in the middle of the desert inside a human zoo, what do you expect?"

"Right, right. It's still a trip to me. Look at how close the moon is."

"The way these prisons are filling up, they going to put a colony of prisons up there."

"That's a cold thought."

"Naw, that's a real thought."

"Who's your celly?"

"This cat named Askari."

"A Muslim cat?"

"No, just a regular Black man."

"How long you and him been celly's?"

"Since I've been on the yard."

"That's cool; I know you got a roster of hoes on the team?"

"Only if you count old flicks and letters. They all fell off, you know how that goes."

"If you're doing a year flat that's too long for most let alone when you got some calendars to do."

"My situation isn't that different, Tanisha is still staying down, but that's only until the money runs out. She brings my daughters on the weekends. I had a couple other hoes on the team but they fell off once they found out I had life. I know you heard about Uzi and Tanisha."

"I'm up on it, that's my lok, but that move he pulled on your wife wasn't cool. There are too many other females to be pressing up on then to be sexing a homies baby momma or main broad. I just don't believe in giving females power over how you and a homie will mingle with each other."

Caught off guard by K-Stone's response towards Uzi sexing his wife, Bone-Tone continued to elaborate on the matter.

"When I first heard about it, I didn't want to believe Uzi would play me that close. I even heard he said something about me never getting out, so he didn't give a fuck. Since he touched some paper he has gotten big headed. I remember when he was a broke dusty nigga hanging out, now all of a sudden he's the man. It's crazy how the script can flip."

As Bone-Tone continued ranting, K-Stone couldn't help but notice a bit of envy and anger inside his voice as he spoke about Uzi. K-Stone continued listening on in hopes that Bone-Tone wouldn't over step his boundaries and bad mouth Uzi to the point of disrespect. Then he would have to smash him. Wrong was wrong, but he wasn't about to allow the disrespect of his lok while he wasn't present.

"I didn't mean to go on a long one K-Stone; I just had to get that off my chest."

"There's nothing wrong with that, sometimes it's needed."

"So what does your daily program consist of?"

"On the yard I workout about two hours everyday throughout the week. In my cell I read and study."

"Read and study! What about the tube?"

"That stays off the majority of the day. I have a few shows I watch on certain days, but that's it."

"The reason I asked is because I fell off my workout at High Desert. The cells are so hot up there that it left me sweaty every time. I know I need to get back on point so I'll hop in with you."

"That's cool as long as you're serious."

"Come on, I've been doing this before you youngster."

"You kind of old BT, I keep forgetting I'm a have to take it easy on you."

"I see all that studying hasn't taken away your jokes."

"Those will never leave, it's the only other way I stay sane in here. If you need anything just come by the cell since you're in the building with me."

"Yard recall, pick it up and take it home!" The officer yelled over the microphone.

"I'll catch you in the morning cuzz."

"Alright, make sure you're ready in the morning."

"Man, I stay ready."

With that, K-Stone walked towards the A-Section of the building and Bone-Tone towards the C-Section.

"Five sets, I thought you only fell off your workout for a minute?"

"Usually I don't have a problem doing dips. I'll be back on deck in a couple of days."

"Probably some weeks, but definitely not days."

K-Stone found it amazing watching Bone-Tone struggle with his workout, after all the bragging he had done on their way to breakfast that morning. When Bone-Tone came out that morning with a fresh white t-shirt, Reeboks, and new sweat shorts on, he knew he wasn't use to real workouts.

"Stone you like a machine, no wonder the homies looked at me crazy when I said I was working out with you."

"Where are you going?"

"To sit down on the curb, I'm through for the morning."

"We've only been working out thirty minutes."

"Look, I'm going to fill the bottles up and hit some laps until you get finished."

"Just give me forty-five minutes."

While walking the track it didn't take long for Bone-Tone to take notice of the other penitentiary ballers that were possible candidates for business and to chill with. It was easy for him to spot his own kind. The swagger that came from playing with paper for a long period of time was unmistakable. Every now and then, Bone-Tone would run across imitators who had just come up on a fat broad who they convinced to bring them drugs. Most automatically assumed they were a baller because they sold a couple of hats and did some mail outs. Bone-Tone never considered selling drugs in prison for real money. It was crumbs to him and he only did it because he liked to blow, and the hustle was just in him. With only so much an inmate could bring in on the weekends, there was only so much one could make. A couple of thousand dollars a month was nothing to a hustler who was used to having cheese. The imitators always gave themselves away, especially when they would get excited about spending a hundred to a hundred and eighty dollars at the store. It only showed they were use to checking minor figures. One-eighty was nothing to him; he spent more than that on a normal day. Although he saw the yard was packed with fake ballers, it didn't trouble him much because he knew it was inevitable that they would fall off and be exposed for who they really were. When the that time came, he would swoop in and steal all their clientele, then find a front man who mingled with all races on the yard to push his product while he kicked back and did his baller thing.

"That seemed like more then forty-five minutes. I can see how you got so big now."

"Somebody got to do it."

"Better you then me. Who's the hustle man around here?"

"This cat named Dice. He's the best hustler on the yard to use if you trying to get your work off quick."

"Where he at now?"

"In the morning he works in the kitchen, so you'll have to catch him on one of his off days. I've been meaning to ask you what's up with M-Rat?"

"I thought you were already up, that's why I never brought him up. The homie got domed by a C.O. in the tower after he stabbed to death a fool from K4 named Bazooka."

"Is that right?"

"You're killing me with that one. I heard about an inmate getting domed up there a few years back, but I never caught any names."

"We were just coming off of lockdown when it happened. Since they both died the homies and Damus squashed it before we came up. From what I heard his own homies were plotting on him before we went on lockdown. If you didn't hear about that you must not have heard about M-Dogg."

"Naw, what happened with cuzz?"

"That fool caught an extra ten years for getting caught stabbing one of the homies on some extortion type shit. He's in Pelican Bay Shu program now with an undetermined shu."

"You are killing me with all this."

"Then this last bit of info is going to make you dig your grave. The boy X-Ray got full blown A.I.D.S. They got him up at Vacaville on a life support machine."

"What about G-Liz?"

"The last thing I heard on him was he turned Muslim and was into it real deep wearing the Kufi and sporting a beard."

"Damn BT! It seems like everybody then took down falls or then done a three-sixty."

"Prison will do all types of things to individuals K-Stone, that's all I can say. So your teacher going to be gone the whole week?"

"Yeah, he's always taking days off, that's the only thing I don't like about being behind the wall. It's hard to grasp the skill of the trade with constant lockdowns and the instructor being absent."

"I hope they don't give me a job any time soon, they can just leave me A.1.A. unassigned."

"You saying that now, you're going to get tired of this yard all day everyday. On another note, make sure you grab a shower when you come out to dayroom this afternoon. Their going to let out your section first today."

"Don't trip, I'm on it, I like sticking to the single man showers."

"Alright then, I'll holla at you then. I'm about to go and hook something up to eat."

"Ivie, is that you baby?"

Looking up from her shopping cart, Ivie noticed it was K-Stone's mother.

"How you doing Ms. Pink?"

"I'm doing fine, just trying to get rid of the flu."

"It's been a while since I've seen you."

"Yes it has, I only come out when I really need to. Is that your little girl?"

"Yes. Her name is Gina."

"She is so pretty!"

"Thank you. Say thank you Gina." After the baby let out a barley audible thank you, they continued talking.

"You come to Target all the time?"

"Not really, I just heard about the sale and decided to come." Seeing K-Stone's mother brought back a flood of memories Ivie had suppressed.

As they continued talking she tried her hardest not to ask about K-Stone but she couldn't resist.

"How is Kevin doing?" Sophia was eager to say write him and see, but she didn't.

She was fully aware that she abandoned her son. Although she didn't know the reason, she still held a little resentment for Ivie even though she always liked her.

"He's doing fine. I saw him a couple of months ago, he's getting big. In fact, I have a picture of him in my wallet he took last year."

Seeing the picture made Ivie re-live all the good times they had. The feelings she had so badly wanting to deny were coming back in full force. Realizing what was happening she quickly averted her eyes looking at the passing customers instead. Noticing Ivies body language become uncomfortable, Sophia cut the conversation short.

"Alright babe, I'm not going to hold you up. I know how babies get."

"Okay, it was nice seeing you. Tell Kevin I said hi."

"Will do." With that, they parted their separate ways in the store.

"K-Stone, I've sat here and observed you since our first meeting. Since then I've seen you go from full out Crippin to breaking out the shield of ignorance. You've made me proud and have inspired me to continue in my battle to bring awareness to all brothers that come through this soul snatching system. Congratulations brother on all your accomplishments, you've done the time it hasn't done you."

Though he held his A.A. degree in his hands, K-Stone couldn't fully grasp what he had accomplished. For the first time in his life he felt truly proud of something he did and it didn't require trickery, physical strength, or anything negative. He did it all with his mind and he felt like a new man.

"We're going to hook us up a special spread for this occasion."

"You the chef, I'm just here."

K-Stone had never seen Askari so excited before. His energy was getting him excited for a minute. K-Stone had forgotten about his degree and just marveled at how proud he had made Askari. He was genuinely happy for him. Not the fake happiness people put on when they really don't care in any type of way. That night, Askari and K-Stone hung out and conversed about everything. The chicken spread he hooked up was his best work since he had been in the cell with him and that's was saying a lot, being that Askari had a vicious cooking hand.

K-Stone wanted to break the news to his mother about his accomplishment, but since his brother's birthday was coming, he decided to wait. With only a year to go in the penitentiary, everything was starting to fall in place. The next morning he didn't go to the dayroom, he just chilled in his cell looking at the pictures on the wall of Toussaint L'ouverture, Nat Turner, Stephin Biko, Malcolm X, Marcus Garvey, and Nelson Mandela. They were strangers to him at first, but now they served as heroes. In their eyes he saw himself within their faces. He found the answer he was desperately searching for all his life. He realized there was much to gain beyond empty reputations and material things. His gain would be the strength Black men had an abundance of before they started hating their women, neglecting their children, and destroying each generation with sincere ignorance.

Jamal Jr's birthday was tomorrow and Sophia was ironing her clothes to partake in her yearly ritual of visiting him at his grave and bringing his baby pictures out of her trunk closet. Butting out her cigarette, she took a seat at her kitchen table. Sophia started thinking about how fast her life had gone by. She couldn't help but wonder where the time went. Looking over Jamal Jr. and Kevin's pictures on the table she made her way to her bedroom. It had been a long day, she thought to herself as she started to untie her robe and climbed into bed. After getting comfortable, she turned the light off. Lying there peacefully, she was violently awakened by a sudden tightness in her chest. Paralyzed by the pain there was nothing she could do. Years of stress, cigarettes, and a broken heart had finally taken a toll on her body. All she could do was clutch her sheets with her moist palms as her heart gave its final beat.

Early the next morning K-Stone was up energized ready to make his phone call to his mother. When he came back from the yard later that day, he knew his mother would be back from the cemetery by the time he was finished. The sound in her voice he was going to hear played in his mind all day. When she didn't answer the phone that afternoon, he assumed she was probably held up somewhere. K-Stone would just call her later that night. Something definitely had to be wrong he thought to himself when she didn't answer the phone that night. Instead of stressing off of her not answering the phone, he decided to call the next day.

Seeing K-Stone's mother at Target reopened wounds in Ivie that she couldn't pacify or cover. She wanted to write him bad, but couldn't remember his address. It was funny to her because she use to know it by heart. After years of placing it in the back of her mind, it wouldn't come to her, but she still remembered where his mother lived. She made up her mind to stop by while she was out the next day.

Going against her better judgment, Ivie pulled into K-Stone's mother's driveway. After ringing the doorbell for the third time without an answer she decided to leave. Turning the ignition on, she started to pull out of the driveway when she looked in her rear view mirror she saw another car pulling in behind her. Seeing that the driver wasn't going to let her out Sophia turned off her ignition and got out her car.

"Is Sophia home?" The stranger asked while approaching closer.

"No, I just rang the door bell three times and she didn't answer."

"That's odd; Sophia rarely leaves her car behind. Did she know you were coming?"

"No, I was just in the neighborhood and decided to drop by."

"You seem a little young to be coming to see Sophia?"

"I was coming to get her son's address. Are you a friend of the family?"

"No, I'm Kevin's father. Sorry I didn't say so earlier, I'm Jamal Sr."

Extending her hand to meet his, Ivie was so caught-up trying to get K-Stones address that she didn't even pay attention to the obvious resemblance K-Stone and his father shared. Now that she was aware, there was no denying he was K-Stone's father. They favored so much that he could have passed for his older brother, Ivie thought as she watched him approaching the door.

"It's unlike her to leave her car. She's probably asleep, I have an extra key. If she's not inside, I'll look around to see if the address is lying around so you can be on your way."

"Thank you."

Walking inside, Jamal Sr. called out Sophia's name but didn't get a response. Proceeding further in the house he came upon her bedroom. Peering inside, he saw that she was in the bed. Making sure not to startle her, he eased in her room but was held back by an awful rotten smell. Holding his breath he reached in to tap her but quickly noticed her distorted body under the sheet as he reached for her. He knew she was dead.

An entire two weeks had gone by and K-Stone hadn't heard anything from his mother. She didn't answer the phone and he hadn't received one piece of mail from her. The last couple of nights had been hard for him to sleep with thought after thought playing in his mind as to what could have happened to his mother.

"Pink, last two?"

"Eight, three."

Looking at the envelope, K-Stone noticed it was a letter from his father that struck him as odd, because his father only wrote on holidays and his birthday. Without hesitation he sat on top of his desk and proceeded to open the envelope. Placing the letter to the side, K-Stone was motionless for a few minutes as he tried to take in what he had just read. No emotion came over him at the news of his mother's death.

Getting up off the desk he took a seat on the stool. Sitting at his desk, K-Stone stared out the window, past the dirt, passed the barbwire and the other buildings into the mountains that were in the distance. Arms folded tightly across each other, K-Stone stayed in the same position for hours, he didn't even walk to chow. As he sat there, his mind went blank as his body emptied of all his emotions.

Anticipation was high amongst the inmates who carried the prisoners label as stalkers. It was the day the new C.O.s were hitting the yard more aggressively than usual. To avoid over familiarity with inmates, C.O.s would swap yards, positions, and building periodically. All the stalkers waited patiently in the cut watching to see if their building would get a female C.O. Age, race, weight or how they looked played no factor in the stalker's interest. As long as she was a female, there would be a stalker for her.

Ms. Evans had only been working in K-Stone's building two days and already had the attentions of nearly every inmate in the building. She was a Black older woman who stood five foot seven inches and appeared to be between her late forties and fifties. It was difficult to pin point her exact age because she took good care of herself and was aging quite well. There was nothing jaw-dropping about her at first sight. She was an average looking woman in the face who wore her hair in a natural ponytail. If the average inmate was on the street he wouldn't even look twice unless he saw her from the back first. Ms. Evans had ass and she knew it. It was the ass that stopped inmates in whatever they were doing, just to get a glance. Trapped in their own personal fantasies, every inmate was left wondering how a woman her age had ass like that. It was unbelievable. In the prison community this made her the talk of the yard from the Southsiders to the Crips. It didn't take long before the other stalkers from other buildings were finding excuses to get a peek at the cheeks that the yard was comparing to Serena Williams.

Wiping the remaining lotion off his erect penis, Bone-Tone stood at his cell door breathing heavily, frustrated with himself for submitting to his desires that were unquenchable. Just the thought of him lavishing over a woman he couldn't acquire made him yearn for his freedom more. Since Ms. Evans started working in the building with her extra tight green pants, he couldn't keep his hands dry. Except for seeing his daughters, his visits seemed like a strange torture. Kissing and squeezing on Tanisha had grown old for him two years ago. Sometimes the visits made him feel like he was one of those teenagers he saw on TV who would go on a chaperoned date with the girl's parents, and he, like the boy could only hold hands with a hard dick.

The thought of penetration had been on his mind lately. Masturbation didn't provide the pleasure it did three years ago; it only served as a stress reliever. He had finally exhausted all of his appeals; he figured he had nothing to lose. His new project would be to bust Ms. Evans.

It was summer time and the smell of hot cement filled the air as K-Stone stood on the yard sweating heavily after a long workout. Looks of frustration filled nearly every inmate's face as fantasies of pool parties and barbeques were drowned out by the one hundred and twelve degrees dry heat. Two months had gone by since his mother's passing. Her obituary was placed amongst the cards he had received from her over the years. From what his father told him, the funeral was nice, and she was buried right along side his brother's grave.

A tear had yet to fall since hearing of the bad news. He often wondered if all his nefarious behavior on the streets destroyed every single emotion in him. He was the same with his brother's death. All her death did was reaffirm that he had to make something out of his life. He refused to let his family name be tarnished any longer by doing what an animal would do.

Four months remained on his sentence, but K-Stone still operated as if he had years to go. He wasn't about to make the deadly mistake of taking it easy, the heat brought with it tension amongst the races. He made sure to hit the yard daily for that reason alone. The Blacks were already short and it wasn't right for him to be hiding in his cell like a coward. Thinking back to when he first came through the gates, he realized he had come a long way from the days of his butt hanging out his pants and saying cuzz in every sentence to validate his loyalty to his gang. These days he prided himself on mastering speech and not putting himself in a communication stigma of what he was suppose speak like. No longer was he stuck in the illusion that talking proper meant being white. Seeing Bone-Tone approaching on the track, he put his thoughts to the side preparing himself in the process for what he knew would be a senseless conversation.

"K-Stone what's happening?"

"Not much, just chilling, waiting on yard recall."

"You not hot out here?" Bone-Tone said dapping his forehead with a damp towel.

"Naw, I'm an African, I'm use to it. Maybe it'll give you some color, and then you can change your alias to Dark-Tone."

"That's the last thing I'm trying to do is get dark. I'll stick with the Bone-Tone."

"Black is beautiful, didn't you grow up during that era?"

"I was a kid then, besides I ain't with all that shit. I'm cool with being a rich L.A. nigga."

"If that's what you choose to label yourself as. With that thinking, you're the reason we don't have any unity, like the other races in the pen."

"You sound like your celly. I think he brained washed you over the years. You saying all that now but as soon as you hit them streets you going to be calling sisters bitches and aiming cannons at your so called brothers, especially when you hook up with your boy Uzi."

"Bone-Tone, you belong on USA Network because you're a real character. You really think this is a veneer you see day after day. You of all people should know that what you see is what you get with K-Stone. I just didn't decide to change a few months ago because I was close to paroling. I've been reshaping my thoughts and molding my character for four long years. For some strange reason you refuse to accept the K-Stone that stands before you. When I was out there shooting my own kind it was simply reactions based on behaviors I learned in my environment. I knew no other way back then, but now another way of life is clear to me, I'm choosing to fall into it instead of a lifestyle that ends nowhere. Besides, I'm not trying to kill or attack them in here when they're just a couple of feet from me. Why would I go out my way to hunt them down on the streets? So I can get life, and then hit the pen again just to walk the track with the same so called enemies doing nothing to them. What sense does that make? Do you see anybody rushing their enemies on the yard? Nothing stopping them and it just goes to show that what we represent is not only wrong but has many flaws within its structure. That is only excepted because boys created it. If anything, I'll attack one of these skinheads walking around with lighting bolts and swastikas all over their bodies."

"I guess K-Stone "

"Yeah, you just keep on guessing about life. Guessing and not knowing about life is what got us all in this predicament. Thinking we knew what was going on in the streets. Thinking we were those dudes. Too much thinking leads to uncertainty which ultimately leads to failure. See that's the main difference in me, you fail to see I no longer think I know life and the situations associated with it. I know how to succeed without picking up a gun or a dope sack."

"Why you so serious all the time? I was just shooting the shit with you."

"Haven't we played enough with our lives? Look at us, just here in the middle of the desert. While life moves on, we're stuck in suspension unaware of what life is really like out there, because we in here. TV and magazines only give us a glimpse of what's going on in the world. People your age and my age are building futures for themselves, preparing for families, retirement, and sharing new experiences with someone. While we sit, stand, and sleep through the same situations daily, masking our pains, setbacks, and what ifs with fake happiness. They say it ended in 1865, but it is hard for me to tell from what I know and wake up to every morning."

"Wait hold up, what ended in 1865?"

"Pick up a book without eye candy and find out."

"Oh, you are going to leave the Tone hanging?"

After a couple of minutes went by, K-Stone seen that he was boggled.

"Since you're looking like you're about to pop a vessel I'll enlighten you, slavery!"

"Okay, Mr. Philosopher lets talk about something else."

"Something like what?"

"Like my girl right here walking down the pavement."

"That's your girl now?"

"Cuzz, you don't know, that's going to be me!"

"I know this time is starting to affect your brain."

"Hold up Killa, I got to holla at my pound-cake! How you doing today Ms. Evans?"

"I'm alright Mr. Tapps, how about you?"

"Fine now that I've seen you."

Smiling without further response, Ms. Evans proceeded to the building while speaking to K-Stone. Turning around simultaneously, K-Stone and Bone-Tone both admired Ms. Evan's back side as she waited patiently for the tower to let her in the building.

"I told you K-Stone, that's my pound-cake! You see how she smiled at me when she said my name?"

"Bone, she smiles at everybody in the building."

"That's where you're wrong. Now you're about to hear my philosophy. Since she started working in the building, I've been observing how she interacts with all the inmates. There are only certain ones she actually smiles at. That list includes me, you, two other Blacks, and three Mexicans."

"Bone-Tone, seriously you trippin. You actually got a list?"

"Hell yeah! I got to keep tabs on mines."

"So if someone on your list so happens to catch her attention before you, what are you going to do?"

"First off, you don't count. You're not going to do anything like that. You're too stuck on your discipline plus close to release for me to trip off you. But then again, you sure were looking at those cheeks rather hard a minute ago."

"I'm a man of course, I'm going to look, their no denying she has cheeks."

"I don't know K-Stone, I might have to watch you too."

"It's best you keep yours on the other cats you mentioned. Besides, I'm cool on that."

"Why is that? She too old for you?"

"Naw, I'm not tripping off the age. I just don't feel her get down. Every time a Black is in the dayroom she goes out of her way to flash the light on them or stalk them, but when a Mexican or Wood is on a door during dayroom she acts as if she doesn't see them. When she started working in the building, I was like cool, a sister in the building. But it didn't take long to see she didn't view the brothers in the same light. I understand that some of the brother be weirdoes especially when a sister is working in the building, but that doesn't give her an excuse to act funny."

"Sounds like you want some special treatment."

"The last thing I want is special treatment. All I'm saying is we both Black people acknowledge that like the Mexicans C.O.s acknowledge their own. Don't go out your way to sweat a Black just to show your partner you're not showing favoritism. Because nine times out of ten they don't care. The thing that irritates me the most about her is she lets other C.O.s change her program when they work with her. Being she's the new senior officer in the building, the program is set by what she forces, not some other C.O. working substitution for a day. Feel me?"

"I feel you on that, I've noticed that too."

"I remember one day they didn't run showers because of some training they were doing. When the program started back up they had enough time to run showers, being that there were only a couple of towels on the door. The fool in the tower was on his period and didn't want to run the shower program for some lame reason. So when Ms. Evans came by my door to give me my mail I asked what was up with the showers? She responded by saying it was the towers program, which made me ask aren't you the senior officer? She said yes, but couldn't explain to me why he couldn't run a total of five showers that day before we went to chow. She just kept shrugging her shoulders, with that sincere ignorant look on her face she gets when you ask her a simple question a child could answer. You probably look past all that because of the big butt and a smile. Her behavior just proves my theory that all Black people aren't actually Black people, she's just an American. Prison has taught me that your people are the ones that share the same thinking."

"Why do you speak to her if you feel that way?"

"Even though she highly irritates me by her silliness, I must keep in mind that she is nothing but a test to what I'll face on the streets in the real world. If I loose my cool and cuss her out, I'm no better then the ignorance she portrays daily trying to fit in with her coworkers who will never accept her. Believe me she has brought me to the point more then once with her foolish behavior, but I find solace in the fact that I control myself so her behavior will never bring me out of my character."

"All that sounds good but that ass definitely brings me out of my character."

"If that's what makes your time easier go ahead and do you. Just keep in mind that smiles are not always friendly and Ms. Evans isn't cool."

"Maybe not for you and those she ignores, but when I look at her I see the opportunity to be a man."

K-Stone was going to respond to the comment Bone-Tone just made, but decided to not further fuel the senseless conversation he was sucked into. Since Bone-Tone's final appeal was shot down the sudden change in his behavior was evident. Ms. Evans had become his new pacifier since the law library was no longer effective. Every conversation they had ultimately led to her. It was unbelievable to him the way Bone-Tone had thoroughly convinced himself that Ms. Evans wanted him. The fact that she chose that approach in her duties in a kind way instead of like an asshole was simply her method of getting inmates to obey her. Bone-Tone had simply over looked her kind gestures for something else. A mistake most males made when confronted by a female. The average male is conditioned from birth to believe that he can have every woman and that thought becomes magnified in prison. From just doing time, K-Stone knew it was easy to slip into a fantasy world and convince oneself of anything especially that a female was feeling them. It wasn't that he doubted Bone-Tone's mack hand, because it was fully possible to bust a female C.O. or any female that worked in prison. That was a fact every inmate was aware of. One rule that Bone-Tone was over looking was the inmates didn't choose the females did. Although Ms. Evans did do some light weight flirting with certain inmates, it was only expected because she was still a female and no uniform could change that. K-Stone couldn't see her risking her job for an inmate. When the C.O. yelled over the microphone yard recall, K-Stone was glad to break away from BT's ranting. All he kept thinking on his way to his cell was it wasn't going to be much longer before he would be released from the human zoo.

Holding the letter firmly in his hands, K-Stone could hardly believe she had finally written him, after all the years. From the feel of the envelop he knew it only contained two sheets of paper. He also noticed the change of address. It had been a long time, he thought to himself. Nevertheless, he could never forget her even though she rarely crossed his mind nowadays. A negative thought of, fuck this bitch, why is she writing, crossed his mind as he picked the staples from the envelope, but was quickly replace with forgiveness. He had realized that he couldn't allow old memories, good or bad, to control his emotions. After removing the two pieces of paper from the envelope, he proceeded to read her letter. Before actually absorbing the words he instantly noticed her hand writing was still the same as it was years ago. This brought back a myriad of memories that he couldn't control nor wanted to.

The first page basically broke down her current situation of the past few years, the death of her sister, baby daddy drama, and the daily drama of being a single mother raising a child. He just took it all in with a deep breath. It was a scenario he was all too familiar with hearing. The second page departed from the negative she had been enduring and dealt with how she was putting her life back together with a little help from others. Lastly, it expressed condolence for his recent loss of his mother, which was still hard for him to accept. In closing, she let it be known that she was there for him if he needed someone to talk to or ease his mind. It didn't take him long to decide that he would write a response back the following day to let her know how much he appreciated her reaching out to him despite her own personal dilemmas.

"Been a while since I seen you drop a letter in the mail box, Stone."

"You know how it gets when you're short timing?"

"Yeah, on my first trip I was hitting like the post office, especially when I got down to my last five months. Now I hardly hear form anybody except moms and the kids. I see you don't have any of your books in the dayroom. Let's shoot some bones."

"I don't mind giving you a few lessons."

While walking to the dayroom tables, K-Stone couldn't help but notice that the Mexicans weren't playing Pinochle or Dominoes on their side of the dayroom. Instead, they were huddled by the benches under the TV.

"You peep, the Southsiders out?"

"Naw, I wasn't even tripping, but now that you brought it to my attention it is odd. There dayroom is empty despite the Woods."

"You haven't heard anything floating in the air?"

"I heard something about the Mexicans and Blacks in the gym were having issues about the Blacks disrespecting quiet time after the TV goes off at night. I didn't bring it up because you know how that gym is. It's like another world inside there and there is always something strange going on inside there."

"Yeah, I know, but you also know the platitude about the straw and the camel?"

"I'm familiar, we just going to have to be more on point the next few days. Then again, you know how this yard is. Niggas don't ever want to clean up their backyards. They rather let the debris pile up until it becomes someone else's problem."

"You know I know the business on how these cats operate, yet it still irritates me to the marrow. Just look at these cats, haven't none of them even tripped off the Mexicans gathering up. They're more concerned about their Pinochle hand and the latest prison gossip."

"I don't even know why you're tripping K-Stone, you like a few months to the tilt. Before you know it you'll be on them streets with some tight on your swipe and a pill in your system."

"It'll be five years since I've had some pussy, a few days or months without it won't make a difference when I touch down. That's the last thing on my agenda; anyways you know the business with me."

"Whatever cuzz, I know you're going to see all those bitches out there with them apple bottoms fits on and you're going to put some of those Magnums to use quickly. The only thing I'm going to be using quickly is these fist and pistols if these cats don't squash whatever trip they got going on in the gym."

"Like I said you'll be out of here so don't even sweat it."

"And like I mentioned before I'm not gone until I'm out the gate on that white van doing fifty out of here."

"I'm starting to think all this talk is some form of distraction to slow down this lesson you're getting, Stone."

"We both know that you can't see me in these bones, so you know that's not the case."

"Then why are you washing the bones for the third time?"

"Sometimes a brother got to warm the engines up," Bone-Tone and K-Stone kept playing on for a couple of more games of Dominoes.

"Skunk, see what you made me do to you. See what happens when you start talking crazy to the K-Stone."

Kneeling down between the bleachers surrounded by Southsiders, Solo was giving orders to his people he received from the top man the day before about how to handle the situation with the Blacks in the gym.

"Speedy, Chewy, and Chubbs are going to bring out the flats next night yard and bury them outside along the curb by the basketball court. The homies in the other building will secure their positions and bury their knives in their disclosed spots too. Make sure you maintain a cool composure, we don't want the Blacks to suspect we're going to attack in a few days. I know a few of you homies are first timers and may be nervous, it doesn't mean you're weak. The Rasa has your back so there should be no doubt in us overwhelming them. Weto, you and Flaco get together the homies who will be attacking the Blacks main heads. Make sure they're the first to get attacked and that the homies know exactly who they are. It's important that we throw off the little structure they do have amongst each other, just incase there is a second wave after the lockdown."

"Done, I've wanted to get me a nigger since I left the streets, especially since the Bloods killed my little homie."

"Well, you'll have your chance Weto, if the Blacks continue to disrespect the Rasa in the gym."

"Fuck those niggers; the homies should've been taken off a month ago. That's the reason they act so hard homes, too many passes."

"You're just a hot head Weto, if it wasn't for the structure you would be fighting every F13 you saw. You must think of the consequences before you act hot headed. With every lockdown we lose money, drugs, and time with our Rasa on visits. So it's wise to make it worth it when we ride."

"No disrespect ese Solo, but I've noticed you function with those niggers comfortably as if you don't have an issue with them. Isn't your barrio beefing with the Crips on the streets?"

"You basically answered your own question Weto. We beef with one Crip set not all Blacks. Before we started to beef with the Crips in my barrio, we use to hang with them, go to school with them, and even did business with them. Personally I don't harbor hate for Blacks because I wasn't raised that way."

"But they kill Rasa!"

"We kill Rasa, probably more then them. There's probably more Rasa in jail for victimizing Rasa then for victimizing another race. I dislike the barrio the homies and I beef with. I don't hate one more then the other because of race, an enemy is an enemy no matter his skin color, ese."

Weto stared at Solo for a while silently stuck in thought at what he had been told. Three years into his thirteen year sentence for attempted murder on two rival Southsiders had left him with a lot of anger and a heroin habit he could hardly afford. Not once since doing his time had he ever considered that he was indeed locked in prison for shedding the Blood of his own kind. Yet, he preached the Rasa motto to all the young homies hitting the system. Solo's words made him feel like a hypocrite for a slight moment.

With all the Bs slashed out on his head, and other disrespectful tattoos he didn't actually know if he even had any confirmed kills on any Bloods. Weto basically shot anything male with Black skin. But he knew that he had killed and attempted to kill plenty of rival Southsiders and that now disturbed him even though he would never show it.

Seeing Weto stuck in thought was nothing new to Solo, he knew he had the tendency to drift off into another zone at any given time, besides he wanted to shift the flow of the conversation. It wasn't always wise to state ones opinion that didn't coincide with the Rasa. The gears from being an attacker to being attacked shifted quickly and with little or no motivation.

"So what's been up with your lady from Baldwin Hills Weto?"

"Nothing much, she's doing her duties and making sure uno ocho Weto is taken care of. Have you heard the new Ice Cube?"

"Nope, but I heard the shit knocks."

"If we still on the mainline after the clashing, I'll slide it to you to check it out."

"That's right, Cube and 2pac is my shits outside of oldies."

"What about that Scarface and WC though?"

"I stay with the Face and Dubb C on the radio."

"Did you read the article in the King I slid you last week. Scarface said he's coming out with a new album."

"I must've missed that part Weto, I was too busy looking at Buffy."

"That's right."

Chapter 16

All the Time

"Just make sure you bring all one-seventy-five of those push ups you owe. I'm starting to think you're starting an oil company BT, because you always seem to be pumping the floor when we come to dayroom. Being that you know the end results of our domino games will end with you on the ground, I'm assuming you either like it down there or you're trying to get swoll!"

Getting up off the floor with sweat beads forming on his forehead, Bone-Tone proceeded to place the dominoes into the box.

"You sure talk crazy when you're up a few games. You seem to have forgotten you've been on that floor plenty too."

"I have to let you win some or you wouldn't ever want to play me."

After giving each other dap, K-Stone and Bone-Tone along with the other inmates in the dayroom made their way towards their cells for the night.

Hearing his custom ring tone go off, baby Uzi answered his phone while backing up into the apartment gates his homies just got arrested in front of.

"They still on the street?"

"Naw, they just pulled off three cars deep."

"What took them so long?"

"They gaffled three of the homies under that punk ass gang injunction for hanging out."

"Cuzz, they starting to take that injunction to another level."

"To keep it real, the only reason they took the homies is because they wouldn't tell them where you were at. The homies kept saying they never heard of you. So that fool Garcia pulled out your mug shot and asked them if they recognize your face since they never heard of you. You know how he gets to going in super cop mode when he doesn't get his way. Cuzz, they on you tough. You should go ahead and bounce out."

"Fuck them; I'm not going nowhere, they not about to chase me off seventy-fifth street!"

"Where you at anyway?"

"Around the corner, I saw them cherry tops when I was passing by and kept it moving. I'm about to park my hoop over at that bitch Tawana's pad and hit the cuts over there. I got some business to holla at you about."

Over the last year Uzi's life had been filled with confusion and a series of come ups with down falls. Too much partying caused him to lack in his hustle. Drinking Remy and Hennessey day after day was taking the little weight he possessed and started causing him to fatigue. Purple Kush and Ecstasy kept his mind clouded and paranoid daily. His paranoia caused him to kill his homie Lil Uzi because he thought his flamboyancy after a lick they hit would've led to him getting caught and snitched on. All elements combined led to the loss of his town house and the repossession of his Benz. He was back to driving five year old, low keys, in hopes of dodging the police who were looking for him again for robbery and murder. To make matters worse, he had a baby on the way by one of his home girls who was constantly sweating him about coming home at night and a list other accusations. Uzi just wasn't trying to hear or compromise on anything. He was concerned with trying to get his money and lifestyle back on track. It was becoming harder it seemed the more he desired it. Being wanted by the Feds and the Seventy-Seventh Division didn't help his plight either. The murder he knew he could beat, but the bank robberies were another situation because they had his face on camera.

"So, what's the business Big?"

"First let me twist the purple before I begin."

Letting the thick Kush smoke engulf the inside of the car, Uzi checked his Mac-11 for the third time in ten minutes to see if there was a bullet in the chamber before he continued to speak.

"When I went out to Bakersfield last week, my partners put me up on a couple of banks out there way. After checking them out, I decided they were easy come-ups. I did the necessary homework before I left. I'm pushing back out there next week to hit them. You with that?" Baby Uzi looked at Uzi with a look that said you know I'm with that, so he didn't even respond verbally.

"That's what I figured; I just had to make sure. Did you hear that?"

"Hear what?"

"Hold up, be still and turn the music off." After sitting in silence for five minutes, Uzi began to speak again.

"I thought I heard some foot steps. Gots to stay on everything Baby. You know how the boys be creeping. Back to what I was saying, the banks are small so it's going to be me, you, and another homie that will hit them. My nigga K-Stone is going to be touching soon and I gots to make sure I'm back right before he touches down, feel me?"

Baby Uzi just shook his head. Even though he got put on the set a few years after K-Stone went to prison, he had heard so much about him that he felt as if he already knew him. He couldn't wait to go put one down on the K4s with K-Stone to further increase his reputation.

Being under Uzi, Baby knew he had to stay active at all times on all levels. With Lil Uzi getting killed by the K4s, he assumed it was only him and big left to keep the name ringing. With Big's name already having much status, Baby knew he had a long way to go to gain the respect Big got in the streets. Living under another's shadow was never his thing, so he knew his gang-banging had to be more violent than Big's to surpass him and be known as Baby Uzi instead of Uzi's little homie.

Three of his killing's had already made the news so he was well on his way to being known for his killing hand. This would be the first time he and Big hit a major lick together. They had done plenty of spare of the moment pocket checks together and liquor stores, but nothing involving thousands of dollars. If things went on point in Bakersfield, he would be the man to the young homies above and under him. The thought made him smirk, because he felt he would get all the pussy that was denied to him by the older home girls who only let the homies with money toss. Hell yeah, he thought to himself. He would be the man sooner then he thought and nobody would be able to tell him shit after that.

"Who keeps blowing your phone up Big?"

"That bitch Cupcake, she don't want shit. She probably can't catch up to another dick so she sweating me."

"Cuzz, I don't know how you got Cupcake pregnant anyway."

"Tripping, drunk off that Remy one night."

"Was the pussy cool?"

"The pussy was light weight bomb."

"Is that right, I thought it would've been beat up with all the homies that then hit."

"Me too, but it wasn't, and I was pounding for a minute, so it wasn't that stay tight for three minutes then go to it's natural form of pussy. To keep it real Baby, it wasn't the pussy that made me go back."

"You don't even have to tell me Big, I've heard about the throat."

"Yes, the throat is magnificent! I would tell you to push up on her and see if you could get a sample but she going to play the "I don't get down like that role" based on the fact you named after me. After you get your hands on this Bakersfield green, all that will change."

Baby Uzi's smirk returned at the thought of that.

"While you over there smirking, why don't you call some of your little hoes up so we can get a toss session cracking."

"I'm already five steps ahead of you on that Big."

"Let's make it happen then," Uzi said turning the car on.

The weather had returned to its reasonable temperature at Centinela during the last week of September. Small tornadoes substituted the normally dry heat, bringing with it an occasional breeze that felt refreshing after a long workout or even during the middle of one fortunate enough to be standing in the right areas when it blew past.

On this day, K -Stone stepped on the yard. There was no breeze to be found or any clouds that would shield the sun. It was afternoon yard and the desert sun wasn't giving up none, but that wasn't where the heat was radiating from. The heat on the yard came from the emptiness of the basketball court and handball wall the Southsiders normally occupied.

The Hispanics huddled together around different parts of the yard in groups of four hitting the track in what seemed like a war strategy. They watched all movement on the yard while most of the yard continued in their normal routines of prison sports, card games, and exercise. It didn't take long for other convicts from different sets to also take notice of the odd formation and lack of routine. Surrounded by his homies, K-Stone knew what time it was. Reaching down between his cheeks, he gripped the handle of his knife and brought it around to the front of his waistline for easier access. Simultaneously, his homies followed the same procedure.

Speedy along with three of his homies and two groups of four more Southsiders trailing behind them, made their way towards the pack that surrounded K-Stone with knives and razor blades in their hands.

With reflexes of a true warrior, K-Stone and his homies met Speedy's attack head on throwing off the small advantage of the sneak attack. In a matter of seconds, Speedy was on the ground curled in a ball holding the remaining parts of his left eye as the blood flowed down his face. Bone-Tone was bleeding lightly from a razor slash he received to his right cheek that he was unaware of, as he stood tall swinging at every Southside that came within striking distance. The first four man vanguard was taken down swiftly giving K-Stone and his homies time to meet the second wave head on as well. In all, it was seven fighting seventeen because more Southsiders had run over in the direction of them while certain Blacks in their area ran in the opposite direction of the action. It didn't make much sense because it was a full blown riot taking place. With every inch of the yard including the buildings going down, it was be a victim or victimizer situation. Three minutes into the riot, a mixture of fatigue, smoke, bloody inmates, and unconscious inmates was what the environment portrayed. Projectiles from block guns began flying, along with an occasional shot from a mini fourteen with orders to get down and stay down being blasted over the loud speaker every five seconds, causing the rioters to stop and start five times. With neither side giving in, the riot continued. Although there were more Hispanics participating than Blacks, the Blacks were fighting more out of a survival than in aggression. The Whites and the Others sat by and watched the entertainment.

"Get 'em!"

K-Stone heard voices saying to his left as he fought two Southsiders who were having a hard time getting him down. He dropped one of them with a hard right across the temple. He then quickly glanced over to see where the voices were coming from as the second Southsider focused on his unconscious homie. His glance found Askari surrounded by three Southsiders who were reluctant to attack. Each one was waiting for the other to attack first. When, one finally did go in for the attack; Askari caught his arm with his left hand and pulled him in so quickly that it was hard to actually see what happened. The sound of a bone being broken was unmistakable. Seeing their homie scream in pain and cussing in Spanish angered the Southsiders causing them to attack simultaneously from the front and back. K-Stone was about to run and assist Askari when he felt a punch to the back of his neck that made him stumble. To prevent himself from falling he braced his fall with one hand which enabled him to get his balance back and

countered the attack which had become unnecessary when a
Black man from out of nowhere attacked his attackers, giving K-
Stone the opportunity to run and assist Askari who was now being
swarmed by five Southsiders. They were trying to drag him to the
ground. Kneeing one in the back and punching another in the
stomach, K-Stone managed to prevent their intentions. With the
Black brother that helped him when he was dazed now helping him
help Askari, they looked around to see who was next; but instead,
saw five C.O.s running their way yelling at them to get down. With
a slight hesitation, all three complied even though they were ready to
spring up if another attacker appeared. In the confusion, K-Stone
didn't even recognize the Black brother that came to his aide, and
when he turned around to extend his hand and a give him a good
looking out, he found it to be the K4 he had gotten down with.
Without hesitation he continued his gesture which was met with an
equal response. It really sunk in more than ever, that where one was
from didn't matter only skin color did. Five hours later two-hundred
Hispanics and Black inmates were lined up against the wall from the
program office all the way to the kitchen. The others were separated
on different parts of the yard all with their hands secured with plastic
ties behind their backs. Most of the inmates were dirty, sweaty, had
torn clothes, were lumped up, and still coughing from the pepper
spray. Those were the fortunate ones five Hispanics came out of the
building, one on a stretcher wrapped from head to waist. Building
four had two Hispanics come out on stretchers with bandages soaked
with blood. Seven Blacks had been stabbed on the yard most near
death. It was so bad that K-Stone lost count of the victims. All he
remembered were the ambulances parked at the facility gate leaving
and returning.

Overall, K-Stone came out alright compared to most. He
had a couple of lumps and a few scratches but no serious wounds.
His nostrils were still raw and irritated from the pepper spray used
on him and the other rioting inmates, but those were the only
injuries. It was going to be a long evening he thought to himself as
he brushed his back up against the wall to stop the itch he was
unable to do himself because his hands were still bonded. The
facility had to make room for all the inmates going to the hole that
night which would be near impossible. From the way it was looking,
every inmate who didn't have visible wounds was taken back to their
cells.

Those chosen few included Bone-Tone. When K-Stone noticed him returning back to the building with another group of inmates he couldn't help but wonder how he was able to stop his face from bleeding before he got cuffed. K-Stone was so fatigued, he didn't spend much of his dwindling energy trying to figure out the mystery, he just chopped-it-up that he got away.

Askari was seven bodies down from K-Stone and he had no one to speak to during his wait to be placed in Ad-Seg. The moon was full providing a blanket of light over the wide oil dark desert night in which Centinela was sunken in an ocean of shallow sand. A wrecked immobile slave ship is what it depicted. C-6 was the equivalent to its smaller vessel, where disgruntled slaves were kept pending a shu term, court case, or investigation by ISU.

Years had passed since K-Stone had been inside of a moving vehicle. The feeling gave him an instant nostalgia of when he used to drive through his turf at high speeds with his music bumping. So close yet so far away was the only way he could describe the feeling in his stomach. A few months to the house could be altered to more time depending on the outcome the committee would come to when he went before them.

Stepping out the white van, he, along with nine other Black inmates were led into C-6. Since Askari and he were celly's they placed them in the holding tank together while the C.O.s filled out their paperwork and organized bed rolls.

Splashing water on his face from the tank sink that needed a decent cleaning, Askari took a deep breath before stretching his body. Multiple hours of being hand cuffed had left him stiff and wanting rest.

"Long day."

"Adventure is all I have to say about it," K-Stone said placing one foot on a small bench.

K-Stone let out a short laugh at the sound of Askari's reply. Askari followed up with a short laugh also to ease the tension. Both had learned that most situations of such caliber could only be eased with laughter, because when the situation ended it all seemed so silly it could have easily ended with a small compromise. Instead, they conducted themselves like savage animals. Both sides would be slammed a mandatory six months or longer.

"Well K-Stone, it looks like we'll be starting that hole program come tomorrow morning."

"Yeah, seems that way. All I'm trying to do right now is to lay it out and think about the rest in the morning."

"Can't help but feel you on that brother. By the way, good looking on the assistance out there on the battlefield."

"Come on Askari, you know how we do it."

"Still, I need you to know you weren't obliged to do that when you had your own neck to watch."

"I know you would have done the same."

"I wish I could extend my thanks to the other brother who was with you. With all that was going on, I might be mistaken but wasn't that the brother from K4 you fought?"

"You're far from confused, that was him. I'm still dealing with how to take that one. I use to kill those dudes on the streets. Yet, one prevented me from getting harmed even though I brought him harm. My so called enemy had my back when my so called homies were nowhere insight on the second jump up, except Bone-Tone."

"Attention on the tier! Ese, Chino!"

"Como estas?"

"Buenos dias!"

"Buenos dias!"

"Gracias!"

"Gracias, de nada!"

Hearing the Southsiders morning role call end, Askari hopped down from his bunk to prepare to answer the Blacks' morning role call. Standing by the door he watched as K-Stone folded his blanket and sheet before rolling his mattress up.

"Attention on the tier! To all my Black Africans, Askari, and K-Stone, Injama-Sue Booie!"

"Injama-sue Booie!"

"Asante!"

It was their third day on H-Pod with C-6 and they had the program down to a science. There were ten cells on their pod. Four were occupied by Blacks and one by some skin heads who were next door to them. The other five cells were occupied by Southsiders.

Breakfast usually came twenty minutes after the morning roll call which gave Askari and K-Stone ample time to get themselves together before it came. The roll call acted as an alarm clock. In the hole there weren't any clocks visible, so it was impossible to know the time. The only exception to this was when the psychologist did their daily check-ups to see if anyone was losing their mind. This was crazy to K-Stone because he couldn't understand how someone could lose something that had already been lost.

C-6 cells were much larger than the mainline cells which allowed K-Stone and Askari to exercise together inside the cell on the days they didn't go to the yard. The cells consisted of ten dog kennels each with a toilet sink combination to take baths, use the bathroom, and drink water all while being monitored by video cameras. The yard schedule consisted of three days a week anytime between six-thirty in the morning to two-thirty in the afternoon. The weeks went by quickly. The other days were used for showers except for Thursdays, they were reserved for committee.

Knowing that he would be going before the committee the following day, K-Stone could hardly stay concentrated on the urban novel he was reading. Realizing that he was barely keeping up with the plot of the book that consisted of sex and violence, he placed it on top of the other novels and magazines that he and Askari acquired since being in the hole. K-Stone then made his way to the toilet to relieve himself of the gas that the prison food never failed to give him.

After three flushes, he sat down on the edge of his bed focusing his head towards the window in the ceiling. Sighing for the lack of seeing nothing but empty skies, he reached underneath the bed and pulled out his paperwork to retrieve his sheet he received from the property officer a few days ago. She had told him that after he went in front of the committee he could receive a couple items out of his property if they decided to keep him. Going over the list he noticed that there wasn't much he could get but hygiene, letters, and reading materials. Nevertheless, he filled the form out just in case they pulled a stunt.

Walking back to their cell with the common look one gets when things don't go the way one had in mind, K-Stone and Askari were both dealing with the decision the committee handed down to them. Both had been put up for transfer and would remain in the hole until the transfer went through.

"It's official that I'll be paroling from the hole now. From what the lieutenant told me at the committee, the transfer will take at least three months," K-Stone said coming out of his jump suit.

"At least the riot didn't affect your release date."

"Yeah, but it's crazy that they found me not guilty but they're still making me sit in the hole pending a transfer."

"You know how these people operate."

"That I do, so they sending you back to the level foe?"

"The riot boosted my points right back up which means we'll be parting ways in here as well."

"What do you mean?"

"Once they adjust my points back to level four, I won't be able to be housed with anyone with lower points."

"So you'll be out of here any day now?"

K-Stone hated asking questions he already knew the answers to, but he couldn't help but let the words trickle out his mouth. His mentor and friend would be parting with him sooner then both had expected. He had come to rely on Askari's teachings, advice, and friendship throughout the years. Change was definite and K-Stone knew he would just have to accept what was bound to take place.

"Don't trip K-Stone, you have my hook up. You will be able to contact me once you get out."

"That's without question. It's just so much has happened so fast in a short amount of time, that I'm just trying to get back on track mentally."

"Let it be a lesson to what's to come once you're released. There will be all types of temptations, let downs, and spontaneous events that will be out of your control. Most will leave you in mental disarray, but you have to stay strong K-Stone, because it's definitely going to be harder for you than the average person. Just never allow yourself to be beaten down by life because it's so easy to give into what appears to be right but we know to be wrong. In short, don't be a sheep like so many choose, be a Shepard and remember to take your time out there. Moving to fast always leaves room for error. Keep in mind that you've been in this environment were we all find failures, society's failures; those who are unable to find their way within a contradicting system that doesn't apply or provide the same laws or opportunities for all members of society equally. Yet, expect for every member to behave accordingly. Though you've been away for five years, you were given the opportunity to deprogram your mind and grow. But at the same time, your absence from society has created a void for you that will be apparent upon your daily dealings. With all your growth, just keep in mind that you will be behind in certain aspects of society."

Shaking his head in agreement, K-Stone listened to Askari without much response besides a head nod. This could possibly be his last day chilling with him and he wanted to take in as much as possible.

Chapter 17

A New Way

"So what's the first thing you're going to do when you touch down?"

"Visit my mother and brother's grave and begin my new life. Basically I'm going to take it real easy and apply my new thoughts to the world."

"Nothing wrong with that sounds like a logical plan."

"What about you? What do you plan on doing once you're back on the foe?"

"Keep my eyes open and stay out the way of preventable chaos. Depending on what level four I hit, I'll most likely be back on a level three next year. Only time will tell and I have plenty of it. No matter how long my stay, I'll remain on my mission of building more warriors who'll stop this cycle of ignorance and hate we harbor for each other."

"Righteous!"

"Mr. Frank," a C.O. said peering inside the cell.

"Yes," Askari said walking to the door.

"Roll up you property, your points were raised after you left committee earlier today and you no longer can be housed with Mr. Pink because you two have different custody levels."

"Do you know where I'm going?"

"I'm not sure, but most likely you're going to G-Pod."
While Askari gathered his things, K-Stone made his way to the door to ask the C.O. a question.

"Do you know the name of the C.O. I'm supposed to give my allowable slip to?"

"Yes, just give it to me and I'll give it to Mendez for you on my way back to the front."

Before cuffing up, Askari and K-Stone embraced.

"Stay solid comrade, in all that you do. This is the easy part; the true test is in on the streets."

"I refuse to let myself or my people down anymore."

"I know."

"Alright Askari."

With that said, Askari made his way down the tier with his hands cuffed behind his back and his property wrapped in his sheet while K-Stone watched him leave for the last time.

The loneliness was felt immediately by K-Stone once Askari left. He suddenly felt a void similar to when he had lost his brother years ago. Nothingness engulfed him as he dimmed the light and placed his back against his rolled up mattress.

It had been two weeks since the riot and the yard was barely getting a shower program. It was already confirmed that the lockdown would last at least four months before talks of withdrawing the lockdown would even be considered. This didn't bother Bone-Tone one bit because he was on a level four. His first few years in prison had more then prepared him for doing a program on lockdown. His celly had gotten caught up in the riot so he was living the bachelor life. There was little movement on the yard and he wouldn't be getting a celly until the situation was put into perspective, which was fine with him. He hadn't been in a cell by himself in years. The benefits were felt daily at all hours of the day and night.

His exercise program had ceased completely. His daily routine now consisted of eating junk food, masturbating, sleep, and watching TV depending on his mood. Ten years or better usually was the time period that the average prisoner was given to break and lose parts of his mind according to prison yard guidelines. It had been about that long and Bone-Tone was already losing the little bit of sense he had a hold of.

"How you doing today Ms. Evans?"

"I'm fine. I need you to step away from the door so I can see if you're still alone in there."

"Ms. Evans, you know nobody in here but me."

"Regardless I need to check Mr. Tapps."

Reluctantly, Bone-Tone stepped away from the door a few feet to allow the C.O. to peak in with her flash light. She knew nobody was in here she just wanted to check him out, I know it, Bone-Tone said to himself. He was tired of playing cat and mouse games with Ms. Evans. He was ready to make his move. Too many days had gone by for him to just keep accepting a smile. He at least needed to grasp one of her butt cheeks to see how it felt in his boney hands.

"So what section are you going to run today Evans?"

"I don't know I have to check the daily assignment sheet. It says C-Section, but I don't know if I want to run it today."

"And why is that?"

"The inmate in two-thirty-five gives me the creeps. He's always giving me those predator eyes."

"Like he's going to attack you?"

"Not attack me, but step out of line one day and say something crazy."

"Say something crazy, like what?"

"That's what I don't know and I'm definitely not trying to find out."

"It's at your discretion to what side you want to run first. Just keep in mind that if you don't run C-Section you're going to hear a lot of whining from a lot of angry grown men."

"I know, I have a headache already and that's the last thing I want to hear is Ms. Evans coming from their section all day."

"Just wait ten more minutes before you run C-section which will give your admirer only enough time to shower and lock it up"

"Sounds like a plan."

"We'll start from two-fifty and work up."

By the time they reached two-thirty-seven, it was 4:10p.m. giving them fifteen minutes to finish showering before count time. During that moment, Bone-Tone was standing at his door impatiently waiting to be let out for a shower. He couldn't understand why it was taking so long for them to run showers. He had his mind made that he was going to drag his feet once they popped open his door.

"Mr. Tapps, you're going to have to hurry up in the shower, you're running into count."

Whatever Bone-Tone thought to himself as he rinsed the last bit of soap off his body. After getting out the shower, Bone-Tone made his way towards the water fountain. While filling his water jug up, he purposely ignored Ms. Evans demands to lock it up.

"Mr. Tapps, I'm going to have to write you a 115 for disobeying a direct order."

"I don't give a fuck about a 115, I got life. You can run it concurrent with my sentence!"

Ms. Evans had no response for what Bone-Tone had just said. Frankly, she didn't care. She just wanted him to lock it up. His disobedience was really working her nerves and she made a mental note to make his program difficult every time she worked his section from this day forward.

After filling his jug, Bone-Tone grabbed his shower bag and made his way towards his cell with Ms. Evans trailing behind him

acting as an escort. Half way up the stairs Bone-Tone stopped
and turned around informing Ms. Evans that he didn't need an
escort.

"Well maybe if you weren't acting like a child I wouldn't
have to escort you to your cell."

At that moment something in Bone-Tone clicked and he
realized that he would never get out and had nothing to lose. Ms.
Evans didn't like him, and he realized that she was just doing her
job. His self imposed illusions had truly blinded him. He decided
then that he could not live like this, being treated like a child when
he was thirty something years old. He would end it now on his on
terms.

"Tower, pop two-thirty-five." Ms. Evans said leaning
against the railing tapping her right hand on her mace.

Walking in his cell half way, Bone-Tone quickly threw his
shower bag in his sink, spun around, and grabbed his jug off the
ground. Seeing that Bone-Tone was stalling, Ms. Evans stepped
towards his door to close it. When she stepped in to close the door,
Bone-Tone grabbed her quickly with all of his strength pulling her
inside his cell. She tried to struggle but he was too strong and the
surprise attack caught her off guard. In the struggle she tried to press
her panic button but forgot she had left it at the podium. When the
thought settled in, her instincts guided her to reach for her mace.
Seeing that she was reaching for her mace, Bone-Tone placed more
pressure around her neck with his right arm as he placed his left arm
underneath her left arm taking away the use of her left arm. It didn't
take long for her to lose consciousness from the strangle hold, giving
Bone-Tone enough time to close his door. Breathing heavily, he
couldn't believe what he had just done as he double checked his door
window to see if her partner heard the commotion. By the time her
partner had finished doing his count for the bottom tier, Bone-Tone
had undressed Ms. Evans down to her panties and hand cuffed her
hands behind her back. Knowing that her partner would come
looking for her shortly, he moved all his belongings from underneath
his bed and placed her body underneath his bunk.

"Hey Johnson, is Evans in the bathroom?"

"No, she should be on the top tier doing count."

Seeing her partner walking by B-Section looking into all the
cell windows he knew he had a good twenty minutes before they
started a real search for the missing officer. Sitting on his bunk,
watching TV, while twisting his sheets up, Bone-Tone played the

role like he was doing his normal program as the C.O. made his way towards his section. Once he passed by, Bone-Tone turned the TV off and tied the sheet he was twisting to his stool making sure it was the length he wanted before he pulled his hostage from underneath the bed who was now conscious.

"Look bitch this could be hard and very violent," he said leaning into her face.

He knew he was going to enjoy taking it to Ms. Evans. To prevent anymore spitting and potential screaming, he placed a sock in her mouth then proceeded to move her from the floor to the bed.

The initial energy from the adrenaline he had when he first snatched Ms. Evans into his cell had worn off. He now felt the weeks of not exercising affect him as he tried to put her struggling body on his bed. When he finally got her on the bed he had to pin her down a few minutes to regain his breath and strength. Gaining his composure back, he quickly turned her around on her stomach to enter her from the back of her vagina. In his twisted mind, he expected her vagina to be wet and warm waiting for his entry. He knew it was an act on her part, but that was quickly displaced when his throbbing penis was met by a dry vagina that couldn't be penetrated. Bone-Tone then reached over to his locker and grabbed some Vaseline. Taking a generous amount from the container, he whipped it on the outside of her vagina. The grease that remained he placed on his penis. Wasting no more valuable time, Bone-Tone was able to penetrate the tight vagina of Ms. Evans. He placed his full erection inside of his hostage and let out a moan of pleasure. It was all he had imagined as he violently pounded away going deeper ignoring the tears sliding down her face. Bone-Tone got so caught up in his sexual assault that he didn't hear the C.O.s down at the podium assembling their cell extraction gear.

"When was the last time you've seen your partner?" The sergeant asked irritated at the fact that one of his officers was missing inside the building.

"She was escorting inmate Tapps to his cell the last time I saw her." The tower commander yelled down.

"I checked all the cells and she wasn't in any of them," her partner said.

"Before we start pulling the inmates out one by one, we'll check Tapp's cell first to make sure he didn't have something to do with her disappearance. What I don't understand is why she didn't push her emergency button?" The sergeant inquired.

"Maybe because it's right here at the podium." One of the surrounding officers answered.

"Let it be a lesson to you all, that to not wear it is dangerous!"

"Stop acting like you didn't like it," Bone-Tone said slapping Ms. Evans on the butt.

She looked at him with disgust on her face wondering when her co-workers were going to come looking for her.

"Well here comes the rescue party coming to save you."

"Mr. Tapps we need you step out so we can search your cell."

"Why do you need to search my cell?"

"I don't have to give you a reason inmate. Just step out your cell inmate." "Talking to me like that won't get you anywhere."

"If you don't come out your cell voluntarily we are going to come in and extract your ass! We're not trying to go that route but you are pushing it. All we want to do is check your cell."

"And all I want to know is why and I'll let you check."

"Look, I don't have to give you a reason. Either you come out or we're coming in!"

"Alright, I'll let you in. Let me put some clothes on. Turning around, Bone-Tone grabbed the sheet he had twisted earlier which he had fastened a noose at the end and placed it around his neck. Then he decided to play some more verbal games with the sergeant. Glancing inside the sergeant saw Ms. Evans' leg hanging off the bed. This sent the sergeant into a rage causing him to give the order to get the cell opened up, without further negotiation he sent his subordinates into the cell.

The cell was so small it only allowed for one C.O. at a time to go inside. Knowing this, there was a slight hesitation on who was going first, causing one of the officers to shoot a gas pallet inside before the first one entered. Coughing while trying to hold his breath, Bone-Tone made his way around the C.O.s shield, outside the cell where he was met by several more C.O.s with shields trying to tackle him down to the ground. They were unable to, as he made his way to the rail jumping over it.

By the time they realized what actually took place, Bone-Tone's body was jerking violently over the edge of the tier and there was nothing they could do but watch in disbelief, as every inmate in the building was watching too. Amidst all of the commotion, they had forgotten about Ms. Evans lying in the smoked filled cell. When they finally got to her, she was coughing, crying, and mumbling uncontrollably.

"Somebody get a sheet!" The sergeant commanded.

"Here's everything you requested out of your property. I'm going to need you to sign right here Mr. Pink."

"Alright, thanks." Walking back to his bunk, K-Stone sorted through the hygiene, pictures, and letters he requested out of his property.

K-Stone noticed that they had given him an old letter from his mother. Hesitantly, he read the letter. His eyes began to water as he read the whole letter; especially where his mother signed off by telling him she loved him. His eyes were watery, but no tears ran down his face. The empty feeling he so often felt when faced with the loss of a loved one hit him hard. Then it happened, tears slowly blotted the words on the letter he was reading.

The realization that he would never see his mother again until he went to her grave, settled in. He cried for her and his situation, trapped away like a caged beast inside a human zoo. The warm salty tears flowed smoothly without any sniffles. They were controlled, soothing tears that cleansed his thirsty soul of a myriad of pains that resided in him.

"What you been smirking all day for?"
"Shit my nigga is about to touchdown in a few days!"
"Damn how long did he do all together?"
"Five years and some change, but that doesn't mean anything. I'll catch him up on everything once he touches. By the way what is your sister going to be doing in a few days?"
"Why?"
"Why you think? The homie is going to need something to pound on when he touches down."
"My sister ain't no hoe, she don't even know that boy!"
"If you don't knock it off. That never stopped her before. She's a toss just like you."
"That's how you going to disrespect me Uzi?"
"If the shoe fit wear it."
"You're a scandalous little dark muthafucka!"
"Then why you with this dark muthafucka?"
"Because of your money stupid!"
"Oh you a bold bitch."

"I'm not a bitch; your mother's a bitch!"

"Tell me something I don't know."

"I can't stand your ass!"

"Then get on!"

"I not going nowhere!"

"Is that right. Baby Uzi, bring some of the home girls to the spot."

"I'll be there in five minutes."

"Come on, I'm going to take you home."

"Good and I won't be coming back either!"

"Why we standing out here? Go get your truck so we can leave."

"Just hold up we'll be leaving in a minute."

"What up cuzz?

"What it do Baby Uzi?"

"Nothing, I brought the home girls, what you got crackin'?"

"I need them to fuck this little bitch up!"

"This is going to be funny."

"I know, so go get them so the entertainment can begin."

"What's up Uzi," his three home girls said simultaneously.

"That little bitch right there is from K-Forts."

It didn't take long for his home girls to jump the girl Uzi pointed out to them. She didn't stand a chance against the roughneck girls who had her on the ground stomping her out until she lost consciousness. All Uzi and Baby did was sit back and laugh.

"Them little bitches is crazy, they'll do whatever! I see you stay with the bitches on your line Baby."

"You know how it is once the money is right."

"Yeah, you know I know."

"Why did you bring a K-Fort bitch over here?"

"That bitch not from K-Forts, she from talk too damn much to the wrong nigga gang."

"Where they at?"

"Everywhere!"

"Know the homie supposed to be touching down this week?"

"You know the business. Once he gets settled then we can start killing more of these snitches around the turf. With us leading and your little crew of niggas, we going to take over Ransom."

"I can feel that!"

It almost felt unreal, K-Stone thought to himself as the crisp cold air lay on his face outside the bus station. For a brief second he thought this day wasn't going to happen, especially with the long process he endured just to get processed out. He kept thinking it would be his luck, he would have an unpaid ticket or something, but none of that happened. He was finally out with a bus ticket in hand on his way to the bus station. Downtown is where his father would be picking him up. While on the bus, his mind was voided of thought. He was just taking in the euphoric feeling he was sensing as he took in the fresh free air that was much different from the stale air of the previous environment he was no longer entrapped in. The three year parole would constantly remind him where his five years had been spent previous to his freedom.

Everything seemed to be going fast for him once he actually departed out the gates which he didn't look back to when he was driven out. The three hour ride seemed like one as he stepped off the bus taking in all the movement with each step he took. Walking out the bus station to the parking lot, it didn't take long for him to spot his father standing by his vehicle.

Upon reaching each other, words weren't exchanged at first. Just looks of finally, as Jamal Sr. looked upon his only remaining son who had grown into a man before hugging him.

"It's good you're finally home son."

"It's good to be home."

"Well, get inside so we can go to the cemetery to see your mother and brother like you requested in your letter. Then we can go to the house so you can eat a real meal."

"Let's be on our way."

The meal his father prepared consisted of fried chicken, macaroni and cheese, sweet potatoes, and greens, and that was just half of the main course. His taste buds seemed to come anew as he savored each bite of food that had been denied over the years. It felt good to not have to scruff his meal down; something he had become accustomed to in the prison dining halls.

After eating and joking with his father they both made their way to the back yard to play a few games of dominoes.

"So what do you have planned now that you're out Kevin?"

"I was hoping you could take me down to the DMV so I can renew my driver's license and California ID. From there, I'm going to enroll into West LA College. Once that is in the works, I'll go find a job. Basically, I'm just trying to set a foundation and stick to it for six months to a year, depending on how things turn out with my schedule."

"Sounds like a solid plan Kevin. It's good you have your priorities in order. I won't be able to take you to the DMV until next week. Until then you can relax here at the house and get use to your freedom. While we're on the subject of jobs, I have some bitter sweet news for you son. When your mother passed away, she had a life insurance policy that I'm sure you were aware of."

"Yes I was, but I had forgotten all about it. I know she mentioned it a few times when I was younger."

"Well Kevin, your mother had a five hundred thousand dollar life insurance policy and you're the soul beneficiary. All you have to do is meet with the insurance company. The paperwork is all prepared; it just needs your signature when you're ready."

K-Stone didn't know how to respond to the news his father laid on him. He just slouched in his chair for a minute thinking to himself what it meant. The money would definitely catapult his life forward in the direction he was heading and quicker than he planned. This meant he would have to rewrite his three year plan the next day.

"You alright son?"

"I'm cool pops, the news you just gave me had me thinking for a minute."

"I'm sure it did. I know I don't need to advise you on what to do with it based on the few conversations we've had."

"Even though I know what to do with it pops, I'm always open for advice."

"Spoken like a true wise man. My only advise to you now son is to just enjoy your first day out and relax. There will be plenty of time this week for advice and important decisions."

"I fully agree, so let's get on with the lesson old man." K-Stone said scrambling the dominoes.

"Old man! This old man taught you the fundamentals of this here game."

Later on that night, K-Stone made himself comfortable in his father's guestroom. It was around 10:30 pm and his father had already called it a night thirty minutes ago because he had to work in the morning. Looking out the bedroom window at the full moon, K-Stone still found it hard to believe he was free. He knew he wouldn't get a decent night of sleep. However he still laid it out on the bed, which felt weird compared to the flat mattress he had become accustomed to. Being able to open doors without asking for permission was awkward to him the first few hours of freedom.

The next morning he awakened to his normal time of five am and did his normal routine. For breakfast he ate a couple of bananas and drank some orange juice. Around seven a.m., he went outside in the back yard and exercised for an hour and a half, and then he caught himself washing his boxers in the shower. Around 10:00 a.m. he had completed all the normal activities a normal prison day consisted of.

This left him feeling restless as he waited for his parole officer to come interview him at eleven, there was a platitude that he was reminded of that said, don't judge a book by its cover. But he knew the platitude to be vague and followed it with caution. As soon as he saw his P.O. stepping out his car, he knew he was going to be dealing with a character. It wasn't his tight black jeans, extra medium brown shirt, and too small black tie that made K-Stone know he was dealing with a character, or more so the look he knew he held behind the sun glasses he wore even though the sun was not out.

Being Black didn't mean a thing to K-Stone; most Black people weren't Black people in their souls. Standing six foot three inches and two hundred and thirty pounds, Mr. Givens made his way to his new case load's house. From what he had read, Mr. Givens knew he was dealing with another hardcore gangbanger who he would be violating for any miss step.

After letting his P.O. ring the doorbell twice, K-Stone made his way towards the door.

"I assume you're Mr. Pink?" Givens said entering the house, sun glasses remaining untouched.

"You assume right," K-Stone said gesturing him towards the living room. While sitting on the couch discussing rules of parole, K-Stone and Mr. Givens mentally sized each other up.

Though his assumptions proved right, Mr. Givens wasn't as bad as he appeared not denying the fact that he was a character.

"So do you have any questions?"

"Yes, I hear that I'm entitled to up to two thousand dollars for food, clothes, transportation, and work related tools?"

Hesitantly, Mr. Givens answered yes, instantly thinking to himself as he let the word yes out his mouth that he was dealing with a gangbanger that could read and did read which was rare to find in his line of business. He would have to watch this one, he added as an after thought.

"Well Mr. Pink, I have other clientele I have to go see. So keep in mind to what we have spoken about. As long as you obey the rules you will not get violated."

"Simple enough."

"Sometimes, sometimes not, Mr. Pink. A slight suggestion before I leave. You might want to get that tattoo on your neck removed. It will be difficult enough to get a job with a felony, let alone a neck tattoo."

"Thanks for the advice, I'll think about it."

Now that that was over with, K-Stone's schedule was clear. He didn't have to worry about seeing his P.O. until the following month. With nothing to do, he called Uzi up.

"My lok, how long you been out?"

"Since yesterday."

"What you got planned for the day?"

"Nothing, just sitting here chilling without a vehicle".

"I'm going to come through and get you."

"That's what you not about to do. My P.O. just left and he ran down all my parole stipulations and the main one he kept going over was no contact with gang members. It's cool if you slide through and come keep a Ransom company."

"Your pops still stay at the same spot?"

"Yes sir!"

"Just making sure, I'll be there in a minute."

Hearing a loud booming sound come down the street, K-Stone knew Uzi was on his father's street. Looking through the screen door he watched as Uzi parked his car in the driveway. He was glad he came alone; he didn't fell like being doubled teamed into going for a ride through his turf, though the thought weighed on his mind.

"Big swoll, what's happening?" Uzi said embracing K-Stone.

"Come in the house so we can go kick it in the backyard."

"You know I got some of that kush on me. I know you're trying to get blowed after doing all that time. This definitely not one of those sticks you had in the pen."

"I'm good, the Stone is drug free."

"Drug free? You out the pen now you don't have to be on that strict discipline no more lok."

"Discipline is the key to reaching my goals so you know that will never stop."

"I guess. You still smoking cigarettes though?"

"I done left those alone."

"Just wait until you're out here another couple of months, you'll need something to smoke on, guaranteed."

"I'll be alright."

"Fuck all that shit though, what's the business K-Stone? You haven't got no pussy yet?"

"Nope, I've been chilling with Pops."

"You not trying to knock nothing down?"

"Not really, when it comes, it comes."

"I think the pen fucked you up cuzz."

"Why you say that?"

"What type of nigga don't want no pussy or drugs when they touch down."

"First off I'm not no nigga, I'm K-Stone, so I can't speak for how the next individual gets down."

"You're not a nigga no more?"

"You definitely fucked up in the head K-Stone. I'm not no nigga."

"Nigga you crazy!"

Listening to Uzi imitate his voice and continue to call him out his name wasn't sitting well with K-Stone.

"Check it out Uzi, my name is not nigga and I'm not a nigga. So respect that lok." Seeing that K-Stone was serious, Uzi kicked back on the nigga word in reference to him.

"Look, I didn't mean nothing by it Big serious. I was just fucking with you."

"I feel you; it's nothing against you Uzi. You'll always be my lok, but I have changed the way I think, so I don't see things the way I use to."

"I feel you too K-Stone, but I still think you'll be back to yourself in a few months."

"I'm myself now."

"I'll let you have that for now. On another note, I know you're going to need some bread now that you're out, so here's something to hold you over until you get on your feet."

K-Stone looked at Uzi as he reached underneath his t-shirt into his waistband pulling out a brown envelope filled with hundreds along with a black pistol that looked like it came from the future.

"It's about ten thousand in the envelope, all you, no payback. The pistol is you too, fresh out the box so the only one on it will be the ones you put on it. It's some new heat that hasn't even hit the streets. So don't ask me what it's called. I just know it cost three thousand and shoots A.K. bullets. Well, that's your starter kit. I know you will handle the rest."

"Good looking out Uzi."

"No problem, you know how we do it. A, was you on the yard when Bone-Tone hung himself?"

"What are you talking about?"

"I thought ya'll was on the yard together!"

"We were, but I got caught up in the riot and was sent to the hole. Bone-Tone had stayed on the yard."

"Oh, so you didn't even know? That fool hung himself after raping a C.O. bitch."

"That's crazy!" K-Stone said shaking his head in disbelief.

"It is, but what's crazier is you haven't got any pussy yet." Uzi said laughing.

"Here you go again."

"You know I had to hit you one more time."

"Yeah, you wouldn't be being you if you didn't."

After going back and fourth for another two hours, Uzi had to leave to take care of some business at one of his spots. Walking in his room after letting Uzi out, he placed the money Uzi had given him on the night stand as he moved some boxes around in the closet before placing it in a corner and putting the boxes back on top.

Looking at the gun on the bed, he tried to figure out a place to stash it. His father's residence was put down as his place of parole, the police could do a random search anytime, and he definitely couldn't be caught slipping. Knowing that they could search in the house, it was out of the question to stash it inside. Stepping outside, he surveyed the yard for a spot. Seeing a nice patch of dirt, he knew he had found his new stash spot until he found something better. After playing Martha Stewart in the garden for thirty minutes, he was satisfied that he had properly hidden all that needed to be hid.

Another day went by without having to hear another man urinate and defecate a few feet away from him. K-Stone thought to himself as he awoke without having to hear a loud speaker announce fifteen minutes to chow.

It had been a month since he paroled from prison and all his plans were falling into place. He took eighty thousand dollars of his money and invested it into two homes. One home he rented out and the other he lived in. Even though he and his father got along well, five years of living with another male in a bathroom had planted a seed that he needed a place of his own where he set his own rules.

From reading in prison, he had learned quite a lot about investing. Being that he now had money, he didn't pass up the chance to start a ten thousand dollar portfolio. He took another ten thousand dollars and purchased some bonds, CDs, and mutual funds. The ten thousand Uzi gave him he separated and sent it to certain individuals he had met in prison that had helped him out mentally in the form of packages, magazines, books, and money orders. In correlation to that, he started up a non-profit organization called HIM IS, which was an acronym for Helping Inmates Maintain in Society.

With all his small accomplishments, the most rewarding thing he received from his money was the opportunity to go to college full time to earn a doctorate in psychology that he planned to use to solve Black peoples' mental issues in hopes of unifying them all over the world.

A year out of prison passed quickly and K-Stone had finally gotten use to being back in society. He no longer felt awkward in his daily dealings and was also adjusted to college life. He was networking with a myriad of different people that advanced the way he thought and used his new ideas. He was living a whole new life that he couldn't have ever imagined before he went to prison. He was living Kevin's life.

His only vise was that Ransom was still in his heart and a constant reminder every time he looked at his body. He still found it impossible to stop thinking like a gangsta. One day he rewarded himself with a three hundred Chrysler and instantly got a stash spot put inside along with a music system. Though he wasn't entrenched in the lifestyle anymore, he still felt that need of the gun when driving through his turf. Hanging with Uzi began to feel like a chore as they related to each other less and less.

"So when you going to hook me up with one of those college hoes?"

"Uzi, like I told you before, they're not interested."

"What bitch not interested in a gangsta? None, you were taking too long to answer. I'll give it to you K-Stone; you've stuck to your square thang for a good while. You not tired yet?"

"Are you tired of being Ransoms number one gangsta?"

Uzi's mouth said no, his heart said yes. Uzi was slightly envious of how K-Stone had changed his life around. He couldn't help but notice how they were drifting apart. He knew they kicked it

more out of familiarity and the fact that they were the only ones
left of their generation on the streets. Uzi was burnt out on living
the way he was, especially when he saw K-Stone who had grown up
the same way he did living the complete opposite. His fantasies of
controlling the turf with his closest lok had faded. They were both
twenty four but on two different levels. He was still showing boxers
while K-Stone was covering them up. It had become apparent to Uzi
that he couldn't keep looking at a reflection of what he could be
when he kept feeding himself excuses that he couldn't be. K-Stone
had become his constant reality of his mediocrity that was felt more
and more. Every time they saw each other, K-Stone was a reminder
that Uzi was a failure in life.

"This must be some bomb Kush because I'm about to ask
you a crazy question. When you see me what goes through your
mind?"

"Before I answer you Uzi, let me ask you a question?"

"What goes on in your mind when you see you?"

"Nothing really, I hardly ever look at myself judgmentally."

"When I look at you Uzi, I see the same person I grew up
with as a child. I also see a person who kills our people and
continues to keep the cycle of genocide going on in our
communities. I see a person who makes excuses for his short
comings. A person who feels he is owed something. I see my best
friend who I no longer can relate to anymore. I see a soul, but most
of all, I see potential that refuses to be used for some reason. What
do you see when you see me?"

"I see the opposite of what you see in me. Dudes like us
don't change, yet you did. At least one out of the crew will live a
life worth living. You will always carry us all within you K-Stone."

"Being aware of your short comings is the first step to
changing your destiny."

"I'm too stuck in my ways bro; I'm 'till death."

"Well today is my cheat day. I'm about to grab something to
eat."

"One of these days, I'm going to have to go hit the gym with
you."

"You've been saying that since I got out the pen. You know
you don't pick up anything heavier than a pistol."

"You know me well Killa Stone."

"Make sure you leave the park the same way you found it, I'm gone." After embracing, K-Stone jumped in his ride, mashed out and headed up Manchester to find a place to eat.

Pulling into Golden Birds parking lot, K-Stone pushed the button underneath his seat to remove his pistol from his stash. Tucking his pistol into his waistband, K-Stone made his way into Golden Bird.

"Let me get the twenty four piece chicken bits, fries, and two sweet potato pies."

After placing his order and paying he walked back to his car to listen to some music while his order was being filled. Listening to his intuition, K-Stone looked to his left and saw a police car entering the parking lot. A slight chill ran through his body as he placed his pistol back in his stash with a slight smirk on his face. Stopping right in front of his car the officers occupying the squad car typed in his license plate. When the information came back saying he was on parole the officers stepped out of their vehicle and approached his vehicle from both sides. K-Stone's car had tinted windows and the police couldn't see inside even with their flash lights so K-Stone rolled down his windows.

"Would you step out the vehicle sir, when we see a car like this in a neighborhood like this, it automatically sends a red flag, especially when the owner is a parolee. All we want to do is check out your vehicle while you take a seat in our car."

Twenty minutes passed before the officers came to the patrol car to talk to K-Stone.

"Well Mr. Pink, we didn't find anything in your car. I see you're from Ransom, have you been hanging out with them?"

"No, that would be a violation of my parole, officer."

"You make sure you keep obeying those rules, Mr. Pink."

Watching the police slowly pull out the parking lot, K-Stone couldn't help but want to grab his gun and serve the police officers. He couldn't wait to get off parole. Walking out of Golden Bird with his meal, he started fumbling with his keys while placing change in his pocket, causing him to put his head down. In that instant, he found himself bumping into a familiar figure out the door.

"Ivie!"

"K-Stone!"

"How have you been doing?" K-Stone asked meeting her as she came in for a hug. Ivie could feel the hardness of his body as she forced herself to break away.

"I see you got out."

"Yes I did," K-Stone said smirking

"I've been out about two years now."

"What are you doing over here?"

"I came to get something to eat, how about you?"

"I stay around the corner."

"Instead of sitting in the open like this, let me give you my number so we can get together and catch up."

"Okay, where is your car?"

"Right there."

"Nice car."

"Thanks. Well here's my number. We can get together and catch up when you are free."

"I'm free now if that's the case."

"Is that right?"

"I see the more things change the more they stay the same."

"Yes they do. What do you have in mind?"

"Nothing much, we can go back to my house and eat together while we talk."

"Sounds like a plan; I'll wait for you in the car and follow you to your place."

Watching Ivie walk back into the Golden Bird, K-Stone couldn't help notice she still had it good, if not better. It was easy to see that she kept herself up throughout the years despite the daily dramas she endured. Seeing her hop in her car, he turned the ignition and followed behind her. Once they arrived at her apartment, he parked his car behind hers in the parking stall and grabbed his pistol once again, tucking it into his waistband as he made his way behind her to her apartment.

Looking around her place, he thought she had a nice apartment which wasn't a surprise.

"You can sit at the table K-Stone. I'll get you a plate and some utensils. So what you been up to K-Stone?"

"I go to college full time and run my non-profit organization HIM IS. Besides that, I stay out of the way and remain on the course of bettering myself."

"How about you?"

"Right now, I'm a registered nurse at MLK. I was enrolled in college for a minute, but raising Gina by myself without help is hard, so I had to dropout. I'm thinking about filing for child support on my baby daddy."

"Where is your daughter now?"

"At her grandmother's house for the weekend. Her daddy just got out a few weeks ago and I don't know where he is now, which is crazy after he ran my phone bill up with his collect calls. I'm sorry K-Stone I started unloading my problems on you."

"I wouldn't have asked if I didn't want to know. That's life you're describing, so it's nothing new or painful to my ears."

"So you haven't had any kids K-Stone?"

"No, not yet. I'm not going to have any kids that I'm not there for. I don't need to have kids to validate my manhood."

"You think that's why guys have babies?"

"That and plain irresponsibility, why else would someone create life they know they're not going to take care of or be an example for. Maybe you should tell your baby daddy about my organization. We deal with a lot of issues including taking care of ones family. I have a card right here."

"Thank you K-Stone. I'm proud you have changed your life."

"Thank you Ivie."

"As much as I know you hate dwelling on the past, I must tell you why I dropped out of you r life for what seemed like no reason."

"It may surprise you, but I know the reason why."

"Do you?"

"I know it had something to do with your sister's death."

"How did you figure that?"

"There couldn't have been any other reason, Ivie. Was there?"

"No, you're right. It's still hard for me to talk about, but I need to let you know that I'm sorry Kevin for leaving you with no explanation. I deal with how I did you daily and I sometimes think that my current situation now is my punishment for leaving you like I did."

"We were both young then and two different people. It hurt when you left me, it hurt bad Ivie. But I have forgiven you and wish you no ill will or anything negative. Losing a sibling is rough especially knowing they suffered and it affects everyone differently. If you want to make it up to me Ivie, just let it go, because I have."

"I can do that K-Stone. All this time I thought you hated me, especially when you only wrote me a few times after your mother's passing."

"So much was going on with me at that time that I kind of went into myself and shut out a lot of people to better myself."

"Do you still hang out with Uzi?"

"Occasionally, but we've drifted apart as you can imagine. I wouldn't be surprised if we stopped talking permanently."

"I know that must be hard on you, being that he is your best friend or as you say your lok."

"It is and then again it isn't only a fool remains the same when they see it isn't getting anywhere. I don't need any fools in my life. Eventually it might rub off on me."

"Maybe I should take that advice."

"If the shoe fits, wear it."

"Let me get your plate, K-Stone."

"Good looking out." Seeing it was getting late, K-Stone knew it would be time for him to leave.

"Thanks for the company, K-Stone."

"No, thank you. I would've been eating alone had I not run into you." With that said K-Stone put his jacket on and made his way towards the door.

"I see you still like burning incense?"

"Yes, I like to keep my surroundings as pleasant as possible."

"Alright Ivie, it was nice seeing you."

K-Stone said hugging her before he left. Instead of breaking apart like he intended, they held their hug longer than both intended, as dormant feelings became revitalized between the two. It was hard to say who kissed who first but there they were embraced tightly mouths moistly locked. Pulling away slowly, K-Stone looked into her eyes that were watery from tears she was shedding.

"I still love you, Kevin."

"I still love you too, but I never go down the same road twice. Bye Ivie," K-Stone said releasing Ivie from his arms then letting himself out as he made his way to his car. It wasn't very difficult for K-Stone to forgive but he never forgot the abandonment.

On his way to his car he saw an individual leaning up against his car and automatically put his pistol in reaching range by instinct.

"Excuse me Black man, I'm about to leave."

"Who you came to see?" Without hesitation he held his pistol to the strangers head forcing him down to the ground patting him down in the process.

Finding no gun in his waistband, he instructed the stranger to be on his way or lose his life. The stranger frantically obliged. Getting into his car, K-Stone felt an old feeling he hadn't felt in a long time overcome him and he didn't like it. Pulling out the driveway parking lot, he heard gun shots and quickly threw his car in park jumping out with his pistol to return fire.

The sound of his gun drowned the sound of the other gun firing at him. Whoever was shooting at him retreated once he returned fire, causing him to be on his way. Calmly, K-Stone made his way towards the nearest freeway. All that kept replaying in his mind was how he had almost gotten caught up twice that day and both were avoidable. He had knowingly put himself in jeopardy. Something he didn't need to be doing when he was doing so well. He realized now that he would have to redouble his efforts in self improvement.

Four weeks passed since the shooting incident and no repercussions had been sent his way regarding the issue. Strangely enough he had bumped into Tanisha and she informed him that Bone Tone's appeal had been granted a couple days after he had committed suicide. It had been a while since he and Uzi actually talked, the last thing he heard about him was that he had been on the run. He took the lessons the universe was telling him to heart. It was Sunday afternoon and he was sitting in his kitchen writing letters to his comrades in prison. He had made a pact to himself to write one or two of them every Sunday. He figured if he was ever too busy to sit down and write a comrade, then he was moving too fast. On this particular Sunday he was writing to his mentor Askari.

Comrade,

As always, I hope this letter finds you strong in all areas of importance. As you know I'm nearing the clipping of the chain that still connects me to the sunken slave ship that still holds you and a myriad of warrior's hostage. Even though the chains of parole will be severed, the shackles will still remain on my soul. As brothers we are still kept to erode in caves like modern day slaves, left on permanent display because society has deemed them incapable of finding their way. So they're punished by being buried alive in concrete graves where the soul can't breathe, and causing despair to spread like an airborne disease that kills dreams of wanting to succeed. All for a system that is fueled off greed and horrible misdeeds that are usually more heinous than those entrapped within its belly. Honor, Love, and Respect,

Always and Forever,

Kevin Pink
aka K-Stone

Glossary

Ad-Seg: Administrative segregation, the "hole" at a prison.
Bad work: Drugs that is not good.
Blues: State issued clothing.
B-hands: Hand signals that identify Blood affiliation.
Berpes: Prison calisthenics.
Crackin: An expression, "What's going on?"
Caught the chain: Bus ride to prison.
Cherry top: Police car.
Damus: Blood.
Dome: Oral sex.
Dap: Hand shake in the form of a closed fist.
Holla: Speak.
Hood Rat: A neighborhood girl who sleeps around.
Hoop: To put drugs up the anal cavity or a reference to a car.
Kick Stand(s): A life sentence(s).
Kush: A strong form of marijuana.
Lok: A respected gangbanger.
L.W.O.P: Life without parole.
Murk: To kill someone.
Mashed out: To push on the accelerator of a car real hard causing the car to kick up dust.
M.T.A: Medical trained assistant.
Mac-Rep: Men advisory council representative.
Off: To kill someone.
Pound cake: A thick attractive female.
P.C.: Police custody.
Philly Blunt: Cigar used to smoke weed in.
Pruno: Prison alcohol.
R & R: Receive and release department at a prison.
Ridas: Someone willing to do whatever whenever.
Slap Bones: To play dominoes.
Shank: Prison knife.
Strawberries: A women who sells her body specifically for drugs.
Sagoony: A transsexual.
Swoll: To be muscular.
Shu: Another term for Ad-Seg.
Sherm: The drug PCP.
Smash out: To press on the gas petal hard and fast.

Glossary (cont.)

Tender dick: A male who falls in love with females rather quickly and often.

Tossing: To have an orgy with females or a one nightstand.

Twelve in a box: A reference to twelve juries.

Y.A.: Youth authority

115: Discipline for prison inmate infractions.

From the Up Coming 2009 book....

House of Failure

II

Escape From Failure

William V. Fields

Chapter 1

Finally

"You sure that's him I'm not trying to waste no bullets on no smokers or has-beens." Uzi said tucking his 357 python into his brown khakis.

"Cuzz I'm positive, I just did a violation with him in CMC where he was pushing a line on the homies." Tall Can said while adjusting his red beanie.

"Pull over on the side street behind his car we'll catch him when he comes out the liquor store. We can post against the gate. I'll shoot him in the head while you give it to him in the body." Uzi said as Baby Uzi pulled behind their victims brown 83 Cutlass Supreme.

Stepping out of their black 97 Honda Accord Uzi and Tall Can made their way to the side gate of an apartment building which set adjacent to an alley on the corner of Figueroa

Usually they would have stood out in the Blood neighborhood, but they were flamed up so they blended into the environment well for their current mission.

"Hey Uzi, you see those kids over there playing jump rope in that yard?" Tall Can asked as he looked down the alley in the other direction at some smokers digging through a graffiti dumpster.

"Yeah I see them, but it don't mean anything, once they here the gun shots they'll start running anyway or continue playing. Besides they hear gun shots all the time it probably want even stop them from playing."

"I'm just putting you up on the kids so no bullets hit them."

"Cuzz, fuck them kids I'm not trying to hear that soft shit. Go join a non-profit if you want to help save the kids, I gangbang."

"Let me get five packs of Cherry berry blunt wraps too." B-Down told the Asian cashier as he paid for the blunt wraps along with the twenty four pack of MGD for his set day on October 9. He had been out twenty six days and was feeling damn good after pulling eight in the pen.

Being away so long had its benefits and draw backs. For one he was the new swipe in the set which meant all his home girls new and old wanted to give him a piece before he got sucked up by the street life. Plus he was looking good with his twenty inch arms that set apart from a pumped out wide chest, but mostly the females were on his extra long hair which he wore in nine French braids that laid against the middle of his upper back. The drawback of course was he had to start from scratch with everything including meeting new Y.G. homies who had only heard about him, but that was the least of his worries, he was going to get a chance to see his eight year old daughter who he hadn't seen since his baby momma received thirteen years for consecutive shoplifting. Since she had went to jail his daughter had to be raised by her parents who lived in Arizona, but had family that lived on Imperial and Vermont.

Bending the corner B-Down quickly noticed the two Black males leaning against the gate not too far from his car.

"Whats up blood?" Uzi said.

"Just bicking it." B-Down replied.

"Dogg you need help with those brews?"

"Naw I'm bool, I got it blood." B-Down replied as he reached in his pocket for his car keys with his right hand.

Opening his trunk he placed his beers inside before he could close it he was thrown off guard by a question from Uzi. "Blood you got a bigarette on you?"

"Naw, blood I don't smoke." Turning back around to close his trunk B-Down heard the sound of sneakers screeching behind him, but it was too late as Uzi placed the 357 Pythons nose to the back of his head squeezing the trigger all in one fluid motion. The blast of the revolver knocked the back part of his skull along with his forehead into the hood of the trunk beating the upper part of his body which quickly followed.

   The thickness of B-Down's braided hair muffled the normally loud python, causing little to no reaction from the kids a few homes up. What did catch their attention were the multiple shots from Tall Can's 45 automatic handgun that pumped bullet after bullet into his hunched over already deceased body.

Uzi, had done this numerous times before and walked away with no regard for what he had just done. With Tall Can right behind him they walked a few feet to their awaiting car which Baby Uzi already had up and running.

While opening up the passenger door Uzi felt eyes on him, when he turned to meet the gaze he saw that it was coming from the children a few feet from them leaning over their gate watching the entire last part of their mission. Without much thought Uzi tossed his 357 into the passenger seat and grabbed his AK 47 that had a hundred round drum attached to it laying against the side of the passenger seat. The kids didn't think much of the man coming towards them in a red t-shirt and hat with a big gun by his side and before they realized his intentions he had opened fire on them killing them all in a matter of seconds with a few sweeps of the AK which ended up hitting more of the house then anything.

Back in the car Uzi lit a cigarette as Tall Can set in shock at what He just saw. He had heard stories about how crazy Uzi was, but he just realized he was in the presence of pure evil.

   "Cuzz you just killed three kids." Tall Can said hysterically.

   "Tell me something I don't know any other quick facts."

   "There was no reason for that."

   "Says who?"

   "Says me, you just murdered some little Black kids for no reason."

   "There was a reason they saw my face."

   "But they were just little kids they wouldn't have been able to identify you."

   "Whatever, besides they would have turned Lanes anyway."

   "Cuzz, that don't sit well with me."

"Then you probably want be feeling this either." Uzi said reaching his arm into the backseat with his 357 pointing directly at Tall Cans head pulling the trigger. The close range of the hollow tip bullet split his forehead as if an axe had went through it as his body flipped forward.

"Damn cuzz, now we have to burn the car. Soft as nigga talking about I killed some kids, nigga please we just killed a man the producer of kids.

* *

"After a five year investigation ten Los Angeles Police Officers belonging to the 77th Street C.R.A.S.H. division have been charged with a string of unlawful arrests, murders, attempted murders, and various other crimes that span over a 20 year period. There will definitely be a public outcry equaling that of the Rampart corruption scandal that happened to the city many years ago." This is Pat Harvey reporting for KCAL 9 News.

Askari was paralyzed in body and soul by the news report he had just seen, he had been following the case for the last year since it begun to appear in the Los Angeles Sentinel. For a while he had thought the investigation on the corrupt police officers would just be swept under the rug like so many suspect shootings, beatings, and arrests. Yet he sat galvanized at the possibility that many of his peers would once again have an opportunity to walk the streets with their families, but most importantly he thought about the twelve years he had been incarcerated and how it could now be coming to an end.

Fantasies of his freedom crossed his mind frequently in the beginning of his term, but after seeing countless board extension, legislatives for three strikes ignored, and appeals denied he had simply put his problems in Gods hand choosing in the mean time to dwell in his on comforts and understanding of life and the way it was supposed to be. Like so many others he had come to accept life in prison as the way it was with a small amount of hope that every human being needed to survive day to day that there would eventually be a light at the end of the tunnel that would set him free. For many years he had known mental freedom quite well it had been physical freedom that had become foreign to him over the last decade yet now he felt a feeling that had only visited him in dreams and while watching the Discovery channel.

This feeling made his eyes slightly water as he stared off into the air that had been his for far too long it was after all a breathless air that lacked life all together. He felt a slight since of shame that he had even allowed himself to have such a foolish feeling he seen this type of scenario played out too many times with the same results, but that inner hope was always there no matter how much he denied it. Nevertheless he reacted like he always did when confronted with such feelings and thoughts bury them inside.

The next day the prison yard was filled with the same gleefulness that usually followed the news of early release bringing with it facts and fiction of what was actually said the night before on the case regarding the police. Askari just continued his daily routine letting the echoes of what was going to be slide in one earlobe and out the other.
It was Tuesday and the sun was shining bright on the inmates skin as they all tried to adjust to the sun that had been denied to them for three months due to a lock down. For some it took a little more adjusting then others to gain their composure reason being there were a lot of youngsters on the yard serving life sentencing for a for all type of crimes, but the majority being murders and robberies gone wrong. This disturbed Askari a lot because he was seeing a cycle of wasted young misguided life thrown away year after year. The ages ranged from 18 to 26 years old and the numbers were increasing. With so much youth placed in prison he often wondered what would eventually happen to neighborhoods without any male influence. From what he had heard there was an increase in lesbianism on the streets do to the fact that the male influence

was so in decline, women had started to take on the role of the missing soon to be link. A day didn't pass that he didn't hear my bitch just left me for another bitch escaping a youngsters lips. Just a few years back the average inmate had to worry about another male taking his place, but now they had double trouble with the women being involved. So much had changed yet so much still remained the same. The death rate in California had dropped over the last couple of years, but the only reason being that the system had locked up the majority of the line pushers from the different sets throughout L.A. county nevertheless brothers were still killing brothers as the new crop of gang members were being born to single mothers in the ghetto.

The rise in black on brown killings were still increasing in Compton, Watts, SGV, Pomona and throughout the L.A. area basically every Black gang was having some type of friction with a Hispanic gang over money ,territory ,misunderstandings or just skin issues. This information was constantly being reported on the news of what was taking place between the two race everyday which did nothing but fuel the tension in the prison environment as well as the county jail.

Most blacks didn't realize the low number of blacks until they reached the jail system then it eventually dawned on them that they needed each other at the end of the day especially when faced with a seven to one ratio in a riot. The word nigga still sounded like finger nails being dragged across a chalk board in his ears whenever he heard it especially when said around different races. He had just gotten two youngstas from 83 Hoover who came from another yard placed next door and they seemed to be having a competitions on who could say nigga the most in one day there had been a lot of bed moves since the last riot which basically meant there would be a whole lot of chaos on the yard for the next few months. Askari would eventually get around to meeting his new neighbors and possibly give them some knowledge in the meantime. One of the youngsta kind of reminded him of his protégée K-Stone who had moved on to the physical freedom that eluded so

many inmates. Even though he heard from him once a
month he still missed being around his comrade who he
lived through vicariously in the form of pictures, letters, and
phone calls.

November 3, 2008 the world felt a united anticipation as they
stood by on all levels of the social ladder waiting on Tuesday
to come bringing with it the results of who would be their next
president. Emotions were running high in Beverly Hills at
Nate'n Al were younger Jews were discussing the possibility
of Obama wining and what it would do for their taxes while
their matzo ball soup cooled downed; over on Hyde Park
behind some rundown apartment building the Rollin 60 Crips
were initiating two brand new teenage members; a little further
down on Crenshaw Eso Won book store was serving Earl
Grey tea from the Coffee Bean and Tea leaf as a group of
people out in the community ranging from early twenties to
late eighties discussed how they could continue to keep the
interest of politics fresh in the community after Tuesdays
presidential results while informing the community how they
could help make the president's job much easier ; Down in
East L.A amongst the hustle and bustle Hispanics leaned
against their vendor vehicles after a long prospers day making
sure their Obama stickers were still intact while talking in their
native tongue about what their children's health care benefits
would be like under Obama's policies. In prisons across
California conversation ranged from "who cares who wins I
got life", "It would be righteous to see a familiar face in the
White House", and "That nigger better not win", but mostly
inmates were concerned with the passing of Proposition 9
which would take away the little rights they had managed to
hold on to. To the inmate it really didn't matter who won on
the free world if Proposition 9 was passed. For that reason the
prison system was on high alert because of talk of a possible
riot on staff if the 9 Bill did pass. Furthermore there was talk in
the air that if Obama did win the Skin Heads and Aaron
Brother hood were going to launch a full scale attack on all
Black inmates within the system. There was also talk about the
Blacks doing a similar attack if McCain won the presidency.

Tensions were just high all around the board throughout the prison complex and the world at large with the recession getting worse, but even with all the distress there was a ray of hope awaiting one inmate in the form of a letter within a mail bag.

From the Up Coming 2009 book....

Unexpected Thoughts of a Felon

William V. Fields

But Life Goes On……..

Pain becomes a companion as more mourning mothers are left standing viewing new dug dirt while experiencing a pain worse than hurt.

As they reminiscence over old pictures and clutches the scent of their deceased baby's shirt. Taking them back to the many months of birth along with new thoughts of was it worth?

When they were taking so easily from earth with a few quick burst by some ignorant twerp who decided to go berserk just to have something to brag about in his turf.

But life goes on…..

Continuous degradation in the form of songs, birth in a world where they are labeled whores finds many women with blacken emotions hidden behind impenetrable doors.

A constant cycle of plight where 20 something inch rims are put above life as chivalry is kept steadily out of sight. Leaving many gasping for the might to keep their perspective of those who disrespect them in the right.

Hard though when attention is only paid when wearing something skin tight.

Time to set off a permanent protest for women rights to prevent the next generation from having to fight.

But life goes on....

For those who have triangle prints in heir pant whom men choose not to understand outside of what's beneath their waist bands.

Respect of the world for their little girls, but send their children mothers through constant peril. Twirling in a confusion of unsettle causing emotions to reach high peaks and plummet to deeper levels.

As she tries to figure out the male specious need to test her mettle.

But life goes on.....

Obviously this non sense has gone on too long the reason I sat down to pen this poem for a young sister named Halee Strong who is the epitome of what women must long to be.

Despite the images and commentary they see in magazines ranging from Maxiam to King.

But life goes on....

Endorsements catered to those who can wear the skinniest thong while performing the lewdest scenes. Frightening how we portray our female beings yet critizes them for any immoral thing.

Laughing platitudes like can't turn a hoe into a house wife, but those we usually choose to date twice. While ostracizing those who don't sex on the first night.

In a civilized world this would set off a light, but it's hard to tell nowadays what is truly right let alone wrong. When people get their inspiration from negative based songs.

I guess eventually we'll come along.

I guess?

Instead of operating off the flesh, money, and violence then we'll all reach a highness, but if not

Life goes on….

www.ingramcontent.com/pod-product-compliance
Lightning Source LLC
Chambersburg PA
CBHW072115270326
41931CB00010B/1567